A MAJOR
OBSESSION

A MAJOR OBSESSION

One Fan, Four Golf Championships

KENNY REID

BIRLINN

First published in 2010 by
Birlinn Limited
West Newington House
10 Newington Road
Edinburgh
EH9 1QS

www.birlinn.co.uk

ISBN 13: 978 1 84158 859 9

British Library Cataloguing-in-Publication Data
A catalogue record for this book is available from the
British Library

Typeset in Adobe Garamond at Birlinn

Printed and bound in Great Britain by
MPG Books, Bodmin, Cornwall

Contents

Plates

For Bob and Moira

Something is missing from golf as experienced on television. The third dimension is missing. The serene space of it all, and the singing flight of the happily struck shot. On television, every shot appears to jump off to the right, like the worst sort of shank. Again and again one is amazed to be told that the shot that just went sideways off the screen is right on line – that, far from a shank, it has wound up 10 feet from the pin. Also, the distances are impossible to judge on that little screen, so that players take 9-irons for what look like targets in the next country. And the greens don't show their slope or swales, so that putts move in a weird magnetic field insulated from the contours that would be obvious if we were there. Being there, really, is much of the joy of golf.

John Updike, *Golf Dreams*

Preface

By trade or profession I am neither journalist nor writer. At heart I am simply a golf fan. I've played since I was a boy, and I love the game.

This book is not the work of a professional author, an established member of the media or golfing insider. I hope it's a book for golf fans and golf lovers everywhere. For years I've watched all the majors on TV, read about them in books and magazines, occasionally listened on radio, and attended a few, too.

I hope this book can take you out of your armchair and onto the courses along with me as I enjoy a golfing odyssey, watching the world's best players on some of the best courses, playing in *the* best tournaments. As in all endeavours, I often came to rely on the kindness of strangers and friends, some of whom you'll meet in the forthcoming pages. In an effort to give the average golfer a look behind the scenes that go into the making of a major, I made various requests; some were granted, others not. It was all part of the experience of trying to put this book together.

To avoid argument and correspondence from the pedants out there, I have chosen to call each of the championships by the names used by their respective organising bodies. So within these pages there will be no 'British Open' in the same way as there will be no 'US PGA'.

I hope you enjoy this journey into the crucible of golf's greatest events: The Masters at Augusta National; the US Open at Bethpage; The Open Championship at Turnberry; the PGA Championship at Hazeltine.

Planet Augusta, Golf's Shangri-La
The Masters Tournament

I was glad Cabrera won, although I'd liked to have seen Kenny Perry win. My husband's from the same small town as him in Kentucky , and it's just a wide bit of the road.

Elaine Harris, Roswell, Georgia

MASTERS WEEK: GO SOUTH, YOUNG MAN

Shangri-La is defined in the *Oxford English Dictionary* as 'a place regarded as an earthly paradise, especially when involving a retreat from modern civilisation', and I was very lucky to be coming to such a paradise, Augusta National, for the second time. After a three-day visit in 2007, Augusta took root in my golfing psyche. It's an amazing venue, almost literally breathtaking.

The Masters is the only Major with a true sense of place; no other Major has that same feeling. With that comes a clear feeling of time and history. If the other majors play in your mind on some mundane multiplex cinema, Augusta National is IMAX High Definition, an assault to the senses with sharp, brilliant colours, near-perfection wherever you look.

For years The Masters has provided invigorating climaxes, drama at every turn. I'd watched it religiously on TV, my first real recollection Ben Crenshaw's long, twisting, 60-foot snake of a putt at the 10th in 1984 that kick-started his drive to victory. Gentle Ben's win followed Seve's second green jacket, and preceded Langer's first. And then there was 1986.

On that fabled Sunday afternoon, Seve and Greg Norman rode into Choke City while ageing gunslinger, the Golden Bear, shot 30 on the back nine and carded a 65. It was Jack Nicklaus' sixth green jacket and an amazing display from a written-off 46-year-old. I still have that round on videotape (remember that format?), and marvel every time I watch.

Of course, before my own real-time memories were the great battles and victories of Ben Hogan, Slammin' Sam Snead and Arnold Palmer. And, lest we forget, the victories of Nick Faldo, José Maria Olazábal, Phil Mickelson and Tiger. Although recent Masters Sundays have bordered on the anodyne, many others at Augusta National have been the benchmark for major golfing excitement. Much of that is down to the course.

Seeing Augusta as I did in 2007, you are smacked in the face by its sheer scale, its vastness, its tranquillity, its quest to be the best course it can be for the best Masters possible, year after year after year. The Masters tries to be the best of all possible golf tournaments in the best of all possible worlds. It succeeds.

On each of my seven days at Augusta – Monday to Wednesday in 2007; Thursday to Sunday in 2009 – I always entered via Patron Corridor, past the golf shop, the exhibit stand and the right of the first fairway. You double-take on seeing the slope that heads from the front of the teeing ground and runs down from the left, then steeply up to your right. This first view of the course is a blow to your solar plexus.

Through the dip, on the left of the first fairway, massive pine trees demand your attention, watching over you, challenging you to believe that they are as tall and magnificent as they seem. Everywhere you turn, similar trees abound, most guarding fairways, some guarding greens. It's horticulture on steroids. Hyperbolic, it grabs your breath and beggars belief.

As you stagger, dizzy with myriad sensations, up towards the first tee, you see the tricky 9th green, the 18th green, the long sweep down to the 2nd green, and beyond, the beauty of the 7th green. Can this really be where some people get to play golf? What perversity of chance or upbringing or wealth allows for such inequity in The Golfing Life?

But then you realise it doesn't matter, because you're here and the rest of the world isn't; you've seen it and so many haven't, and most never will. The bigness – a clumsy word, but it seems right – of Augusta National is there at every turn. When Bob Jones first came to the old and dilapidated Fruitland Nurseries in the spring of 1931, he saw immediately that the land was perfect. So much so, Jones was hard pressed to believe it wasn't specifically designed for his purposes.

Visitors to Augusta National get a sense of what Jones saw. Rolling hills, the flora and turf, the humps and hollows; Jones sensed which areas demanded tees, fairways and greens. It comes as no surprise to learn that when routing the famous 13th – the boomerang par-5, 'Azalea' – Alister Mackenzie designed it seconds after first seeing the creek and sweep of the land. Hidden in the mists of time, the 13th had been there for centuries, waiting to be discovered. Of these things legends are made.

The more you drink from the fountain of Augusta's beauty and grandeur, the more you start to notice some of the paradoxes. The greens are large, but somehow they feel small. Then you realise the humps and the hollows, the swales and the steps on many of the greens mean that landing areas require precision, the utmost skill, the correct shot choice. You notice that each green is a different shape, the generous parts often presented at less than straightforward angles to the approaching player. Bunkers and humps beside the green eat and cut into the green contours, nibbling away at the target areas.

You begin to understand the illusion of smallness is a trick of the eye, the large greens dwarfed by the scale of everything else. There are 18 greens, but at Augusta National these cover over 110,000 square feet, more than double that of traditional US courses of the 1930s. The course is set among trees as high as the ancient cathedrals of Europe. And you also know that this coming Sunday, there will be more worshippers at the church of Augusta National than anywhere else on the planet.

Augusta National is beautiful and energising, a supermodel of a golf course. Augusta National is a rush, a golfing high. But first you have to get there.

My Tuesday morning flight via Paris was smooth and punctual, and once I was through the pain of Atlanta airport, I grabbed a cab to Ansley Golf Club, a lovely, picturesque 9-hole course almost in the heart of the city. After a game and some food, I am given my ticket for The Masters. The Tournament Badge (or Series Badge, Thursday to Sunday) has a face value of $200.

So, this is the hardest ticket in sports? Literally that's certainly true, as the ticket is laminated plastic. Perversely there's a mere safety pin affixed to the back to secure golf's greatest spectator prize. I am transfixed; this is where my journey really starts, and the next few days all hinge on this small and ultimately ephemeral thing in front of me. I feel like I am holding the winning numbers in the lottery, or a golden ticket to Willy Wonka's Chocolate Factory. My whole trip depends on this, and if I lose it a replacement could cost me $5000.

For the next 36 hours, much of my focus is on not losing the ticket, checking my pockets every 15 minutes to ensure it's still there, all of which obsessive compulsive behaviour probably greatly enhances my chances of losing it. By the time I get to my Atlanta hotel I've been awake for around 24 hours. I'm told not to go walkabout in this part of town, but I'm heading for only one place: bed.

The next day it's Wednesday, the day of the Par-3 Contest, played only hours ahead of the main event itself. I'd been to the contest, unique in all of golf, once before, in 2007. There are no tee times, and people start lining the holes long before the one o'clock start. Tiger doesn't usually attend. First staged in 1960 when it was won by Sam Snead, it takes place on a course measuring 1,060 yards and is played over DeSoto Springs Pond and Ike's Pond. Scenically, the course is an oasis of the sort that will lie just beyond the pearly gates. The course record of 20, seven under for the nine holes, is held by the late Art Wall and the late Gay Brewer.

Waking from my slumber, I realise that the past champions will also be stirring after the night before at The Masters Club, more popularly known as The Champions' Dinner. Each Tuesday of Masters week since 1952 – when defending champion Ben Hogan chose to host a meal for fellow champions – the current holder hosts and chooses the menu. Notable dinners include the one held to be the least popular, Sandy Lyle's (which featured haggis); the most unique for all the wrong reasons, Tiger's (cheeseburgers and milkshakes. I'm not sure if there was a drive-thru option); and the one many considered the best, Vijay Singh's Thai option. Just reading his menu makes one salivate.

Seafood Tom Kah
Chicken Panang Curry
Baked Sea Scallops with Garlic Sauce
Rack of Lamb with Yellow Kari Sauce
Baked Fillet Chilean Sea Bass with Three Flavour Sauce
Lychee Sorbet

I was looking forward to a great four days of golf, and although my long journey via continental Europe had been a bit trying, it could have been worse. That morning the *Atlanta Journal-Constitution* newspaper reported that the FBI had charged a passenger on a flight from Honduras to Atlanta with a felony charge of 'interference' for manhandling a flight attendant. Unfortunately the passenger in question, one Joao Correa, had eaten something dodgy before boarding the plane and was facing a very public evacuation of his bowel. He claimed the attendant wouldn't let him use the Business Class toilet during the plane's ascent. He'd faced a nasty choice – a felony or crapping himself in public.

Having never been to Atlanta, I decided to take a look downtown. To the untrained eye the centre doesn't appear to have any particular focal point, but its avenues are leafy, and as almost all the buildings are new, there isn't much of a feel for the Antebellum Deep South. There appeared to be only one sign of the credit crunch – a retail unit was for let, although how it had failed was beyond me, as it clearly catered for a highly specialised clientele: CIGARS – SCREEN PRINTS – ICE CREAM.

I passed the tall, cylindrical Westin Hotel. In March 2008 a tornado swept through the city and the 73-storey hotel lost use of 320 rooms, with windows blown to smithereens. The curved glass had been custom-made, is no longer in production, and 81 rooms remain closed. Rumour has it that the insurance company has been paying the full nightly rack rate on each. The hotel is due a makeover to bring the whole structure in line with new building codes, and all 6,000 windows are to be replaced. Glaziers, get your tenders in now.

After meandering through Centennial Olympic Park, which salutes the city's achievement of hosting the 1996 Olympiad, I reach The World of Coca-Cola. The famous brand has its headquarters in Atlanta, so I felt a visit would be appropriate. As with most US attractions, it's done very well. The guide, perhaps predictably, knew a lot about Coke and its 2,800 other brands. Among the fascinating facts we learn are that Fanta has 200 versions, 80 of which are orange, and the first diet drinks produced by Coca Cola were TAB and Fresca, both notable because, as a young boy growing up in 1970s Scotland, I thought they tasted like old shoes.

In the shop I purchase something I'm not likely to find in Scotland, and perhaps is only available in the South, a Coca Cola toothpick holder. The kind of handy thing a redneck would have next to a bedside photo of his favourite cousin. With my purchase I head off to pick up my hire car, anxious to get across to Augusta and put the 150-mile drive due east behind me.

The laneage to Augusta was excellent. Laneage (*lane-age*) was the newest word in my vocabulary, courtesy of the traffic announcer on 97.1 The River, 'Atlanta's only classic hits station'. The word has yet to reach the *Oxford English Dictionary*, but this can only be a matter of time, because every time I use it people laugh and give me strange looks.

My hotel was just off the Bobby Jones Expressway, and once checked in I focused on tomorrow's golf, facing a conundrum. On TV and on the Masters website the first published tee time is 08:00. But nowhere, not even by googling, can I find the time Arnold Palmer would hit the ceremonial tee shot. Every published time for the gates' opening was also 08:00. It didn't add up that people would just be coming onto the grounds as play began. And what of Palmer, was his drive just for members, guests and invited officials? I booked my slot for the first shuttle in the morning, 07:00. I turned the TV off and hit the pillow.

Drifting off to sleep, I was excited about the days ahead, especially at the thought of seeing Augusta National again. Heightening my anticipation, Tiger had continued his return to form. Overturning a five-shot deficit with some stellar play, in his last outing he had shot a final round 67 to win at Bay Hill. It was his sixth victory at the Orlando club and his first since the US Open at Torrey Pines. Woods was back.

MASTERS THURSDAY: CHAD CAMPBELL IS COLLECTING BIRDIES WHOLESALE

Masters Week had already seen inclement weather, but when I went for breakfast at 06:20 it was balmy enough for a golf shirt and shorts. I was the only passenger on the first shuttle bus, arriving at the course 15 minutes after seven, and was delighted to see crowds already streaming towards the gates.

I recalled 2007, when my heart had quickened as I began to realise that I was on the verge of something I had never fully imagined – I was approaching the grounds of Augusta National, the famed golf course of Bobby Jones and The Masters, something I had watched on TV since I was a boy. Goose pimples formed and the adrenalin started to pump, I got the kind of feeling when you're about to phone a girl, hoping she'll come out with you.

Turning left off Berckmans Road I walked in past the big green gates of Gate 6, up to the turnstiles, and then another 80 yards to the metal detectors.

'Morning, Sir.'

'Good morning, welcome to Augusta National.'

'Welcome to The Masters.'

'Enjoy your day at The Masters, Sir.'

Every guard made eye contact and greeted me. It's a special place. I was back in Shangri-La.

7

The Patron Corridor – which houses the tournament golf shop, exhibit area, merchandise shipping and checking, toilets and the first concession stand – was teeming. By the time I got to the gates of the course, I delightedly found myself only six rows from the front. Barring an unforeseen hitch, I would have a good view of Arnold. I could relax. As I waited at the gate, it was all as I remembered it. Sky-scraping pines, the fresh scent of spring flowers, and the laser-sharp green of the fairways. This was Augusta National.

Belying the advertised opening time, the gates parted at 07:40 and in minutes, briskly walking – no running at Augusta – patrons scurry in all directions, heading to the holes of choice to plant their chairs for the day. Like multicoloured ants, lines of people head from this gate up to the 1st green and onwards down the hill to the likes of the 2nd and 7th greens. Others, on the opposite side of the course, stream in through Gate 10 to make for the picture postcard scenes of the 12th and 16th.

I'm delighted that I have got up and come down early. I'm in the first row of standing patrons at the teeing area and, with three rows of seated patrons in front of me, my view of The King will be unimpeded. The standing patrons are ten-deep for the first 100 yards of the hole, and at 07:50 Arnold Palmer is announced and walks on to the tee to great applause. Smiling, he turns to Augusta National Chairman Billy Payne and says, 'There's one thing wrong this morning, Mr Chairman, I ordered fog,' and everyone laughs, tension lifted before his single shot of the day.

Arnie stands up, has a couple of waggles and smacks a lovely fading tee shot into the bright blue sky, much to the delight of the assembled fans. The Masters is underway, and just like that it's on with business. Without any fanfare, it's down to golf.

'Fore please, Ian Woosnam now driving.'

No mention of his 1991 triumph. Today, on the tee, he's just a slightly podgy Welshman who played a lot of great golf back in the day. Augusta National and The Masters are, paradoxically, all about understatement. One friend of mine, who played representative golf for Scotland and was at Augusta in 2008, was taken aback at the basic, routine nature of the announcer on the first tee. But that's how it is at The Masters. Keep it simple, keep it nice, keep it perfect.

It's already a beautiful Georgia spring day, a cloudless sky, pleasantly warm and everywhere the luscious green of the course, the sparkling sugary-white[1] bunkers. The sky is a piercing pale blue. I've been here just an hour and already it feels like golfing heaven.

The second game out features lone Scot and 1988 Masters Champion, Sandy Lyle. Although now 51, Sandy still possesses serious firepower and I follow him for two holes, firstly to see if he makes the 2nd green in two, and secondly to see one of my favourite parts of the course – the view from the middle of the fairway at the 2nd, down to the green, bringing into view the 7th green, framed by five bunkers. For me it's one of the few sights in golf that can take your breath away.

Sandy's first drive is a quick pull, and he's in the pine straw left. Amazingly, as one of the spectators remarks, Sandy walks up to his ball, has a quick look, then plays a punch-hook that makes the green but runs through the back. He must know the course and his swing like the back of his hand – Lyle takes all the time over the shot that you'd expect from a 12-handicapper trying to sneak in a few holes before his wife discovers he's left the office early.

Watching Sandy and playing partners Billy Mayfair and Tim Clark go about their business at the first green, hardly anyone speaks. Those who do, do so in hushed, almost inaudible tones. Birds chatter in the trees. A private jet tears across the sky, heading for nearby Daniel Field and disturbing our contemplation of golfing serenity. These hushed tones are not the exception, they are the rule. Sandy starts with a double bogey, pumps a big drive 320 yards down two, then hits another quick hook. It could be a long day.

The breathtaking panorama from the crest of the hill at the 2nd typifies so much of Augusta National. You feel as if you are looking down into a vale of golfing perfection, with so much space, greenery

1. The bunkers at Augusta National do not contain sand, but a form of feldspar. See your local library's Geology section for a definition.

and golfing excitement to come. Imagine the scene in some old Western when, after months of struggle, the settlers' wagon train comes to the head of an escarpment, and below lie the pure and rich lands of their future. I have never seen anything quite like it on a golf course.

The terrain feels like some massive golfing homestead. In overall area, the course is more than twice the size of the Old Course at St Andrews. St Andrews is notoriously compact in the layout of its 18 holes, all holes contiguous with another, but imagine if there were only nine holes on that hallowed strip from the Auld Toon to the Eden estuary: that would be a lot of room for each hole, and thus it is at Augusta.

The course and its holes have been so well documented down the years. Thousands of articles, books and television hours have burned it onto the armchair viewers' psyche, but you'll never be prepared for your first view of it in the flesh. Augusta National is unique in other ways that are not immediately visible to the naked eye. Very rarely do consecutive holes have the same par: 9, 10 and 11, and 17 and 18, are the only two stretches where this happens, all par-4s. On every other stretch consecutive pars differ, providing a great test and much variety. Similarly, from exact tee to exact green, no two consecutive holes go in the same direction. It's the ultimate examination.

I walked back to the first tee as Greg Norman, Bernhard Langer and Lee Westwood appeared. You'd think from his reception that Greg was a multiple winner of the green jacket, instead of a guy who three times had one arm in the sleeve of sport's most coveted piece of clothing before Jack Nicklaus, Larry Mize and Nick Faldo ripped it off his back. Norman smashed his tee shot right down the middle, delighting the fans. As he walked from the tee, cheers and shouts rung out. This would happen for the rest of the day, every time I saw Norman. Apart from the top players like Phil and Tiger, the only other players who were consistently encouraged and greeted by the majority of fans were Greg, Fred Couples, Rory McIlroy and Rocco Mediate.

I'm equally mesmerised by Norman's reception and the awfulness of Bernhard Langer's golf shirt. It's black, fawn and red, and looks like something a Formula One driver would wear on his day off. Or the kind of thing a mother would put on her seven-year-old son – in the 1970s. Langer has won The Masters twice, but the encouragement he receives compared to Greg is miniscule. Maybe a better choice of clothing would help.

The starting time of 10:01 is left free, a gap to allow play to get away smoothly, so I head to the golf shop.

On my first trip in 2007 I made a beeline for the shop, but this time I was only buying for friends. Just as well, because my last three visits went $900, $400, $200 spent: very easy to do in an Aladdin's Cave of kit with golf's most famous logo, the yellow badge in the outline of the USA, pin placed at Augusta. Although the logo is instantly recognisable, many accept it without knowing what it represents. One Masters Champion of yesteryear referred to it in his autobiography as the 'funny little badge in the shape of Augusta National'. Oh dear.

Although most people interested in golf recognise it, the same cannot be said for others. A few years ago my dad was accosted by a lady in the local garden centre, asking where she could find a certain plant. The lady took his Masters slipover for the logo of the store. A mildly ridiculous incident, although there's a nice charm in the thought that the former Berckmans' nursery is still showing up in horticultural outlets around the globe.

The shop was mobbed, kit flying off the shelves. Just as well it is restocked on a half-hourly basis. Just about the only thing they didn't appear to have was something I saw in the University of Michigan shop in Ann Arbor – a musical pizza cutter. I'd like to see this added to the merchandise, provided it plays the CBS music used for the broadcasts, or perhaps the dulcet tones of Jimmy Nantz, CBS sportscaster: 'Here we are in the Butler Kitchen for the green pepper ceremony, with my good friends, cheese and tomato'.

The other item they don't and never will sell in the shop is the coveted green jacket, the most prestigious piece of clothing in sport. Although personally I wouldn't normally be seen dead in a $250 sports coat, never mind a bright green one (it's pantone 342 for all you chromophiles out there), I would make an exception for the Hamilton Tailoring Company of Cincinnati's tropical-weight wool jacket, even with its nasty rayon lining.

Leaving the shop and temptation behind, I checked my purchases and went to grab some food, another unique experience at Augusta National. The prices are stuck in the 1950s and it's an open secret that the food is sold at a loss. The Tournament Committee wants everyone to have a great time, nobody is ripped off. You can spend more in a day on food at the other majors than you'll spend all week at The Masters.

Being at Augusta National each year, The Masters is a five-star symposium for all of those involved in the world of golf, and the old oak next to the clubhouse is the meeting place of choice. As I stand under it, a member's guest appears from the lawn enclosure, wearing tatty combat shorts and even tattier sneakers. It was good of him to make the effort, I thought. Quite the dandy. The spectator mix is surprisingly diverse. The mysticism surrounding tickets encourages the expectation that most patrons will be silver-haired, perma-tanned, minty-breathed billionaires wearing cashmere, and Rolex Yachtmasters. While that is true of some, the spectator profile is much more heterogeneous. Some look rich, many look as if they couldn't afford the bus fare to the end of the road.

I watch the world go by and games tee off, content to soak up the sun and listen to the quiet babble of excited patrons. As I contemplate how lucky I am, I spot Bob Rotella making his way down the first hole, off to track Padraig Harrington's progress. I own all his books, CDs and even a putting DVD featuring Brad Faxon (I need to get out more). I notice Dr Bob's wearing a pass that reads, 'JERRY BELLIS', in an effort to stop fans pestering him. Bellis is the President of Titleist Golf Balls. I wonder if Dr Bob would be able to stay in the moment if I went up and said, 'Hey, Jerry, great to meet you finally, we've only ever spoken over the phone or exchanged emails'? Maybe next time. Realising I have now been meandering for the best part of five hours – the beauty of Augusta does that to you – I decide I need to get out onto the course again.

As I watched the field begin this year's Masters, out on the course some were lighting it up. With little or no form to speak of, Chad

Campbell had broken a Masters record and birdied the first five holes. Hunter Mahan had made gains at two of his first six, and Englishman Ross Fisher had birdied four of the first eight. The consequence of a small field – 96 players – is that it's packed with quality. After Norman's game, I watched, in succession, Rose, Stenson, Cabrera; Vijay Singh, Ogilvy, Els; Weir, Harrington, Imada; Mickelson, Villegas and Furyk. No wonder I wasn't in a hurry, as each one sent that pristine white ball into the flawless, sharp blue sky, before returning it to terra firma, the rich, deep green of the first fairway.

Wandering down to Amen Corner, I'm thrilled to see the most famous stretch of golf on the globe. It's a popular place to be, so I take a seat in the Observation Stand. Winston Churchill[1] described Russia as a 'riddle, wrapped in a mystery, inside an enigma': he might as well have been describing the wind down at the lowest part of the course. It's not uncommon to see the flag limp at 11, fluttering at 12, and then five seconds later the opposite is the case. With a green only 10 yards deep in the middle at the 12th, it's your worst golfing nightmare.

Norman, Langer and Westwood come to the tee. Again, Norman's greeted like a champion and I decide to follow the group for a while. At the 15th I notice two gents sitting in chairs, apparently with a theodolite at their disposal, as well as a clipboard containing a set of notes that would put Mission Control during the Apollo 13 crisis to shame. I ask them what they are up to.

'We're just doin' a bit of work for the club,' one replies in the friendly but direct tone of a policeman at work. I get the message. I move along. I follow Norman's game down to the 15th green, walk round the back of the stand to the 16th tee, and find myself with a perfect view straight up the length of the short hole. It's a beautiful sight and one of my favourite holes on the course, as much for its look as its playability.

It's an outstanding golfing arena in a natural amphitheatre, with water, the green and three bunkers flanking the front, left and right, towering trees and a lot of people: beautiful. And what you see is basically what

1. Churchill also described golf as being like chasing a quinine pill round a cow pasture. Eh?

you get. A big green, severely sloped from front to back with a ridge that runs virtually across the middle from right to left. In my dreams I hit a nicely drawn 7-iron that finds the middle of the green and bleeds down into the hole for an ace. In reality, I'm likely to come up off the shot slightly early – looking for the ace – and hit a necky cut into the front right bunker, leaving me with a world of pain. Given it's the third last hole of the tournament, it has to be one of the greatest arenas in sport. A guy comes past, asking if this hole is 6. 6 is a par-3 down the hill at the back of the 16th green. As we know, 16 is one of the most famous short holes in golf. Okay, they are next to each other, but so are Manhattan and New Jersey.

A friend had put me in contact with South African Richard Sterne's caddy, Ritchie Blair, so I head back to the clubhouse to catch his game playing the back nine, hoping to gain some insight into how the players approach golf's most famous holes. And as luck would have it, Chad Campbell is in the game behind.

I cross from 16 to 17, over 7, across 3, 2 and 8, and as I get through the trees and round to the 9th, the Dane Soren Kjeldsen, Sean O'Hair and Sterne are walking down to their drives on the bottom right-hand side of the fairway. There are some marshals trying to identify who's who. These gentlemen are part of the scoring and stats teams, collating shots hit, fairways found.

'Is that O'Hair or Sterne?' one asks the other.

'I'm not sure, not too sure,' comes the assured response.

O'Hair was all over TV a fortnight ago, surrendering a 5-shot lead to Tiger at Bay Hill. There wasn't exactly a dearth of coverage on this. O'Hair is also a blonde, 6ft 2in. In sharp contrast, Richard Sterne was not all over the media recently, has dark hair, is 5ft 7in and is South African. As if this is some sort of comedy routine just for me, they now focus, having left the previous conundrum unsolved, on Soren Kjeldsen.

'How do you pronounce THAT name?'

'It's Kenjerson.'

Nobody's perfect, but that's not even close. I leave Abbott and Costello to it and continue onwards.

The 10th hole blew me away when I first saw it. The hole encapsulates what Augusta is all about – vastness; precision; change; ornamental beauty. Running from virtually the practice putting green, away from the clubhouse, straight down a steep hill with a drop of about 100 feet, banking to the left towards the green, the 10th is massive in every sense. It started life as the 1st hole, a relatively short and easy par-4, the original green nestling in the trough beyond and below the large fairway bunker. However, a combination of early, damp starts and the green's location saw it moved by architect Perry Maxwell up onto the plateau where it currently resides, nestled in a natural amphitheatre of tall, majestic pines. The morning dew also meant the hole became the 10th in 1935, and the new green was first used in the Masters in 1937.

Those who govern Augusta National have always embraced change, but they also understand a good thing when they see it. The relocation of the 10th green renders the fairway bunker useless for the pros, it's too far back from the putting surface, but the ornamental, variegated splash of feldspar is the perfect counterpoint to the massive green fairway. It's one of the most beautiful parts of the course. About 100 yards shy of the bunker the fairway tilts dramatically, a slingshot towards the green.

I followed the three-ball down the 10th, hoping that Ritchie, Sterne's caddy, would be able to enlighten me on some of the playing secrets at Augusta National. Raymond Russell (1996 winner of the European Tour's Cannes Open) had put me in touch, and I'd managed to grab Ritchie before proceedings started. I wondered how he'd come to caddy for the world number 56 who'd finished 25th in his first Masters the previous year. Disillusioned with his job working for a large Japanese electronics firm back home near Glasgow, Ritchie was about to resign but was made redundant instead. This gave him the opportunity to do some looping on the local Scottish circuit, making his way onto the European Tour where, after a few years, he picked up Sterne's bag. From a drab factory in Scotland's industrial heartland to the hallowed fairways of Augusta National: sweet.

Sterne was down the middle at the 10th, having driven with a three-wood, the extra loft allowing a bit more control and the ability to turn the ball right to left down the dogleg, landing at the ideal spot, 250 yards out, giving the desired kick down and round the corner. Par. At the 11th the pin is cut in the very front tongue, only a few yards on the green. It's a very narrow target to be going at with a long iron on this devilish 505-yard hole that will play the hardest all week. Just missing the green right, he faces a very slick pitch, water behind the hole, and although he hits a good chip, Richard makes bogey.

At the next hole, the 12th, the wind is, as ever, a key factor. Gauging what the others did and how the wind affected them, Sterne hits a hard 9-iron, but there's very little room for error and his ball travels further than he anticipated, landing long and left in the flowers and shrubbery behind the green. Fortunately, after a few minutes of searching, O'Hair's caddy finds the ball. Double bogey.

By now Sean O'Hair is 2 under and moving nicely. This is ideal, as I've placed a small wager on him this week at fairly long odds. Although pumped at Bay Hill by Woods, O'Hair's swing is modern, highly repetitive, and he's one of the few under-30s to have multiple wins on the PGA Tour. I believe he's one day destined for a major. As O'Hair and co. make their way to the 13th tee, I watch Campbell play the 12th. He's still at 5-under after his electric start, but he stripes his short iron, emailing his ball straight into Golden Bell's inbox – a matter of feet away, he taps in for birdie and moves to 6-under.

At the 13th Sterne hits a good drive but it's up the right side, not a boomer down and round the corner, so it's a cautious shot or a very risky tonk onto the green. He lays up, hits a good pitch that's pin high but fails to feed down the slope left of the pin, otherwise he'd have been close. He almost holes his 20-footer for birdie but has to settle for par. It's not Richard's best stretch, and the simple equation of missing the green at 11, going long at 12 and failing to birdie 13 means he's played the famous Amen Corner in 3 over. He's now level for the tournament. Poor positioning and hitting the wrong shot at the wrong time kill you at Augusta National.

O'Hair birdies to make up for a blip at 12, and they proceed to the 14th tee behind me and to the right. Again I hang back and watch

Andres Romero, Boo Weekley and Chad. Romero is having, at best, a mixed round. He bogeyed the eagleable 2nd, holed his second for eagle at the 3rd, and bogeyed 6, 7 and 12. He birdies 13, as he did 11. The Argentine's scorecard is like a high school maths exam, while Weekley must be dreaming of huntin', shootin' and fishin': he's plus-2. Campbell birdies the 13th to get to 7-under, and the fans are going wild, getting right behind him, urging him to go really low.

I follow Campbell up the 14th, the straightaway, bunkerless, 440-yard par-4. He hits a lovely drive, a great approach into about eight feet and he strokes it in; 8-under and hotter than a phosphorous grenade. He's now picked up quite a following as news of his peerless golf continues to spread.

At the 15th Sterne's hit a big drive of around 300 yards, leaving around 220 to the middle of a green that is well downhill and very shallow, only 15 paces deep at the left side. Coming in high to the green is always good, the softest possible landing, and initially they discuss a 5-wood, but soon reckon this is too much club. After debating the relative merits of a 3 or 4-iron, Richard hits a 4 onto the green and makes birdie. Back on track. Unfortunately, at the next Richard goes straight at the pin, which is cut front left, and his ball catches the slope and drops into the pond. It was merely a yard or two from being a great shot, but again he pays the ultimate penalty.

At this point it's time for me to stop following this three-ball, as the game behind has history in the making.

Would I have the chance to see history made on my first major day of the year? Campbell had continued his flag-hunting at the long 15th, picking up his ninth bird. After starting with five in a row, he's just had four on the trot. Finishing on his current tally would equal Augusta National's course record, 63. Going one better would give him something nobody had ever achieved in a major: 62.

The hillside left of 16 was packed with anxious fans waiting to see if Campbell could maintain his form. I stood on the walkway left of the pond, between the two sections of seated patrons, making sure I wasn't impeding anyone's view. Although there were thousands surrounding the green, there was absolute quiet. Even the female friend of Andres Romero stopped her incessant Spanish chatter and watched.

Campbell took the tee and flushed a 7-iron, his ball on a frozen rope, right at the stick. I watched the ball shoot from my right to left, tracking its progress against the backdrop of the trees. It landed right over the flag and stopped 12 feet beyond the pin. A treacherously quick putt, but makeable to get to 10-under.

'There's some 70-year-old men going to be pissed off tonight,' says one patron next to me, referring to the low scoring and the Tournament Committee. The crowd is all on its feet, clapping and cheering, acknowledging Campbell's play so far and what may come. Chad leaves the tee, tips his hat and nods, almost embarrassed at the attention. I'd met Campbell two years before at Prestwick, and asking him how his round went, you'd never suspect this modest guy was a world-class golfer. It'd be nice if someone so unassuming could make history.

You could cut the air with a knife, it was thick with expectation.

'Go, Chad, get it to ten, baby,' shouted one beer-fuelled patron.

The crowd willed his birdie putt into the hole, but it wouldn't drop: Chad just missed. There were still two holes to go.

Sadly Chad pulled his next two tee shots and made bogeys on both 17 and 18. The dream of a 62 was over, but he'd played great golf and was in the lead at 7-under. If he could continue that form, he was going to have a good week. As well as money on O'Hair, who finished minus-4, I'd also wagered on Jim Furyk, who stamped his own brand of excellence in round one with a 66, one behind Chad. US young gun Hunter Mahan was also there with a 66. Tiger had eked out a 70, tucked in nicely behind the leaders on the first bend.

Later I get chatting with a few caddies and have the chance to congratulate Craig Connelly, Paul Casey's bagman, on victory last week in the Houston Open, the Englishman's first win on the PGA Tour. Most of the caddie chat is around how easily the course played today, something borne out by the excellent scoring. This is revelatory; Augusta National demands utmost accuracy. It becomes clear that top caddies have a very different perception from the fan, and even from some very good players. They see golf in a totally different light. Some of the pins that look tricky to me are considered rich pickings.

Recently, some tell me, the experience at The Masters has not been a happy one. Although much talk in the press is of the course's length and how it is 'destroying' the tournament, the consensus among the caddies – and presumably the players – was that length wasn't the issue; it was the fiery greens that were problematic. When the greens were hard, any approach not landing within a foot or so of where it needed to be spelled misery for player and caddy. Shots that were just off perfect finished on the wrong tier, on the wrong side of a swale, off the side of the green, in a bunker – it was just *too* penal. And to add insult to injury, this often strained relations between caddy and boss.

As I told one of them, I could in a small way relate to this. When I watched players hit their seconds into the final green, the pin cut on the back tier, in 2007 practice rounds, I could hardly believe what I saw. Of the dozen or so balls that landed on the upper step, all pitched, skidded and ran well beyond the pin, usually off the back of the green. Anything that landed on the bottom of the green or on the upslope was in the lap of the Gods: some skipping up, others checking and staying on the bottom level. To me, sitting and watching this, the test at this one hole alone appeared too severe, especially when most were coming in with long to medium irons.

Leaving the guys to finish up for the night, I decide to head home, hoping to beat the Tiger Rush. As I cut up a walkway parallel to Patron Corridor, Condoleezza Rice passes, saying hello in the process. I'm flabbergasted. As the US Secretary of State she used to be the most powerful woman on earth, and she's surrounded by a handful of associates whom I presume to be a mix of close protectors, friends and colleagues. She looks like a very nice lady, and you wouldn't peg her as someone to sanction hours of torture, although I could imagine her sternly telling me to tidy up my bedroom.

It's just before seven o'clock, I've been at Augusta almost 12 hours, and I haven't even had a single beer. I collect my purchases from the merchandise-checking area and head for the shuttle. Between the receptive greens, the great weather and lots of fine play, especially Chad Campbell's brush with major destiny, it's been a great day of golfage.

MASTERS FRIDAY: EVERYBODY LOVES ROCCO

Getting back to my hotel on Thursday was a total bind. My focus on getting down to see Arnold Palmer in the morning had meant I hopped off the bus without taking note of when the uplifts were.

To exacerbate my angst, I didn't have a phone. After I had hung around for the best part of an hour, a kind gent lent me his. The shuttle driver told me he was on his way back through the diabolical traffic, so Ray and I got chatting. He'd been coming to The Masters for a decade, always buying tickets in the open market from the same supplier. This year he'd paid $450 per day (later in the week I'd meet others who paid $1,000). Not cheap, but not a king's ransom for anyone looking for a once in a lifetime trip.

Ticket prices had definitely been credit-crunched. Ray said 2002 was the height of Tiger Fever, when four-day badges were being traded for around $5000. In 2008, while shadowing Tiger for his entertaining book, *Follow the Roar*, Bob Smiley pitched up at Augusta without tickets and paid a total of $4,100 to get in Tuesday to Sunday. Out of interest I'd taken a look at prices on the web a couple of weeks prior to the tournament. I found some tickets at $1,300 plus tax for four days, and some at $5,000 plus tax. Ray and I agreed the latter were hoping to snare the unsuspecting.

Many packages advertised come with accommodation, transfers, some golf and The Masters bundled up, taking the pain out of travel. Many include hospitality, food, drink and flat screen TVs at houses nearby. I am told that some of these houses are actually bought just for the week of the event.[1] In these pavilions – as the houses are grandiosely called – food

1. At the time of writing, there is a three bedroom, two bathroom, four car garage house for sale at $499,000. It's one block from Augusta National and the whole advert by the vendor is focused on The Masters and the house's potential for hospitality (the garage has an upstairs section for entertaining).

and beer flows freely. I put a call in to one company, explained what I was doing and asked if I could come along for a look. I don't think they quite got it... it'd be $250. I asked if I could pay for half a day. Brian said he'd call me back. I never heard from him again.

I'm sure these packages are great for corporate and frequent visitors, but in the two visits I have made to Augusta, I've spent all my time at the course. And the food at The Masters is ridiculously cheap. Some companies will try to take advantage of you. One golf travel company was charging customers $65 per day for a Masters chair, and it wasn't clear to me if it was theirs to keep after the event. In the shop they are $29 plus tax.

In terms of accommodation, don't be afraid to slum it. Ritchie, Sterne's caddy, was staying in a house at $1,000 for the week. Sleeping on the couch were two Italians, there with Ritchie's housemate and fellow caddy. No big deal usually, but one was Daniele Massaro. Part of the 1982 Italian World Cup winning squad, he also scored two goals for AC Milan against FC Barcelona in the 1994 Champions League Final. Sadly, along with Roberto Baggio and Franco Baresi, Daniele missed a penalty in the 1994 World Cup final, gifting the World Cup to a Brazil team led by Romario. I'm guessing that his nights on Ritchie's couch at $750 for the week were not his first or last sleepless ones. If he can slum it, so can you, especially when, as everyone floods to Augusta for the week, the local economy has a captive market and hotel room prices go up by a multiple of five.

On Friday morning I arrived 30 minutes before play, so headed round to the practice area. En route I passed a van delivering flowers to the clubhouse. The company name, Floral & Hardy, gave me a chuckle, although I'd have much preferred if they'd been called Stamen Corner. The seats at the range were wet with dew, so I didn't stay long and wandered back to the first tee. Wandering at Augusta National is one of the perks of attendance. Meandering and walking mindlessly are also fun, it's just so beautiful.

I watch as Badds, Bubba Watson and Graeme McDowell tee off. I decide to walk up the 1st with the next game, watching Mark O'Meara,

D.J. Trahan and Pat Perez, golf's current answer to an improvised explosive device. Perez won the Bob Hope earlier in the season and has a lot of heart, but he gets so annoyed he makes Colin Montgomerie look like Mother Theresa. He told *Golf Magazine* the PGA Tour suggested he attend anger management therapy; surely enough to piss anyone off. Annoyingly Pat pars the 1st and doesn't helicopter any clubs into the trees, snap his putter over his knee or strangle any junior patrons.

Watching D.J. hit his approach off a beastly 320-yard drive, the guy next to me provides encouragement. Jim, along with his buddy, Allen, from Clemson, South Carolina is, like Trahan, a Clemson alumnus. He doesn't know D.J., but his son does, and it turns out that this is Jim's 47th straight Masters. He barely looks old enough to *be* 47, never mind a patron of such long standing. His first tournament was in 1962, Arnold Palmer's third green jacket. Just a boy then, Jim was watching Palmer play one of the short holes, and as he saw Arnie discard his cigarette butt, asked a marshal to pick it up and give it to him.

A few years ago, Jim ran into Arnold up at the clubhouse and told him the story, and how he still had the cigarette butt.

'Really? What was I smoking?' teased Arnie.

'L&Ms.'

'You got it,' replied the great man.

D.J. secured par and went on his way. In a recent edition of the TV magazine show, *Inside the PGA Tour*, Trahan stated a wish to win majors. Compared with some US players' unwillingness to compete in all the majors available to them, I like his style. And he's obviously not daft. He described the putting test at the Bob Hope as a challenge 'in and of itself'. I love that the 15th club in D.J.'s bag is a book of idioms.

Walking down the left side of the 2nd, I run into O'Meara's coach, Bruce Davidson, formerly of Kings Links in Aberdeen. I last saw him in a bar in Machrihanish on Scotland's west coast about ten years ago; he had a Scottish accent then. He's surprised to learn I've twice heard him mentioned on TV as O'Meara's new coach. I tell him the last time was just over a week ago, when Keith Fergus holed his second shot on the penultimate hole of the Champions Tour Cap Cana event to beat O'Meara and Andy Bean by a shot. I commiserate with him on the narrow miss: and he tells me he also coaches Keith Fergus. Nice work.

Bruce continues to follow O'Meara, but I stay and watch Freddie Couples, Rocco Mediate and amateur Jack Newman. The 2nd green is a mini-amphitheatre, the bank behind the green allowing all patrons a clear view of the green and the wide, lush fairway beyond. Rocco's birdie putt drops, and he shrugs and shudders his shoulders, looking skywards to indicate his good fortune. In a world of mainly anodyne, faceless pros, this amounts to extreme histrionics in modern golf. That's why we love Rocco, the golfing everyman.

I follow the game up the 3rd, one of my favourites. The hole remains virtually as it was when the course was first built, and at a mere 350 yards, it's arguably the most old fashioned, and it's the shortest par-4 on the course by 90 yards (both the 14th and 17th measure 440 yards). From the tee one can see the crest of the fairway and the complex of bunkers to the left of the landing area – four bunkers flank the left side and run for around 30 yards. The fairway is narrow by Augusta standards at this point, and trees and rough hog the right side. To take the bunkers out of play it's a 233-yard lay-up or a 280-yard carry up the hill. Then the problems can begin.

This green is an isosceles; the narrow end to the left is 11 yards deep, it's 19 in the middle and 29 yards on the right side. The pin placement dictates how to approach, and demands accuracy. Anything long or big presents a very tough up-and-down for the pro, never mind the Average Joe. Unless the ball is directly below the cup on any given day, there's probably not an easy straight putt on this entire green. Over the bunkers and down to the left the fairway falls away sharply, so any chip from there is both blind and challenging, up a steep bank. It's a superb hole that shows that length doesn't have to be a factor. On meeting Bobby Jones during his early Masters years, Gary Player remarked that he found this hole, despite its length and apparent innocuousness, very difficult to birdie. Mr Jones replied that was because the hole wasn't meant to be birdied. Simple. This comment alone sums up the strategy put into Augusta National's design.

Rocco handles the 3rd well, almost chipping in for a birdie, and it's pars all round at 4. Standing at the 5th tee, I'm next to a mixed group. One of the guys says, 'Wouldn't it be great if I took a temple shot? The ball hit my temple and I got the ball from Freddie?'

He tries again, 'Hey, guys, wouldn't that be great?' I detect zero irony in his voice, and he's not getting any response from his friends.

We're 150 yards from the tee. The Temple Shot would take less than two seconds from club-head to skull, travelling at 170 miles per hour. It's likely at that speed, and assuming a small brain within his cranium, to do a lot of damage. Unable to get the image of the exploding cantaloupe from *Day of the Jackal* out my head, I silently agree it would be good if he took a temple shot, and his friends could get Freddie's ball and mount it on his casket.

I wait at the 6th tee, and watch Sterne, O'Hair and Kenjerson come through. Next up it's Chad Campbell, and again his golf game is leaving scorch marks on the turf. Shaking off his two bogeys of last evening, he's birdied 2 and 4 and is back at 9-under. I watch as he strikes a nice iron, but Chad merely finds the green, the first tee shot I've seen him hit at a par-3 that's not all over the target like a smart bomb. I leave the excitement, drawn to the beauty of the 16th hole. I walk down the hill, and as play here is an hour away, it's a spot of tranquillity and cleansing calm.

Sitting in the front row at 16, in a prime spot, right behind the teeing area, a gentleman reads *USA Today*. I love that he's immersed in the news, as if not ringside at one of golf's greatest holes. He's clearly been down early to grab the spot, and I end up chatting to Roy, and his two sons, Matthew and Graham, three Englishmen by way of Sydney, Australia. They'd been down at Gate 10 at 07:20 to grab a small piece of prime real estate for the day.

The day before at Gate 10 had been a bit of a scrum, so on Friday morning, a marshal gave the amassed fans a pep talk. There would be no running, no jostling, everyone was going to get the chance to walk to their desired spot. It had been recognised that on Thursday the opening of gates had been asynchronous, and some people had been able to get down from the 1st, moving across the course at speed. This would not happen on Friday. On Thursday night a 16-year-old runner had been timed sprinting from the gates at the 1st, down across the course to the 16th. The young, fit and healthy speed merchant without a chair could not beat an orderly walker who started at the same time from Gate 10. Welcome to The Masters.

Leaving the guys to wait for play to come through 16, I walk up to the 7th and stay there a while, as it's yet another great location to watch the golf. It's a narrow, arrow-straight par-4 of 450 yards, and the drive and second shot afford no room for error. It's a stern test, and standing behind the green is a superb spot. The hole's straightness allows a view all the way back to the tee, clear shots of the incoming seconds, and if that isn't enough, to the right and looking further right, there's the 3rd tee, 2nd green and 8th tee. Plenty of variety, but there's never any danger of boredom.

It's a lovely day still, but the wind is freshening, out of the players' right and slightly into their faces. At least some will have the chance to hold their second shots up into the wind, giving a better chance of finding a green that's only 14 yards deep at the right and 16 on the left. As I arrive, Yong-eun Yang, Robert Allenby and Hunter Mahan, the tenth game of the day, are playing up. The pin's cut front right, a tricky place to get to, especially if you miss the green, which is better protected than a Barack Obama motorcade.

Mahan had started today with yesterday's great form, birdying number 1. But then his game had imploded, and although he parred 7 as I watched, he'd taken six at 2 and 3. Still, this was better than O'Hair, and my bookmaker was laughing. Suggesting he was born of the cloven hoof, O'Hair notched three sixes on the front nine. My £300 payday was now a long way off.

Every game that comes through, oozing quality, has something to get excited about, even though there are not many birdies in store: in quick succession I see Zach Johnson and Robert Karlsson; Olazabal, Martin Kaymer and Brandt Snedeker; Choi, Alvaro Quiros and Kenny Perry; Trevor Immelman, Adam Scott and US Amateur champ, Danny Lee. As

25

I watch all these great players pass, there's a continual stream of patrons heading down to Amen Corner and the 15th and 16th, play there now getting underway. There also a lot of chatter behind the 7th, most people stopping, realising it's a great spot and staying for a number of games.

One gent and his wife tell me that they've been coming to The Masters for years, and the best part of a decade as patrons. He'd been on the practice-round lottery list for years, and back in 1999, out of the blue, received a letter asking if he'd like to be considered for full patron status. Excited, he wrote back confirming that of course he would. Then he waited. Three months later, without further communication, an application arrived for the tournament days' tickets, and he's been coming ever since.

Just as he finishes his tale, Tiger Woods, Jeev Milkha Singh and Stewart Cink are playing the hole, and most people are focused on Tiger, his first major back since knee rehab. Needless to say, a seething mass of humanity is following Woods, and the crowds lining the fairway are much bigger than before. Woods has birdied 6 to get to minus-3, but is now 7 back; Chad has birdied 8 and 10 to get to 11 under par.

Tiger has hit a horror story of a drive, tugging it way left into the trees. Our eyes follow him as he ducks into the trees and reappears, gauging the challenge ahead, talking with caddy Steve Williams. He settles in behind his shot, out of full view, and his ball when it appears is a surface-to-air missile, a rapid, darting movement; first low and hooking, then climbing as some of the hook spin decreases. It's a bit of Tiger magic, the most dramatic ball movement I've seen in two days. The ball lands at the front of the left bunker, hops over it and runs up to the back of the green. The crowd go wild, acclaiming an exhibition shot for our consumption only. Never say die, just one of Woods' many mottos.

Annoyingly for Tiger he has a tortuous third, as his ball has rolled onto the back fringe, just left of the back right bunker which now impedes his line for any putt or running pitch. Now he must chip his ball down to the tight right pin. If you put 25 6-handicappers in this position, I doubt two of them would keep it on the putting surface. For 99.8% of all golfers in the world, Tiger hits a good chip, but for him and the rest of the field it's relatively poor. He's 12 feet away and misses the putt. Bogey, and a bit unlucky, but he was way off piste from the tee and that's going to wear you down at Augusta National.

The next game along is the three young guns, and I hook onto their game for a spell. I follow Ishikawa, Kim and McIlroy up the 8th and back down the 9th. While it's almost impossible for a first-timer at The Masters to do well (although Fuzzy Zoeller won on his first outing), I'd also put some money on the young Irishman. I thought he could be young enough to do something spectacular before he'd even realised what was going on. Smiling, chatting and laughing, they look like juniors in a bounce game at Average Hills Country Club. The ambient noise is nothing more than a susurration, so that even for a spectator, it's almost possible to forget there's a major golf championship being played. The three juniors birdie 8 off three very different drives – trees left for Ryo, mid-fairway for Rory, and right-hand bunker for Anthony Kim. Down 9, Kim hits a massive pull off the tee and finishes on the 1st fairway. He's so far left he actually has a line in to the green, as the hole curves like a banana from right to left.

McIlroy is on the correct fairway, and although I am about 30 yards behind him when he plays, I can tell from the rasp of ball on club-head as it fizzes towards the pin that he's hit a good shot. It appears he's about six feet from the stick. Just then the ever-freshening wind shows its teeth, and the guy in front of me has his hat blown off. Those out in the afternoon are going to have a challenge on their hands. As McIlroy fails to score a consecutive birdie, but turns in minus 2, I decide to grab some food before heading out of the gates to Washington Road. I'd heard John Daly was selling merchandise from his RV.

En route to the concession stand, I spot Irishman Graeme McDowell leaving the final green, and I note he's 2 under par for 36 holes, so is likely to be on BBC TV. I hang around behind him as he's interviewed, not sure if I am in shot. Then, heading up round the side of the media positions, I physically bump into a green jacket, a member of the club. I excuse myself and instinctively check his name badge: Lou Gerstner (former head of IBM). I think no more of it, but assume he and Bill Gates do not have a regular four-ball.

Yards from Gate 6, I come to the junction with Washington Road. Along to my right are the famous Augusta National gatehouse and the fabled Magnolia Drive. The sidewalk is awash with street vendors and proselytizers, a curious mix of people handing out free golf magazines, selling water or preaching the word of God (the real God, not Tiger Woods). Almost immediately I spot an RV with an orange sign in the front window, JOHN DALY MERCHANDISE FOR SALE.

I ask if Big John is around, and at that moment he appears. I tell him I'm over from Scotland and shake his hand. I had hoped that he was for chatting, but the look on his face is one of steely indifference: he's not up for playful badinage. I buy a large coaster for $10, which he signs; if my beer doesn't taste good off a John Daly coaster, it never will. I noticed that John was looking a lot slimmer, and shamefully I assume this is down to boozing. It's only later that I learn he's had a gastric band fitted. It'd be good to see Big John back in form someday soon. I wish him the best and shoot back to the course.[1]

It's approaching four o'clock, and I head back for just an hour, keen to avoid being stranded again. Standing at the 10th, I take in some class players passing through. Norman et al are heading up on to the tee from the 9th green while Kenny Perry almost holes his second shot at the last, his ball coming to rest 18 inches beyond the hole. He receives a rousing reception as he walks on to the green. He's 8-under, 4-under today, and, after some dropped shots from Campbell, has this putt to tie the lead at 9-under. There's a lot of movement at the 10th and up at the clubhouse, all oblivious to what's happening below. Perry rolls in his putt for a 67 to tumultuous applause from the gallery.

I turn my attention back to the Norman 3-ball, and I'm only 12 feet away from the players as they play. As Westwood, the last of the three

1. I'd encountered Daly previously, not that he would recall. I was caddying for my brother in the 2003 Scottish Open, when there was a significant rain delay and I was trying to dry the clubs in the locker room. John appeared, damp and disconsolate, and lit a cigarette. I looked him in the eye and then glanced to his left shoulder. Giving me a curious look, he turned and saw the NO SMOKING sign. He reached over, tore it off the wall, crumpled it up and threw it away. You can do that when you're a maverick who's won two majors. I laughed.

to drive, addresses his ball, Bernhard Langer, his caddy (son Stefan) and Norman's caddy (son Gregory) are fishing into a cooler for water. Lee shoots them a look, but they are totally oblivious. He squeezes the trigger anyway, pulling his ball so far left over the boughs of the trees that it has to be in the boonies. He picks up his tee and starts walking down the hole. He appears in no way annoyed, but I'm sure if I'd been moving like that in the crowd I'd have been told to settle down.

In quick succession it's quality central – Justin Rose, Henrik Stenson and Angel Cabrera – each of whom only hit a 3-wood from the tee, supporting the caddies' thesis regarding length. Next up it's a game that features seven major victories between them – Geoff Ogilvy, Vijay Singh and Ernie Els. A glance at the board shows me that Singh is doing quite nicely at 4 under par, and only then do I notice that Cabrera is 6-under. The leader board is shaping up nicely, like Masters Tournaments of old.

Just before that, a frisson of excitement had fluttered through the crowd at the last green. Tiger was on his way. The Great One had jumped all over his tee-shot, crushing it 340 yards straight up the final fairway, and up a hill that makes the drive feel more like 370 yards: immense. Perhaps betraying his long recuperation, Woods then pushes a wedge into the greenside bunker, leaving a very nasty explosion to the pin, which is cut tight right.

Dressed in black shoes, hat and trousers, his blue shirt, flapping in the wind, delineates the torso and upper arms of Evander Holyfield. Tiger's used his time away to work on every facet of his body and game that his knee condition would allow. As he walks onto the green and looks right, to the trap, exasperation is splashed across his face. Playing partner, Stewart Cink, likewise adorned with the magical swoosh of Beaverton, Oregon, is also in the bunker, and plays right, trying to bring the ball back down the step, towards the hole. Instead it stays on the upper tier, his worst nightmare.

The crowd is reverentially silent as Tiger walks into the bunker, eyeing up a similar challenge. He, too, plays at a 45-degree angle from the pin. He's hit it slightly long, so although the ball feeds down the slope, he's about six feet beyond the hole. The gallery claps and acknowledges a good shot, and Tiger thanks them, hand up, countenance unchanged, steely eyes still focused on what he hopes is his last blow of the day.

Woods gives the putt his utmost attention, and when he strokes it, it looks perfect, tracking towards the left edge, moving right. His ball takes the hole and the crowd gasp and exclaim as it dives down, round and back out, missing right. Tiger can't believe it, taps his ball in and walks up the middle of the green towards the back. He keeps his head down and does not look up, does not even recognise the crowd. It's fair enough to say he's a tad miffed. Shortly after, Tiger appears behind the 18th accompanied by about nine close protectors – two Richmond County Sheriffs, two personal bodyguards and five Securitas guards. This doesn't strike me as a nice way to exist, but 14 majors might just be worth it. He's finished on 2-under, 7 behind.

Next, back at the 10th, it's the best drive I think I've seen, further de-bunking the length myth. Despite standing only 5ft 8in, and outside the top 150 long drivers on tour, Ryuji Imada only hits a three-wood, but with his textbook swing he toes the club head in a bit and fizzes a bullet, straight down the middle with a slight draw. Playing with Imada, Mike Weir hits a lovely, penetrating driver, fading down the hill.[1] The last shot of the day I see is a popped drive from the current Open and PGA Champion, Padraig Harrington. He's been struggling of late, and his near-skied shot would put a few five-handicappers to shame, although an enthusiastic Irishman behind me cheers words of encouragement.

Leaving the grounds, I pick up my mobile phone and coaster at the check stand. I turn my phone on and walk across the parking lot, feeling a repeated buzzing in my pocket, and I don't have to check the messages to work out what's going on. It's ten o'clock at night in Scotland, and the BBC's Masters coverage will be in full swing. About 15 different people have seen me meandering behind Graeme McDowell during his interview – wouldn't it have been great if I'd taken a Temple Shot on national television.

1. Worth noting that although he's an inch taller and about fifty places ahead of Imada in driving distance, Weir hit driver. The simplistic idea that a lengthened Augusta National needs full power all the time just doesn't hold true.

MASTERS SATURDAY: THE TRIUMPHING OF THE WICKED IS SHORT

Saturday began bizarrely, when I woke up in my hotel room at 02:30, wondering why all the lights were on. I'd often been in this position early on a Saturday morning, usually because I've come in after a hard night and collapsed straight into my bed. It took me a few seconds to recall that when I returned to the hotel around ten o'clock after going out for pizza, a tornado struck and there was a total power failure. I'd just climbed into bed and gone to sleep.

Later, when I actually got out my bed for the day's golf, there were no signs of destruction in the area near the hotel, although the local newspaper, the *Augusta Chronicle*, did mention it as one of the areas hit. A total of 11,000 homes – and a few hotel rooms – were without power in Richmond and the adjacent county, Aiken. Sadly, a couple of people were reported dead, and damage in Augusta alone would be around one million dollars' worth. Given that multiple tornadoes had swept across Tennessee and Alabama, it was going to be quite an insurance bill. Naturally, my main concern was the future of the golf.

When I got back to the hotel on the Friday night I had decided to tuck in to the free beer, a treat for this one week of the year. I like Heineken, and it always tastes better when it's given away: it's one of the Universal Laws of Beer Drinking. I got chatting to a fellow patron, an Irishman from Dublin called Graham. I was telling him of my TV appearance and he laughed and said, 'Join the club. I was on TV yesterday, behind Ian Poulter, waving into the camera and a whole load of mates said they saw me. I had a 100 Euro bet at work that I'd be on TV, and they all said I had no chance. Who's laughing now?'[1]

Graham went off to his room to catch up with his brother and I enjoyed another tasty beverage. Another shuttle appeared and four guys came in for a cold one. I recognised them from breakfast and we fell into

1. Sure enough, when I returned from my trip I made a point of watching the recorded coverage and there was Graham on Poulter's shoulder, 100 Euros to the good.

easy conversation. Although the people of Augusta may not all enjoy the golf and the week, for the visitor there is no shortage of fellow enthusiasts to talk to. Conversation and camaraderie come readily.

John and Steven were from Minnesota, Bill from Atlanta and Steven's dad, Greg, was based in Wisconsin. We shot the breeze, enthusing about The Masters set-up and the idyllic nature of Augusta National. As a rule I didn't automatically tell people that I was doing a book on the year's majors, but when it became clear that I was on my own, I felt I had to justify my solitary existence. I explained the trips ahead of me, and like most golfers who enjoy the idea of a good-looking adventure, they settled into the idea of the book and what I was trying to achieve. In the long term it was some kind of golfing travelogue, and in the short term it was another free beer.

With the PGA Championship being held in Chaska, Minnesota, I wasn't going to be too far from John and Steven in August. Steven said, 'I live only a five-minute walk from Hazeltine, literally a five-minute walk. Come and stay with me. My house is fairly big and it's just me, my wife and my daughters. I'm sure they'd be excited about having a writer as a guest.' I was amazed. And I'd never been called a writer before (or since). Nobody in America lives five minutes from anywhere, never mind a five-minute walk. Flabbergasted at Steven's generosity, I said that I was sure that I could take him up on his offer and we'd exchange emails. In another great gesture, the guys then asked me to join them in town for a pizza, and off we went, getting back in time for the blackout. Free beer – what a great way to meet people.

With the cut made, the 2009 Masters Tournament was taking shape. After getting back to the hotel, I'd kept one eye on the TV as I supped my beers. Perry and Campbell remained in the lead. After seeing Cabrera at the 10th, he covered the back side in 1 under to be three shots back. Unlikely candidate Todd Hamilton joined him, and within four of them were the likes of Kim (who'd shot 75 and 65), Tim Clark, Sabbatini, Furyk – at least that bet was still looking promising – Garcia, Stricker, Mahan and Phil Mickelson. McIlroy had taken a 7 at the 18th and was almost disqualified for brushing the sand at the last with his feet. My bet on him was looking none too clever, either.

Some big guns had missed the cut. An out-of-sorts Ernie Els was one shot too many, as were Goosen and two-time champ, a favourite of mine, José Maria Olazábal. Greg Norman's challenge had withered on the vine after a second-round shocker, 77. Langer had slumped to a Friday snowman (80) and was no doubt on his way home to firebomb his wardrobe. And Gary Player had finished his final and 52nd Masters with a classy 83. He should have stopped playing at Augusta National years ago, but just had to beat Arnold Palmer's record for the most appearances.

On the shuttle bus for the last two mornings, the drivers had been telling me how they were all involved in education, two being teachers, the other a college professor. Each year they drove a shuttle for the Masters, as the schools were shut for the week. Kevin, the driver on Saturday, told me he was a science teacher at an Augusta school, and that he enjoyed his job and its challenges. He and other teachers had been brought in because the school had been failing and needed to be reenergised and refocused under the No Child Left Behind legislation passed in 2001. Although it's just a week, The Masters has a massive impact on the area's economy. According to the Augusta Convention and Visitors Bureau, in 1997 the tournament pumped $109 million into the local community.

When we pull into the retail parking lot at the corner of Berckmans and Washington, I notice that the free parking is almost totally full. The day's golf is due to start in 30 minutes, Ryuji Imada and Stuart Appleby at the head of play. Alighting from the van, I spot Ray, the Good Samaritan who lent me his mobile phone on Thursday. He's been down since 07:00, was through the gates just after 08:00 and placed his chair in a spot just to the left of the pin on the 18th. We exchange a few thoughts on getting down early the next day, and I decide that doing the whole chair thing has to be part of the Masters experience and there's no better day than Sunday. We shake hands and I say that I might see him down at the course tomorrow. We also swap email addresses in the hope of hooking up at the US Open.

By the time I get to the turnstiles and scanners, the air is serene and a little bit cooler after the previous night's storms, but there is no sign of damage in and around the club. Although the carnage wrought by the storms is unfortunate, the forecast rain came later than envisaged, having been expected late in the afternoon on Friday, and now we seem set for another clear, bright, sunny and warm day at The Masters.

Once through security I head straight down to the shop for a chair. I shell out my $29 plus tax, but rather than use it today, I immediately check it in for uplift later. Unless I sleep in and/or get very drunk, I am committed to an early start on Sunday morning.

The Masters chair is one of the badges of honour from the tournament. You see them everywhere, at the airport and even at other tournaments, a subtle nod to past events. Like many owners I'll stick my business card in the back of mine, while others write just a single name or nickname on the back. Etiquette means this alone will ensure no one sits on your seat when you're away. Some chairs have the business cards of travel companies inserted in the plastic pouch, many chairs all in a neat row, suggesting that something may be rotten in Denmark . . . local youngsters can be paid to run chairs into the grounds in the early morning, allowing the patron a long lie. It was even suggested to me that by finding the right tournament volunteer, a chair can be on the grounds really, really early for the correct price. The word on the fairways this year was that nobody gets preferential treatment when putting a chair out, not even members, and any left overnight will be shipped home, provided name and address are on the rear.

Between the checking area and the course, I stop to go to the WC. I can't think of any sporting event where this would be of note, but about a dozen different people had suggested I pay a visit to see how it's all done in inimitable Masters style. WC staff usher patrons to use urinals available, and those who need a more substantial evacuation are met upon exiting their stall by an employee who sprays some fresh scent into the air, saving the next desperate patron from noxious odours.

It all ran like clockwork, although I was a tad uneasy at so many non-users hanging around. For me the best thing about the experience was simply the name on the badge of the bespectacled youth who welcomed us in at the door – Robert Hancock. I wondered about the name of the attendant in the ladies?

Walking back onto the course, I notice a slightly crunchy sound and mild tingling sensation underfoot. The undulations of the ground, having taken a bit of a battering from last night's rain, have been covered with a gritty substance that's the same colour as the fairways.

Standing up at the first tee, deep with patrons watching the initial games play away, looking down to the landing area there are just four main colours one can see, as if in some painted golfing paradise regained – the sky is a light, bright blue and cloudless; the shades of the trees' foliage and bark, along with pine straw, make for a darker greeny-brown; below that is the rich green perfection of the fairway, and the final colour on the palate is the platinum blonde splash that is the fairway bunker up on the right. It's a beautiful day and a joy just to stand and watch the snow-white golf balls soar into that bright cerulean ocean of sky.

In the third game out, Rory McIlroy is supported with continual encouragement. I ask one of his acolytes, a man old enough to be McIlroy's grandfather, what's the attraction. He's young, flamboyant and made the cover of *Sports Illustrated's* Masters Preview edition (with a reputed readership of 23 million each week, *S.I.* holds much sway in the hearts and minds of the US sports' fan). Rory makes an easy par and, as I've now been on my feet for two days and not done much sitting, I take a seat in the stand behind the green.

The guy in front of me alternates between the golf and his Sudoku puzzle. In the already baking heat, sun beating down, I'm sorely tempted to close my eyes and lie back, but that would be worse than Japanese number games, so I snap out of my fugue and watch the golf. Most players coming up the 1st will be facing shots between 190 and 130 yards, so anything from a strong wedge to a 6-iron is likely to be the stick, depending on the player.

Luke Donald, playing with Ben Curtis, misses the green way left, then plays a beautiful soft lob with a spot of check that comes to rest four feet away. It's greeted with appreciation from the gallery, especially those who've been *in situ* for a while, watching the challenges on the innocuous but subtly tricky pin placement back and middle right. This subtlety is not lost on the guy in front of me who's looked up from his puzzle to suggest Donald will miss. He does. Luke can't quite believe it didn't break in as he expected. At 9 shots back, he needs to be making more of those.

As Dudley Hart and Paul Casey march on to the green, two large strapping manly types make directly for two seats left of the people beside me. They are a somewhat focused in their mission and attract a bit of attention.

'Sorry folks, we're Army guys. Hi, I'm General Jeffrey Foley,'[1] and he shakes the hands of the elderly couple beside him. He looks far too young to be a general. While they all quietly chat away, I notice that now Sean O'Hair and Andres Romero are hitting in. Romero comes up short, and a few minutes later lags his approach to almost the same spot as Donald.

'Now he's screwed,' intones the guy in front of me. Unlike Donald, Romero holes and it would appear that my fellow spectator's sage-like spell may be broken. Still, I'm quite enjoying his brand of cynicism.

Sartorial elegance is next up; pink Bubba Watson and all-black Ian Poulter. Poulter chips up within a few feet, encouraging the resident cynic to chime, 'I've got news for you, he's not in yet'. Poulter holes, and the cynic's stock is suddenly dropping quicker than shares in Fannie Mae (which, incidentally, would be a great name for the ladies' toilet attendant). Next Camilo Villegas and Larry Mize appear, heading to the green after their approach shots.

---

1. It transpires that Brigadier General Jeffrey Foley is the commanding officer of nearby Fort Gordon. Each year The Masters gives hundreds of tickets to the local military. A nice touch, especially in times of war.

By coincidence the gentleman next to me was ex-Navy. We discussed if Foley looked old enough to be a general. The gentleman, Bob, said, 'Hell, I'm a retired US Navy Commander, but I didn't want to say that, I'd have to have gotten up and saluted.'

'Is that Camilo? I'm pretty sure it is. Pretty sure,' says a guy to my front left. Camilo's the most ripped man on tour, has longish dirty blonde hair, and, these days, Larry Mize is looking more like Leslie Nielsen. I'm starting to believe some of the crowd would have trouble distinguishing Vijay Singh from Steve Stricker. Augusta National is the most beautiful of places, but the experience must be undermined if you walk around in a state of perpetual confusion.

After enjoying sitting down for a while, I have to head down to the 13th, where I'm due to meet up with an old boss. One great thing about having been to The Masters, is when I hear of others going, I get really excited for them, knowing that whatever their most extravagant expectations, they have no idea what will greet them. Derek had given me a call to get the lowdown, and when we meet at the concession stand between 13 and 16 he said I was right, it was better than he could ever have imagined. It's like trying to explain the Grand Canyon to someone – 277 miles long, up to 18 miles wide, one mile deep. The figures cannot and will not do it justice, you need to be there.

We sat in the stand looking across the 13th green, a vast expanse of lush green grass with the azaleas in many shades of pink and dark red forming a beautiful backdrop. The sun was beating down and there was an air of quiet and relaxed calm down in Amen Corner. Derek told me he'd been here the day before when McIlroy carded eagle and Kim made bird. After chatting for 20 minutes, I was heading off to meet a couple of friendly marshals to see if I could understand what they did and how they got their positions (I'd heard there was a waiting list of six years, and it's rumoured one guy on it even had his own private jet), so I wished Derek the best for the rest of his trip.

Diligent nepotism was how one of the marshals described the volunteering system at The Masters – he had been a volunteer for many, many, years and while the other had also been in the position for quite a time, he was a relative newcomer. Many marshals, once they get their position, stay on volunteering for decades, and often positions are passed to other family members. Volunteers come from all over the United States and some from abroad, although key positions tend to be held by those local to the town of Augusta, as they are required to attend a number of meetings throughout the year.

The main volunteers in the playing arena were the Gallery Guards (32 on the 1st hole alone) who marshalled patrons. There were the Secret Service guys with the theodolites.[1] And then there were the Scoring Teams who, via a range of walkie-talkies and wireless communications, fed back to a main team who collated scores and stats on fairways hit, greens hit in regulation etc. The Scoring Teams operated what was called a Silent Scoring System. It was almost invisible, too, as the job was done from within the stands or at the ropes, not on the field of play. Within seconds of them transmitting the data, it's available around the world. Daunting, and quite an incentive to the marshals to get it right first time. Occasional mistakes are made, and I suspect the role involves as much pressure and cold sweat as a downhill 20-foot putt at the 9th. Having a player-identification system was key. Something the guys who couldn't tell O'Hair from Sterne on Thursday had yet to master.

As a great reward for their hard work, each volunteer gets to play Augusta National one day in May, when they are also given the run of the clubhouse and treated like kings. They can also play the Par-3 Course as many times as they wish and take a guest on there, too. A just reward.[2]

As I chatted with the volunteers, we walked to an impressive concession stand hidden in the trees right of the 2nd fairway. I remarked that when I'd been at the tournament in 2007, the catering had been in large, green, bivouac-type tents that formed massive semi-circles and

1. They monitored driving distances etc. not for the purposes of scoring or the collection of playing stats, but rather to provide input into decisions on future course changes.

2. Visiting for the first time in 2002, Andrew Cotter of the BBC – a low-handicap golfer out of Royal Troon – was a first-time winner of the press lottery that allows some of the media to play the course on the Monday after the event. He dumped a couple of balls in the water at 12 and hit it to two feet at 16. He played solidly, although not all holes were off the back pegs. The downside of winning the press lottery is that for the next seven tournaments you cannot enter. Cotter will be eligible next year: I'm sure he'll bring his clubs.

were camouflaged among the trees. Now the catering was housed in impressively-appointed cabins, measuring roughly 30 yards by 30 yards, with bay windows and fans, that were so nice I'd be happy to live in one, never mind have it as a food stall. The guys tell me they were specially designed by an architect in California and are erected just before the tournament and dismantled immediately after it. The queuing within them is totally linear, everything you need in a straight line from start to finish, so it all runs like Swiss clockwork – why can't all events arrange their catering like this?

I'd had a really great day on the Saturday, mostly focused on speaking to various people I'd met and sharing experiences. I'd watched quite a bit of golf, too, but it almost seemed secondary. Thursday and Friday had been about making the cut or pushing out in front, and while Moving Day is key around the golfing world, Augusta is the place where they say it doesn't really start until the back nine on Sunday. When I left the volunteers, it was time to catch the leaders and see how Sunday would shape up.

I take a seat to the right of the 15th, another dell of golfing nirvana. The green slopes subtly, right to left, away from me, a gentle, continuous slope made treacherous by lightning quick greens and a double freaky cut, slicker than your coffee table. To my right is the beautiful 16th hole, lined on three sides by thousands of fans. Behind the green it's party time, lots of young patrons enjoying a beer or choking on big stogies. An annual meeting place to soak up the sun, the alcohol and the atmosphere. It had been the first place that I'd seen anyone at The Masters told to be quiet during play.

Sitting at the 15th I am reminded of my first view of the hole in 2007. At 530 yards it's now a ball breaker, but using the crossing, roughly from where players will hit wedge, you see the water at the front, a sliver of green, and then the water behind, at the 16th. You see nothing of the grass behind the 15th green. It gives the terrifying illusion of being the shallowest island green in the galaxy. Just crossing the fairway and looking down to the green is intimidating.

So far, at The Masters, apart from being close to Chad Campbell's game on Thursday, I'd paid almost no attention to the leaders. The golfers and their scores seemed, somehow, secondary. And standing in one part of the Garden of Eden was surely as good as the other, regardless of whether Adam was coming in to a tight pin placement with a high, cutty 6-iron. At home, watching on TV, I'd be craving sight of the leaders and their every shot. On the grounds themselves, everything was much more relaxed. Campbell and Perry still led at minus-11, and hot on their heels was Cabrera at 10, with Stricks, Furyk and Tim Clark a distant 6-under.

As I sat at 15, the back end of the draw was coming through. Nick Watney and Stephen Ames provided an immediate treat when Watney, just over the back fringe in two shots, knocked his third in for eagle, much to the delight of the crowd. Mission accomplished in five minutes. I hoped I'd see an eagle at this classic par-5, although it only took Watney to 3-under.

Shortly thereafter, with his third birdie in a row, Jim Furyk goes 8-under, and eventually the penultimate game with Angel Cabrera and Todd Hamilton appears. Cabrera goes long, over the right half of the green, well away from the flag which is cut down on the left side. Cabrera then executes a delicate lob, especially for a man set like a prize fighter, that almost sits stone dead on the second bounce, but gently releases to four feet. Making birdie after a bogey at 14, Cabrera is one back, and I am being treated to flourishes that set the scene for the final day.

The final game is Chad Campbell and Kenny Perry. Campbell played short at 15 just as Cabrera holed for bird, every inch a world-class up and down. Perry, blocked out by the trees left, had also knocked an iron down the hill, shy of the pond. He then hit a great pitch all over the pin, but it spun back and away from the hole. He missed his 15-footer and Campbell didn't make from just off the back fringe. Both had failed to birdie or eagle 13 or 15, missing the opportunity to put some golf between themselves and the field.

I decide to follow the last two groups, so leave the stand, the sun starting to set but the air still balmy and comfortable, and walk down to the right of the 16th. Just as I get down and round, Perry hits a tee shot that fails to make the back shelf, where the pin is tucked. His ball bleeds down to the front of the green. Chad then misses the green right and long, leaving a near-impossible bunker shot to that minuscule shelf.

Both players are looking tentative, and this is emphasised when Campbell gets too cute and leaves his ball in the bunker. Another poor one, and he'll be staring at a double. We watch in total silence as he plays a good escape shot, coming to rest five feet beyond the hole, staying on the top side of the putting surface. Perry two-putts from 40 feet, but Campbell misses, a double-bogey disaster. He should have taken his medicine and at least have had a long putt for par. As I walk up towards the 17th there's a loud cheer from that green. Angel Cabrera birdies and joins Perry in the lead at 11-under.

Having followed the golf for three straight days, and then back to the hotel, free beers, dinner then bed, I haven't really had time to contemplate who might win. The top of the field is packed with quality; eight players, the last four groups, are within five shots, so it's wide open.

As part of a group waiting to cross at the 17th, we're joined by a young guy who has clearly enjoyed himself, although he hasn't overdone it. With young Asian good looks and a couple of diamond studs in his ears he immediately engages the attractive young blonde also waiting to cross.

'Hey, how are you doing, d'you want a sandwich?' he asks, as he pulls a pimento from his pocket.

'Oh no, it's okay, I have a tuna one I've still to eat,' she replies, giggling.

'Oh, I love tuna, d'you wanna swap? C'mon let's swap.' I'm impressed at his approach and rakish attitude.

'No, thanks, it's okay,' says the girl, taking it all in her stride.

From just behind Loverboy, a Securitas guard appears. 'Excuse me, ma'am, do you know this gentleman?'

'No, sir, I don't.'

'Okay, YOU GO THAT WAY', says the guard, pointing down the fairway to another walkway. Loverboy drops his head and heads off, without protest or argument. He knew he was on the cusp of being escorted out. No harm done, but it was a bit harsh. Loverboy was chancing his arm, but the young lady was totally in control. It was a non-threatening situation until a eunuch in a security uniform appeared. As we crossed the walkway I took the egg salad sandwich from my right pocket and made a beeline for the young blonde.

Egg salad still intact, I walked up to the 18th to watch Cabrera finish, and then waited for Campbell and Perry. I was lucky to get to see the final brushstrokes added to Saturday's portrait. Cabrera and Perry finish at 11-under, with a faltering Chad Campbell and a resurgent Jim Furyk three shots back. Furyk, along with Steve Stricker, Sean O'Hair and Ian Poulter, has typified Moving Day, advancing up the field with a 68. O'Hair and Poulter are joined on minus-4 by Tiger Woods and Phil Mickelson, who would play together on the final day. A pairing that promised so much: would it deliver?

Later that evening I was a guest at Augusta Country Club, where I had been invited by a couple of members. The surroundings and its inhabitants were as you'd expect from a classy American country club, and the ambience was gentle yet busy, quiet but bustling, everyone was having a good time and it was nice to experience some wonderful Southern hospitality. But before I left Augusta National that night I saw another side of the tournament.

Within 10 minutes of the final game finishing, the supporting cast sprang into action with military precision. A battalion of lawnmowers advanced down the hill and swept across the course like Patton's Third Army, heading down 17 and 14 presumably into Amen Corner at the 13th, headlights marking their progress across the ever-darkening green of Augusta National. As the gloom continued to gather, a handful of greenkeepers on foot appeared at the 18th, and began to water and rake the sand in the bunkers. A photographer was at the 9th, taking shots of the green and the pin as the sun set. At that point a green jacket and helper appeared, carrying a long silver and black pole with an elliptical dome on top. They placed the device in the hole, stopped for a few seconds and then walked towards the front middle of the green, just left of centre.

'What's that?' I asked the photographer.

'GPS. Everything out here is done by GPS. Every single stake is positioned in the same place every year, all using GPS, plotted on some master plan. After all, why not when you have Bill Gates as a member?'

'Amazing, eh?' I thought out loud.

'Yeah, it's crazy out here. This is the best major. And the worst,' he said.

I headed off to grab a cab to Augusta Country Club. As I crossed Berckmans at Gate 6, an old-style truck, the kind that the Beverly Hillbillies would have been proud to own, passed by. Emblazoned on its side, in gold letters on a dark brown background, the words THE TRIUMPHING OF THE WICKED IS SHORT, *Job* 20:5. Let's see who gets the job done tomorrow, and then we can all be the judge of that.

MASTERS SUNDAY: NOT QUITE ANY GIVEN SUNDAY

For the first time on my trip, I'm in a deep sleep when my alarm goes off at 05:00; great. By the time I hop into my car it's 05:42. Soon I am on Berckmans, the tricky fifth hole somewhere just over the fence as my car winds down the road towards Gate 10.

Passing that gate at 5:58 I'm not surprised to see around 100 patrons on their chairs, sitting patiently on the sidewalk. Soon I reach my destination, the free parking opposite Gate 6. As I begin to turn left I see that it is roped off, but this doesn't make sense in my head, so I am mildly panicked, as I don't know any other roads and I don't have a map.

I park, jump out the car and run the 200 yards back to the car park.

'What's the deal with parking here, why can't I get in from this side?'

Asking the question, my brain instantaneously formulates the answer. No access from Berckmans.

'No access from Berckmans.'

If I've heard or read this once, I've heard it a million times. Shit. It's almost a mantra on the radio, a *caballeta* sung by every local traffic announcer. A fugue of Anglo Saxon words explodes in my mind.

'How do I get in then?'

43

'Access from Stanley. It's round the back,' the attendant kindly tells me.

I'm already thinking about how lost I could end up getting, the worst case being that I have to drive back to the hotel to take the shuttle in an hour's time. Behind the parking attendant there's a steady trickle of cars.

I slowly walk back to the car, realising that jumping behind the wheel in a state of high anxiety, in the darkness, looking for a road I've never been on, is hardly the best foot forward. I pull onto Washington Road, heading left and away from the course. It's 06:10, and although it feels daft, my heart is pounding, I don't want to have been up before dawn and for it to be a total waste of time.

Quickly I'm able to see Stanley, and it is festooned with police and traffic cones. There's no left turn from the west. However, using the First Hidden Rule of International Driving – I'm from overseas, so can execute any manoeuvre I want – I do a quick u-turn over double yellow lines in the middle of the road and head back towards Stanley.

As I approach the junction I prepare in my mind the First Hidden Statement of International Driving – Sorry, officer, I'm not from around here. I roll down my window in anticipation of some form of grilling. Nothing is said, and I continue down to the car park entrance; my parking mission soon to be complete. Free parking: yet another courtesy that The Masters Tournament extends to its patrons.

Just before 06:20 I get to Gate 6. There are around 60 others there and I speak to a group at the front of the queue. They've been there since 04:40. Borderline madness. Within fifteen minutes there's a steady stream of cars on Berckmans. The 90-minute wait passes quickly, testament to quality organisational skills at The Masters. The main doors at Gate 6 open at 06:30, and at regular intervals further barriers are opened and we move forwards incrementally. At no point do we get restless or anxious. There's a lesson here for sporting events around the world. By 07:15 I'm down at the gate adjacent to the 1st, about eight rows from the front.

The next hour flies by as I chat with Ken and Chuck from Minnesota. Ken's been coming to The Masters for years, and they are heading with their seats for the right side of the 18th green. I'm heading to the left side to get a view of the players and approach shots as they round the corner and come up towards the green.[1] The gates begin to open and we go our separate ways, hoping to meet up at the PGA Championship in August.

'No running. No running allowed.'

I try to get some sort of quick walking rhythm going, like being in a three-legged race without an actual partner. I canter across the first fairway, and when I turn up to the 1st I'm disconcerted to see a mass of chairs already there, people streaming into the seating area. It looks like any number of rules have been broken, but I'm happy when I get my spot, back left with a good view of the fairway and the entire green. I wouldn't see my chair for another ten hours.

The morning passes in a kind of blur. The first game is out at 10:25, Kevin Sutherland and Mike Weir, and the area around the first tee is mobbed. I'm glad to see Sutherland is out first. His coach doesn't like to fly, so they drove to Augusta National. It took four days. At least he'll get to beat the traffic on his way home.

I stand at the tee and watch the first five groups. Pint-sized Andres Romero smashes the longest drive of the lot. When Bubba Watson appears on the tee he goes through the pleasantries, chats to his caddy and then starts executing some daft practice swings, both left and right-handed. Sunday golf.

Like the worst creature of habit I wander down to the 2nd green, taking in the first half of the draw. As I stand and watch various groups pass by, a tallish, lean man in a blazer, grey slacks and black leather shoes walks just inside the ropes. I check his name-badge: Dow Finsterwald, someone steeped in the lore of The Masters and major golf.

Finsterwald would have tied Arnold Palmer after 72 holes in the 1960 Masters, but for a bizarre 2-shot penalty for having a practice putt on a green during play; back then the tournament was run under Augusta National, not USGA, rules, and this was not allowed by the club. He was penalised, although after his card had been handed in. He really should

1. The next week I see that the guys did get the spots they were after. In a *Sports Illustrated* photo they're behind Kenny Perry.

have been disqualified, but maybe he was cut some slack for reporting his own transgression. Two years later he and Gary Player lost in an 18-hole play-off to Palmer.

Finsterwald had come real close, twice, to having a green jacket, not a navy blazer. Prior to his Masters misses, he'd almost done something in a major that no one before or since would have the chance to do. In 1958 he won the first PGA Championship played under the stroke-play format, but the year previously he'd lost in the final of the final PGA played under match-play. Winning back to back majors in different formats would have given him something not even Tiger could have a crack at, and a unique place in golf history books.

As Dow walks on, I start back up the hill towards the first fairway. Thereafter, the next couple of hours really need to be focused on two players: Tiger Woods and Phil Mickelson. I can't believe they've been drawn together. God obviously knew I was doing a book, but would He go so far as to allow one of them to win?

As Tiger and Phil come on to the 1st tee at 01:30, the entire length of the hole is deep with patrons; everybody wants to be ringside at this clash of the Titans. Phil is dressed in black, and it's no surprise that Tiger's in his Sunday best – red. Tiger drives and I cannot quite believe it when I see people racing from the left side of the 1st fairway towards the 9th. That's miles left. I'm standing 300 yards out, to the right of the fairway bunker, and Woods' shot is roughly in line with me, but about 100 yards away. Shocker. Seconds later I automatically drop to my knees as Mickelson's ball caroms into the branches above, and about 50 people reactively duck and protect their heads. Phil's ball is spat out into the front of the long bunker, just in front of me.

From my vantage point I get a feel for Tiger's approach to the green – not great, but not bad, and it looks as if he may even be as far up and left as the 8th. Meanwhile, Phil is right in front of me, makes a good swing and the ball starts towards the green, although because of the trees up the right I can't see it finish. The guy next to me shouts some encouragement.

'C'mon Phil! C'mon Philly! C'mon Philly cheese!'

In many ways we appear to have entered a parallel universe, where Phil and Tiger will be engaged in their own battle while the others play out a sideshow. I watch as both players par 1, birdie 2. I wait next to the 3rd fairway as both smoke their drives, coming to rest adjacent to each other, just in the rough, 300 yards from the tee. I'm standing about 20 yards away from their balls.

As they approach, Phil looks to be in a state of calm focus. Tiger, also calm, looks more intense. I realise at this moment the world's greatest sportsman is so close to me that we could be playing in the same game. I have a daft notion that maybe I can draw off some of his intensity and skill, capturing it for myself. Is this normal when one stands close to greatness? I'd been this close to Tiger before. But somehow, now that he'd won at Bay Hill when just back from injury, and on a hot, sunny, clear day at Augusta National on a Sunday, Tiger's spell seems crystal clear and more alluring.

The players have almost identical shots, a 50-yard chip to the pin from the rough, but up a steep slope that must be about 20 feet high and not at all obvious from one's armchair. Tiger walks up to the pin, visualising and feeling his shot, decoding the challenge and loading it into his mental and muscle memory banks. Amazingly, despite facing a shot up a steep incline, Phil does not go up to the green as surely 99% of professionals in the final round of a major would. His caddy, Jim 'Bones' Mackay, paces it out and walks up to the pin. This might be target golf or golf by numbers, or whatever you want to call it, but the target and numbers have to be so precise that the image and shot in Mickelson's head must be like a flawless diamond.

Tiger plays first and there's barely a reaction. Phil then pitches and I can see from the flight and first bounce that it could be close. The crowd cheers wildly, and for once Tiger is getting a taste of his own gallery's medicine. I watch from the back of the green as Phil makes his birdie and is now two below the card. The day already has a special feel. I walk down to the back left of the 16th green and the dip at the bottom of the 6th.

Both players parred the 4th, and as I look up I can see them through a large gap in the trees way up on the 5th. There's a substantial roar as

47

someone hits it close, and a few minutes later another one follows a birdie. The 5th green is in its own corner, so the cheers and shouts bounce and reverberate towards me. The scoreboard soon informs us that Phil is now 3-under for the day, while Tiger maintains his position at 1-under.

The 6th tee is set back from the crest of the hill, so I cannot see the players, but can tell from the movements atop the slope that they are on the teeing ground. It's Phil to go first. I use the patrons' heads as my cue, and when I see them turn from their right to left, I try to pick up Phil's ball in the air but cannot, so at once I look directly, hopefully, at the pin. I see the ball plummet from the heavens at what looks like the bottom of the cup. The crowd go wild, and I feel that Phil's ball must be stiff. Up at the green I see Phil hole from about four feet. I was praying he would make it, as the excitement, tension and expectation are already starting to gain real momentum, and goose pimples start to form. Phil has lit up the first six holes and is now 4 under par. And I'm very glad I took the time to fuel up on cola, pimento and egg sandwiches. It could be a long afternoon.

Despite the massive crowds and excitement, both growing with each new hole, I never fail to have a view of the action, always able to see the players and their shots, and usually the results, too. Down the 7th hole, Lefty pulls his drive.

'Spit it out, spit it out,' implores Mackay, the ball tree-bound.

We see Mickelson's ball come to rest in the rough down the right side. He'll be impeded by trees for his next, the pin cut front right. The green is ludicrously shallow, and surely Mickelson will now struggle to make par. Or at best, par is all he can hope for. I start to cross the 7th fairway heading towards the 8th. About 100 yards ahead, Phil plays his approach shot. I cannot see the flight of the ball, but almost defying the law of physics it appears out of nowhere right in line with the pin. Apart from teleportation, I cannot fathom how he got it there. One patron hits the nail on the head.

'Wow. He hit a big-ass hook.'

By now the cheers will be heard on every single part of the course, and the players in contention will see that Mickelson has started to break the front nine in two. He's got it in a stranglehold, and looks to be keen to smother it into submission. I continue crossing, people around exchange glances and words of astonishment and praise. The flawed genius of Phil Mickelson is shining bright.

We watch from afar as he makes his birdie, and then we walk through the trees to the left side of the 8th fairway, a 570-yard par-5 up a hill and round a corner. As I walk, I chat briefly to Joe, a Manchester United fan from Birmingham. Birmingham, Alabama, that is. I tell him it's no surprise to bump into his ilk here, Man U fans are everywhere, like rats.

Phil outhits Tiger up the 8th, about 320 off the tee, up the hill. Four black guys next to me remark on how Phil is smokin' Tiger today off the tee. I head up to the green, hoping to see the approach shots. Tiger's ball appears, 30 feet left of the stick, and Phil's almost comes off the slope to the right, but chooses to stay just off the green. I walk round the green to the same side as Phil and the 9th fairway, always trying to get in position for the next hole.

Tiger arrives with a thump. Eagle 3, aggressive delight scorched across his face, he pumps the air and the crowd goes wild, including myself – we now have two players at this golfing party. Phil makes his birdie putt and is now a cool 6-under for the first eight holes. It beggars belief, a mixture of the sublime and the miraculous since the 2nd green.

Both players miss the 9th fairway with their tee shots, and I hang around long enough to see both play exquisite recoveries and make putts for par. Mickelson has covered the front side in a mere 30 shots, while Tiger is out in a comparatively mediocre 33. Can these standards possibly be maintained?

Rather than traipse down 10 and 11, two holes that exist almost in splendid isolation from the rest of Augusta National, I head to Amen Corner. The last day of The Masters: the 12th hole where every tee shot brings excitement, every outcome uncertain until the ball lands. This is a cauldron of world-class sporting endeavour, a crucible of pressure and fear. Commitment and belief are the twin leitmotifs of success at Golden Bell.

By the time I get to the 12th and look up the 11th I can see Tiger, wracked with indecision on what to hit. He seems to change his mind about three times before hitting a great shot into the green, not far from the pin. As I walk to get a slightly better vantage point, Elin Woods – Tiger's wife – passes right by me, almost brushing my arm. She, too, is wearing Sunday red and appears to be alone, although I know this cannot be the case.

'If he holes this, everyone's going nuts,' says one of the guys next to me.

Neither player makes birdie. Tiger left his 8-foot putt short, and they head to 12. Despite the fact that this is the final round of a major and the world's two best players are going at it, at no point have I been unable to see the action; until now, that is. I'm probably at the most famous par-3 in golf, but it is so deep with people that I just can't see the players, can't even see the tops of their heads or swings.

Tiger finds the green, and disastrously Phil knocks it into the water. Tragic.

'That was pure Phil,' remarks one patron. We've all seen something like this before from Mickelson.

I decide at that point to stop following them. As Phil was over the ball I scanned the holes for a clue on the dreaded swirling wind, and I noticed that as the flag at the 11th went limp, the one at the 12th wafted on the breeze. A few seconds later this was reversed. Then both flags flutter – discombobulating enough during a Sunday four-ball, never mind Masters Sunday.

I wait for the next two games to come through the 12th. Ian Poulter and Lee Westwood are up next, and they are almost inconveniences for the crowd, who continue to chatter and laugh. Westwood's caddy shouts loudly for hush and raises his hand. Again, like the 16th, this corner is a big social gathering for many, especially the younger patrons. 'Why do they need quiet, they know where the hole is?' a girl asks her boyfriend. Obviously she and many others have not grasped the finer nuances of golf, especially top-flight golf.

I notice on the scoreboard that Tiger and Phil both birdie the 13th. It occurs to me that birdies and eagles at the 14th and 15th will put them right in amongst it. I decide that I need to tag onto their game again. Both players hit the 14th green as I wait to cross to the 15th fairway, and Westwood and Poulter approach their drives.

'Can we cross yet? Why can't we cross, what are we waiting for?' says some idiot behind me. Maybe because the two players right in front of us, but who aren't Tiger and Phil, would like us to wait.

Once I'm across I see Elin Woods again. But this time, as I am walking side on and am 25 yards away, I see that she has around ten people with her, some in black, some in red, and a mix of males and females. She has more close protectors than Condoleezza Rice.

Still with the honour, courtesy of his par at the 12th, Tiger's tee ball appears first, and he's smashed it. I check my yardage chart and reckon his blow to have been in the region of 337 yards. Minutes later, Phil detonates his tee shot, pitching almost at Tiger's ball and on for another 15 or so yards. Mickelson, who's continually outhit Woods, has thoroughly smoked his 350 yards. The adrenal gland is now really starting to pump as we get to the business end of the tournament.

I'm about 20 yards abeam the players, as close as one can possibly be at this point on the course. By my calculations the T-Man has about 183 yards to the front and another 20 yards to the pin which is cut back right. The chat on the ropes is that he's hitting a 7-iron. Although it's sharply downhill for much of the shot, it's still a long way. In a controlled flash Tiger's ball leaves the club head and disappears behind the trees to my left, heading for the green. Tiger watches the ball and the noise of the crowd at the green increases, suggesting the ball is heading to the target, although it's still mid-air. I don't see the ball land, but the crowd at the green provides a massive roar. A good shot at worst.

Next up, it's Phil. He too smashes his iron, high and handsome. When his ball lands on the green the crowd goes absolutely, utterly ballistic, a roar that could surely be heard outside Richmond County and a noise the level of which I've never heard on a golf course; the crowd has flipped. I walk down the left side of the fairway and stop to ask a gentleman with binoculars how close Phil is – three feet, he tells me.

As I walk across to the right side of the 15th I gaze down at the water, the crowds lining both sides of the fairway, and then beyond, the 16th hole, thousands of people lining that hole, too. A mass of shimmering silver water, islands of green-jacket green and splashes of pure white sand, thousands upon thousands of fans, dressed in myriad colours, like someone's lobbed a hand-grenade into a paint store, brilliant splashes everywhere. This has to be the number one golfing theatre in the world.

All of this, plus golf that feels like the game is being taken to new levels of dashing brilliance. Goose pimples shiver along the length and breadth of my body and my pace quickens, hopeful of yet another view of these two great players going head to head. I take my spot and get the chance to see Tiger fail in his eagle attempt. I slightly reposition myself to get a good view of Phil and the hole at the same time, but the viewing is so good at Augusta, I get greedy and decide to walk swiftly 15 yards down. I watch and Phil misses. Painful. Phil is 6-under for the day, only two shots back at 10-under for the week. Tiger is a shot back.

At 16 I have a clear view of Tiger, and after the pre-shot rituals he hits a crisp iron which has to be good, the noise level of the crowd increases as the thousands who can actually track the shot amplify their acknowledgement while the ball is mid-flight. The ball falls at the pin and a wave of hysteria shatters the air; like a thousand panes of smashing glass, one marvels at the noise while arrested by its intensity. People everywhere exchange glances, looks of incredulity and almost exhaustion. Tiger says he loves the back-nine burn, and all of a sudden the burn is a raging forest fire, capturing every single person within two hundred metres, all scorched by the intensity of what we're witnessing. Two hours ago a Tiger victory and possible Grand Slam were nowhere to be seen: now it all seems possible. Tears are almost forming in my eyes, as much at the quality and majesty of golf as at the intensity of a shared experience with thousands upon thousands of total strangers. This has to be better than a Moonie Wedding. Are we really on the cusp of historic golf like no other? Down in the cauldron of the 16th, only the most hardened cynic, the most ardent hater of either Tiger or Phil could think otherwise.

Phil makes par but Tiger makes his birdie and the crowd explodes in cheers, claps, cries, shouts and applause, and that was just the guy next to me. I'm not even a massive Tiger fan, but just as I had shouted and cheered as he made eagle at the 8th, I do so again in appreciation of his stellar play and never-say-die attitude.

And then it is over. As quickly as great things can happen in international sport, bad things can also happen: Phil misses a very makeable putt for birdie at 17 and bogeys the last. Tiger finishes bogey, bogey. Both players run out of steam and the dream is finished for another year. I hadn't gone up the 17th, instead heading to my chair next to the 18th green.

Finding it at the final green would be one true litmus test of Master Chair Etiquette and general honesty. Although it took me a while to swim through the sea of people – I couldn't even find the walkway into the Seating Area – I did locate my chair ten hours after I had left it, mainly thanks to a maroon Oakland Hills PGA windcheater that I had placed over its back. I sat down in time to see Tiger play pinball in the trees down the right. In relative terms, he was hacking his way up the 72nd hole.

As they finish, Phil acknowledges the crowd, smiling with a slight grimace, a look of knowing what might have been. Tiger also acknowledges the applause, but does not look up; his eyes stare intensely into the heart of his own failure. The man who does not accept second-best and wants always to win – two of the many qualities that make him so great – is fizzing. The Masters would now appear to be down to just three men: Angel Cabrera, Chad Campbell and Kenny Perry. It's all to play for.

Despite their human failings at the end, the star of Tiger and Phil's golf will burn brightly in my memory for a long, long time.

It's now approaching 18:00, and for the first time I get the chance to sit back and reflect. It's been a dazzling day of golfing brilliance, the sun is shining brightly, starting to set, and a light aircraft buzzes overhead. The scoreboard reads Kenny Perry 12-under, Chad Campbell 11, Angel Cabrera 10. Sporadically, from the TV towers above, we can hear the sweet tones of Jimmy Nantz, calling the final holes of this Masters. A gentleman greenside in a red jacket provides some mild entertainment. He chats and jokes with the crowd, although this is a sideline for him. As each game approaches he walks the ropes, giving brief summaries of each player's career. At one point he announces the Masters Sunday Trivia Quiz, and asks the crowd to name all the major winners with the letter 'z' in their names.[1] This is a nice touch; another small piece of the Masters jigsaw designed to make your experience unique.

There's a massive cheer as Kenny Perry goes to minus-13 on the scoreboard. From the chat around greenside and on the media, plus the fact that Perry's looking to become the oldest Major winner of all time, it's clear he's the favourite among most of the patrons and others gathered nearby. But of eight players that I have now watched approach the final green, only Shingo Katayama found it in regulation – and although Steve Stricker does so in the next game – it's clear a par at the last isn't certain. Further intrigue is added as Shingo rolls in his birdie putt. I get a keen sense that it isn't going to be over until it's over.

In a nice touch of *Bushido* – Japanese for Way of the Warrior – Katayama walks up the green, turns to face down and across the rest of Augusta National, doffs his distinctive hat and bows to the course. The crowd warmly cheers and applauds, and the Japanese sitting all around me go wild, almost as wild as they did when he made birdie. By now the scoreboards show that Perry and Cabrera birdied 16. Kenny Perry has destiny staring right in his face. He hasn't made bogey for 22 holes and he has one arm in the green jacket. Minutes later he bogeys the 17th.

In anticipation of the unthinkable, for Perry at least, Mr Red Coat pipes up, 'The Sunday Announcement, folks. Any playoff will take place over the 18th, the 10th, the 18th etc., but we hope it doesn't go that far. You're all invited. The presentation will follow thereafter on the putting green.'

As the penultimate game heads up the last fairway, rounding the corner and coming into view, a couple of people in front of us stand up to look, even though they have chairs. Someone asks them to sit down, but there's no response.

'Sitting area,' says one patron.

1. Azinger; Mize; Sarazen; Olazabal; Zoeller; Zach Johnson; Vic Ghezzi (who he?); Lee Janzen; Roberto de Vincenzo. Sadly, neither Zoran Zorkic nor Richard Zokol broke through into the Major-winning circle.

'SITTING AREA!' barks another. The people sit down and others chuckle.

Chad Campbell, with Angel Cabrera, is now 12-under, a shot back of Kenny Perry. Chad becomes only the third player of a dozen to hit the last green, lofting a beautiful mid-iron just above and to the right of the hole. He walks up onto the green, glances over his right shoulder at the leader board, and is faced with the stark reality that maybe, just maybe, this putt could win him a green jacket.

'Oh, he took a peek,' says the guy next to me excitedly. Chad marks his ball and begins to eye up his date with destiny. It is a beautiful, warm evening, a wonderful way to spend a Sunday. I wonder how Campbell feels?

'Chad, you got this!' a hopeful patron shouts.

Chad settles over the ball and puts a nice stroke on it. The ball is never going to be far away, but it just slides by, a tad strong. Under the circumstances it was a very good putt, and he's the first in at 12-under. All to play for. Campbell left the green to warm applause and cheers. He'd been in the mix since Thursday afternoon and it still wasn't over, especially as we could now see Kenny Perry was in the bunker back down the left of the fairway – could he pull off a Sandy Lyle? Even a par could be good enough, depending on Cabrera's actions.

I'm excited but don't actually mind who wins. The guy next to me wants Kenny Perry to win 'so bad'. He also tells his buddy he likes his Masters Champion speaking English. I divine from this that he's not supporting Angel Cabrera.

The final hole of Masters regulation play: could Perry win it here? The answer to that came four times in the space of 15 minutes. First, he drove into the bunker. Secondly, his bunker shot wasn't the best, coming up short and left, leaving a nasty uphill chip with not much green to work with. Thirdly, his chip verged on the mediocre, and although there was massive tension and suspense as he stood over his putt, he stroked it weakly and it never made it to the hole. Perry had missed his chance, and after his bogey at the penultimate hole, there seemed to be some inevitability about this closing black mark.

Of course, in real time, the events unfolded much more slowly and with more possibilities and hope, but in the grand scheme of things, as if in a medal at the local club, the leader had bogeyed and his score was on the card. Extra time was required.

Much more delighted at this turn of events was Cabrera. Having missed the green short and right with his approach from the middle of the fairway, the man from the Argentine holed a 5-footer to make it into the playoff. With some minor fist-pumping and delight on his face, he knew the tournament wasn't over and he still had a chance to become the first man from his country to triumph at Augusta National. He may even have felt that he was the favourite to win. Perry had missed a golden opportunity, and Campbell has missed a putt to win. Could Cabrera come from behind?

He'd walked up to the final green and his impending chip with all the insouciance of a hung-over scratch player just looking to par, hand in his card and slake his thirst in the club bar. Any one of the three players could take home the green jacket, a cheque for $1.35 million and, more importantly, a big fat chunk of golfing history.

The play-off starts on the 18th tee again. Mr Red Jacket kindly tells us the players are hitting, the dogleg at the last obscuring any view of the first 250 yards of the final hole. We all looked down the hill to see the two Americans walking up the fairway, but to spot the Argentinean we had to squint into the trees. As he played his shot we heard a loud thwack. He had ricocheted off a tree trunk, squirting out into the middle of the fairway. Clear advantage, Chad and Kenny. Cabrera's ball could have gone almost anywhere, but he got a lucky break.

Before the playoff had started, a phalanx of green staff appeared, raking the bunkers and tidying the final hole.

'Way to go, Mr Sandman,' shouted one patron, and the guys received a standing ovation for their raking efforts. Campbell puts a poor swing on his second shot and finds the bunker. Even from 180 yards I can see his swing was less than perfect, and the same goes for Perry. Kenny spins out of his shot a tad early, coming up just shy of the right-hand bunker. Cabrera still has some skin in the game.

Cabrera then hits a fantastic pitch shot. I can see his ball clearly the second it leaves the club head, and can instantly tell the length is not far off and the direction is excellent. It pitches at the pin and comes to rest around eight feet away. A great shot and potential lifesaver, and he may even have the chance to win if it goes wrong for Perry and Campbell.

Perry hits a brilliant pitch that stops two rolls from being in the cup and certain victory. He bends his knees and throws his head back, looking to the heavens in search of what might have been. It was a superb shot in the most pressurised of situations. Campbell hits a good bunker shot that runs about four feet past the hole, and he looks good for par. If Angel can hole, all three will progress down the 10th.

For the second time in about 40 minutes, the 2007 US Open winner rolls in a putt at the last to stay in the Masters. To say Cabrera is delighted is an understatement, as he plays out the same emotions as before, drawing strength from yet another clutch putt. In contrast, and sadly, Chad Campbell misses. Downcast, he leaves the green almost immediately, graciously accepting the commiserations of his two opponents and the patrons, and disappears up the hill towards the clubhouse.

I had been convinced Chad would make his putt, and of the three players heading down 10, that surely at least two would reappear at the 18th for the third extra hole. I now had a decision to make: stay in my chair or head down 10? I chose to stay put, convinced there'd be another hole. I was wrong.

After being at The Masters for almost every hour of play, I missed the final curtain call. Kenny Perry went into meltdown and Cabrera won at the second extra hole. News filtered up to the 18th shortly after. There was no fanfare, no massive cheer to tell us The Masters was over. I should have known it would happen; no Masters playoff has ever gone to the third extra hole. And the guy next to me, who wanted Perry to win 'so bad', said, as the players went down 10, that he'd stayed at the last when Mike Weir beat Len Mattiace at the 10th, the first extra hole that year. But this minor glitch in no way impacted my enjoyment of the previous four days. Another unforgettable week at Augusta National was at an end.

I watched the green jacket ceremony on the putting green, the Tournament Committee and visiting dignitaries hearing the words of Chairman Billy Payne, before Angel Cabrera received his jacket, a smile as wide as the 10th fairway on his face.

It had been a superb Masters Tournament and the organising committee had set up the course in a way that recaptured the spirit of the great Sundays at Augusta National. It was fitting that it turned out to be the most watched Masters in eight years. According to Nielsen Media Research, 35.2 million watched some or all of the playoff on CBS.

On the Monday after the event, having managed to sustain the hotel's free bar into the wee small hours, I awoke with a slightly fuzzy head. As I ate my breakfast I contemplated the golf I had witnessed the day before.

I didn't feel hard done by at not seeing the final play-off hole. Kenny Perry's response to his loss was admirable, gentlemanly and very sporting, not least when he said that if that was the worst thing to happen to him in his life, he'd done not badly. A harbinger of this reaction was Perry's applause and high-five at the back of the 18th, when Cabrera holed his tricky putt to stay in the play-off. I honestly hate to tout the familiar story of golf being the ultimate gentleman's game – the image is hackneyed and overplayed for any number of reasons – but it's hard to think of too many sports today when one competitor would encourage another in the heat of battle for one of the greatest prizes.

Most of my Monday thoughts were of the immense golf and atmosphere that surrounded Tiger and Phil: it was McEnroe versus Borg, Nicklaus and Watson, Ali against Frazier, with one dazzling difference, neither was victorious. As perverse as it may seem, had either of those players won, it might have felt too good to be true, too much beyond the realms of possibility.

All of this and a whole lot more ran through my mind as I took a last drive down to Augusta National. The town was returning to normal, like any midsize American city, people going about their daily business. Clean-up was in full swing, trailers and greenkeeping vehicles restoring the place to 'just' Augusta National Golf Club.

Driving back towards the highway I was caught in a reverie, reliving the heroics of Phil Mickelson. At the end of Berckmans I missed my turn onto Wheeler Road, continuing onto Highland Avenue. As the lights changed, I turned quickly and mounted the sidewalk, the metal corner of which instantly punctured my tyre. It was fully deflated in about ten seconds. Through gritted teeth I had to laugh. It was all part of the spectator experience, a reality check after the momentous golf of the previous four days. I pulled over, rummaged around in the boot and found the jack. The Masters was truly over for another year . . .

Golf in the Free World: by the People for the People

The US Open Championship

These are heady times for Lucas. If he can keep his head about him he can win the largest prize of his young career; a life-changing week for him either way.

Jim Douglas, Clemson, South Carolina

US OPEN WEEK: HEY WANG

The New York Yankees and the New York Mets; the New York Giants and the New York Jets; the New York Knicks and the New Jersey Nets; The New York Rangers, the New Jersey Devils and the New York Islanders; New York even has its own soccer team, Red Bull New York. NY is awash with sports teams and legendary tales of competitive heroics.

The Masters was the ultimate golf event, the red-carpet experience. The US Open would be different. It was for the golfing everyman. A survey by a New York TV station asked what events interested people on the weekend of the Open – 66% answered the Yankees and Mets; for 16% it was the professional hockey and baseball drafts; 18% said the final round of the US Open. Just 2% fewer people had more interest in picking teams than they had in the exploits of Tiger Woods, but that still left thousands of New Yorkers to flood to the golf.

Sport in America runs through the heart of society, and in his cracking book *Friday Night Lights*, H.G. Bissinger charts the season of a high school football team in an economically shaky part of Texas. He tells us of the agonies and the ecstasies, the bonds made, friendships shattered. In that season over 20 years ago, $70,000 was spent chartering jets for the team. Before one game, the coach told the team it wasn't going to be a party, it was a business trip.

The US Open would be as much a sports experience as a major golf one. The second leg of my journey was to Long Island, New York, and the fearsome Bethpage Black. It was designed by legendary golf architect Albert Warren Tillinghast, and in an article entitled 'Man Killers' in 1934 he'd called the course The Black Leopard. I envisioned a week of hard and demanding golf, and hard and demanding socialising. With four of the last eight US Opens being held in New York State, I was going to get a real taste of the national golf championship in the world's biggest sporting nation. Bethpage had held the championship in 2002, and it delivered intense golf and raucous crowds. It was the USGA Smackdown, with Mexican waves, singing and chanting. It wasn't going to be another Augusta National.

I was only eight miles from my flat, and in the first 90 minutes of my week-long trip when I had my first brush with Major golf. Not bad, considering I was in Edinburgh, Scotland. I spotted D.J. Russell, the youngest player to record an ace in a major,[1] in the departure area, heading for a European seniors' event in Wales. And snoozing in the airline lounge next to me was John Huggan, former senior editor of *Golf Digest*, who was heading to Bethpage to write for the US mag, *Golf World*. He'd been at Bethpage's rebirth in 2002 and told me it was a big golf course, a vast golfing hinterland in the middle of Long Island.

Flying Continental to New Jersey was a quick hop across the pond, made slightly more enjoyable by one of the attendants, our in-flight comedian.

'Ladies and Gentlemen, if Newark is not part of your travel plans, it's too late now, the doors are closed.'

1. The Postage Stamp 8th at Royal Troon, 1973, aged 19.

Levity doesn't go amiss when you're with hundreds of other human beings, shoe-horned into a tube of metal packed with flammable liquid. On the previous weekend, Continental Express had taken two minors to completely the wrong destinations. On Saturday an eight-year-old girl travelling from Houston ended up in Arkansas, not Charlotte, North Carolina. The next day, a ten-year-old ended up at Newark, not in Cleveland, Ohio. Newark was my destination. I just hoped it was also the pilot's.

Not part of my itinerary was the awful movie selection. *Paul Blart: Mall Cop* is not my idea of fun, and I recommend the CIA start showing it on rendition flights, it'd break even the most determined terror suspect. The rest wasn't much better, so I spent the flight reading *All Quiet on the Western Front*, the seminal account of the futility of war. Little did I know then that I was destined for my own horrendous battle on horrifically muddy terrain. I shudder to think what might have happened had I read *American Psycho*.

When the plane landed, our own Chris Rock declared, 'Ladies and Gentleman, welcome to Newark Liberty Airport. We are early, so please remember that for the next time we are late.'

I was just glad not to be in the boondocks. It was my fourth trip to Gotham – once again to wonder at the hustle and bustle of the world's ultimate city, its wide streets, towering buildings and the worker ants of the global economy always in a hurry.

After a shower, I took a walk around town, captivated by its vibrancy and diversity. I strolled down Fifth Avenue past the Flatiron Building, through Chelsea, SoHo, TriBeCa and into Chinatown, where I browsed the fake-watch stalls on Canal. Things had changed in the last 18 months; many of the serious Swiss brands had disappeared as the result of a crackdown. Tourists from around the globe hustled to catch a glimpse of this or that handbag or timepiece. Imposing African men whispered 'Rolex, Rolex,' as I passed, slipping into alleyways to retrieve their contraband. I had promised a friend that I'd look out for a particular brand of watch, but those available were such poor imitations that even Paul Blart would have sniffed them out.

In the evening I met up with Rob Matre, a golf photographer based in Atlanta. Rob and I had been swapping emails since we'd missed each other in Georgia, and he'd been out at The Black shooting on the Monday and Tuesday. The grounds were soaking, and the fans blowing the greens were a near-futile effort to reduce the moisture.

An art-gallery owner in downtown Atlanta, Rob came to golf photography by accident. In 2003 he went to watch practice for the WGC-American Express Championship at Capital City Club in Atlanta. Leaving his car, he noticed his camera in the backseat. On impulse he grabbed it, and a few minutes later he saw Tiger teeing off. A superb picture at the top of his follow-through later, Rob had discovered another talent. Looking at his black and white photographs from various events, at Lake Nona in Florida and across to Cypress Point in California, Rob strikes me as golf's answer to Ansel Adams: creator of beautiful images that bring out the best in their subjects.[1]

Rob, me and Doug, a tennis partner of Rob's who was in town for business, chatted on all things golf. This more than made up for my two crab cakes, six scallops and lone Amstel costing me $100. In stark contrast, the last meal I'd had on US soil was on the final evening of my Masters trip, in Hooters. Unlike the restaurant in cosmopolitan Manhattan, I was served by a young lady in orange hot pants and clinging white top, who described my choice of cheeseburger and fries as 'awesome'. She also pointed out the Training Burgers, a great way to start my meal. This explained why the guy opposite had the build of SpongeBob SquarePants, and his resting heartbeat was that of a cross-country skier at full tilt. In New York our meal was almost awesome, and worth every penny. But fighting jet lag, I had to get some shuteye.

As I walked downtown, Times Square was awash with visitors looking for a meal or a show in the perpetual electronic haze of innumerable neon signs – each flash, every pixel, promising a slice of the American dream. One street promoter asked me if I liked comedy and free beer. Silly question, but I continued onwards, thinking of the US Open. For years it had been a TV spectacle that I didn't enjoy too much. The

1. For Rob Matre's work see *www.robertmatre.com*.

rough seemed horrifically penal, the greens obscenely hard and fast. My hero was Seve, but his never-say-die attitude and attacking play meant his chances of victory in America's golf championship were a statistical error factor. Former USGA president Sandy Tatum said of the US Open examination, 'we're not trying to humiliate the greatest players in golf. We're trying to identify them.'

Tales of course preparation are legendary and verge on the zany, like the work of nutty professors high on hashish. At Inverness in 1979, Lon Hinkle cut 60 yards off the long 8th by driving down the 17th fairway; others followed. Overnight the USGA planted a tree to stop the short-cut. Another tale has an official dropping a ball onto the middle of a green, and not being happy with the green's speed until the ball rolled off. Ridiculously fast greens at Shinnecock Hills and Olympic had quality players hitting 3-foot putts 30 feet past. In 2004, Shinnecock's 7th green was slicker than a bobsleigh run. *Golfweek* columnist Jeff Babineau said it was 'a Coney Island carnival on a golf course that got away'.

However, the championship seems to be moving away from this lunacy. Last year's denouement at Torrey Pines was perhaps the greatest ever. The world's greatest athlete – effectively a cripple – against Joe the Golfer, on a day that twice went into extra time, only for Goliath to defeat his David through sheer determination. It had been a long time since I'd jumped off my chair and punched the air as I did for Rocco Mediate's putt at the 15th. What would this year bring? With all the rain and more forecast, purple greens and putting lotteries were not going to be factors.

I'd booked a hotel no more than a block from Penn Station, the starting point for the Long Island Rail Road out to Farmingdale, where shuttle buses would transfer us the few miles to the course. The 05:00 alarm signalled the real start to my second major, and crossing to the station, the city was starting to wake up, people pounding the streets to their daily hell. It was warm, almost muggy, and the few clouds in the sky suggested a bright, sunny day. In the station I bought a ten-journey ticket and grabbed a fission-heated coffee to perk me up. I'd tried the coffee machine in my hotel, but succeeded only in producing a toxic sludge that would kill even the most hardened cockroach.

While I waited for confirmation of the track number, US Open-specific announcements played on the PA system, wishing us a good day, informing us of the transfer protocol at Farmingdale and advising of prohibited items. No weapons were allowed, and we were told this wasn't just limited to firearms and knives. I presume the caveat was for those with the inclination to bring machetes, death stars and flame-throwers to tournaments. John Rambo never looked good in a Pringle sweater.

The entire transit system for the golf was smooth. There are Americans who should be regularly nominated for Nobel Peace Prizes purely for queue organisation. If, like me, you've seen some of the antagonism, aggression and grief in European queues, you'll know exactly what I mean. They are psychotic episodes waiting to happen, where even world-class exponents of Brazilian Jujitsu linger in deep, primal fear. In contrast, US queues are jolly, social affairs where one is never static.

Alighting from the train, we filtered past ticket collectors and to the security barriers for the golf. We were scanned for prohibited items – a stand nearby awaited mobile phones and machetes – and boarded the transfer bus. Within minutes we were on our way, and during the brief journey I chatted to an older gentleman from Windsor, Ontario. His wife was spending her days in Manhattan while he was at the golf. The bus dropped us next to the clubhouse ten minutes later, and with my ticket scanned I entered the course. The range opened out to my left and the massive merchandising tent reared up in front of me like a benevolent Transformer, huge and imposing.

Despite the hour, hundreds had already turned out, the bleacher at the practice area was full and the railings along the range were inundated with keen New York golf fans. I watched as Phil Mickelson was welcomed with claps and cheers. He shook the hand of Butch Harmon and laughed and joked. A perennial favourite in these parts, his appearance this year was all the more poignant due to his wife Amy's recent diagnosis with breast cancer. I cheered and shouted, too. A Phil win would produce golfing bedlam.

I spent the day walking the course. The first thing to strike me was the elevation changes at many holes. Arriving at the top of the hill at the

18th, one fan screamed to his buddy, 'Where's the frickin' tow rope?' If he was totally honest with himself, losing about 100 pounds would have made his walk a bit easier, but he did have a point. Parallel to the final hole, the 1st dipped straight down the hill, the corner of the dog-leg about six storeys below. The massive 4th hole was on four different levels, a tasty layer cake of golfing majesty. These variations gave some holes Augusta-like qualities, and apart from holes 10, 11, 12 and 13, The Black allowed for generous viewing. This was a relief, as I'd feared watching Tiger or Phil at a US Open would be like the opening scene from Gladiator.

The vastness of Bethpage Black was breathtaking, a golfing Manhattan. It was a big golf course in every sense, and hacking round in level par 70 wasn't going to happen. The State Park itself is huge, just over three times the size of Monaco, although the Park doesn't have a casino, Lamborghinis and Ferraris everywhere, and there weren't many Euro hardbodies wearing Prada. But for public golf it is a paradise. As beautiful as one of Eliot Spitzer's high-class hookers, the Black has a reputation for being meaner than a junkyard dog. Three hundred thousand rounds are played at the Bethpage complex each year, and over 70,000 golfers are registered to play.

As well as the five public golf courses – Yellow, Green, Blue, Red, Black – Bethpage plays host to one of the most elite sports on the planet. The famous polo field is home to Meadowbrook Polo Club's Sunday chukkas and was the venue for the 1994 polo US Open. Not even Tiger could win that. It was here that Gonzo master Hunter S. Thompson started the research for his novel, *Polo Is My Life*, and no doubt in a haze of narcosis, mistakenly interviewed a local dentist he'd taken for one of polo's legendary Gracida brothers.

One well known golf writer criticised Bethpage Black in 2002 for having no stretches worthy of memory, but this smacks of the modern need for instant gratification over the slow burn of quality. The 4th and 5th holes are two design classics, a colossal par-5 and a very tricky par-4. The 15th to the 18th offer a variety of challenges and opportunities and include two of the best holes in major golf. The 15th is a ball-breaking

458-yard par-4, uphill to a severely canted two-tier green. And the 17th is a stadium-like, big par-3 that will be the home of as much theatre as the 71st hole. Not bad for a public course that was born during a New Deal work program in the Great Depression.

The weather was great – unlike the foreboding forecast for future days – and I overheard one fan say he'd never seen the Open so busy during practice. At the 6th hole, Jeff Sorg asked me if I was a photographer and I told him of my project. I bumped into him again at the 14th. Tall and thin with long greying hair, and sporting a casually bohemian look of jeans, shirt hanging out, it wasn't surprising Jeff was a songwriter for children. He wouldn't have looked out of place strumming with Buffalo Springfield. Jeff told me that he'd been at a few US Opens, but his memory of 1980 at Baltusrol stood out. There, a golden-topped Jack Nicklaus won his 16th major, only his second major in a five year spell during which he was continually written off. Jeff said Jack's gleaming hair was like a halo, as fans literally climbed trees to see a golfing angel back at his major best.

I asked Jeff if he'd ever played The Black. 'No, maybe one day. With a cannon.'

I didn't see Tiger. Woods tends to be up with the larks for his practice sessions, so I wasn't surprised. The course was vast, so it'd be quite possible for him to be on the back nine as I walked the front. Apart from The Masters in April, I'd never made the effort to follow Tiger, and I was keen to see him practise. That would have to wait until the Open or the PGA.

Via my hotel I arrived at my next sporting event of the day, the Washington Nationals at the New York Yankees. On paper this fixture was so one-sided it was like Evander Holyfield v. Macaulay Culkin, or Roger Federer v. Stephen Hawking. At Wimbledon. The cheapest ticket was $14, but I splashed $56 for mine, which meant I was fairly high up in the stadium, but not quite in the ozone. I could have paid as much as $2,625 plus the $59.70 Convenience Charge. That's the kind of convenience, and euphemism, I could do without. Who said The Masters was the hardest ticket in sport?

The cost of New Yankee Stadium was about $1.5 billion. A sobering thought, as a prominent billboard downtown advertised that 22% of New Yorkers have to choose between medication or food to survive. Many Yankees fans were in need of medication – playing one of the worst teams in baseball, they lost 3-2. Striking out against jet lag, I was prone to nodding off. If the Yankees keep losing to the likes of the Nationals, the whole stadium will be asleep.

Some of the team's poor form had been attributed to the starting pitcher from Taiwan, Chien-Ming Wang. In fairness to Mister Wang, his wife had had their first baby the night before, so his mind might have been elsewhere, although at a salary of $5 million, maybe it shouldn't. I had no trouble understanding the rules of the game, but I had trouble seeing where the skill was in some areas. The throwing between fielders and basemen was pencil-straight, rapid and impressive, but I couldn't detect with my untrained eye much of a difference between a swing that produced a strike-out or a batted ball.

I took a wander around the stadium and determined that with an infinite supply of Indiana limestone anyone could throw it up. Although it was designed by one of the world's leading stadium architectural firms, I was pretty sure a four-year-old with ADHD and a pack of crayons could do just as well. Two things stood out in the store. If you sold baseball bats in the team shops of Scotland's national game, carnage would ensue. Secondly, perhaps there was a lesson for even The Masters Golf Shop. The most ardent Yankees fan, or agronomist, can purchase the same seed used in the stadium, a trademarked proprietary blend of Kentucky Blue Grass. This sounds like insanity, but on reflection even I'd buy bent grass from Augusta in the hope some would take on my apartment window sill.

The result of the loss to the Nationals was that Thursday's big story was not the weather or inevitability of a Woods victory, but the efficiency of a certain Mister Wang. For my part, however, I wanted to see Tiger at bat. It was time for golf's Hank Aaron to improve his major slugging percentage.

US OPEN THURSDAY: BLACK DAY AT BETHPAGE

I was awoken around 03:00 by a hellish racket. Torrential rain was battering my window, and I had trouble getting back to sleep, with a combination of jet lag and the fridge in my room clunking like a Romanian chemical plant. This was not an ideal combo, something that became patently obvious when I had to get out my bed to catch the 06:18 Tiger Express, scheduled solely to cater for Woods' tee-time at 08:06.

The train was twice as busy as Wednesday's despite the *New York Times* carrying the article, 'Preparing for a Deluge, and They Can't Build an Ark'. This kind of pessimism is usually the preserve of British weather forecasts, and it echoed the Biblical scale of the rain I had already heard on my windows in the early hours. Drawing on Scripture was appropriate, as Bethpage is a reworking of Bethphage, the place in the Bible from whence Jesus sent his disciples to find a donkey and colt for his triumphal entry into Jerusalem.

As I watched the cloudy, dark and patchy sky, we flickered past sodden streets and soaking industrial units. A wet and tired fun fair at one stop looked portentously miserable. It was not what I had envisaged for New York in summer. Already the state was on track for its second wettest and seventh coldest June on record.

As we waited to filter onto the transfer buses at Farmingdale, lumpy, cold rain lashed our faces, legs and arms. I had on cargo shorts and a short-sleeved waterproof jacket, but already something extra was needed, probably an umbrella. I was going to have to be one of those multi-armed Hindu Gods to hold a brolly, take notes, walk and watch Tiger all at the same time. Despite the downpour, a father behind me was tempting his son with tales of professional golf.

'Wait till you see these guys hit the golf ball. You'll hear it sing overhead, the ball actually sings in flight.' Clearly he was a tinnitus sufferer, or mixing up golf balls with incoming artillery shells.

Rain bouncing off my head, I ran from ticket scanning to the golf shop, where a lady stood on the steps handing out ponchos for purchase.

I instinctively grabbed one, then ran inside for cover and an umbrella. I baulked on seeing the price of a brolly, so decided to take my chances with my fetching, new, royal blue poncho. Like a cross between a Mexican peasant and a keen but disorientated hiker, I scuttled round to the first tee. Hundreds of people were filing along the narrow pathway left of the clubhouse, and a thousand fans were waiting for Woods to appear as rain battered us from our left.

As holder and 2002 Bethpage victor, the Golfing Messiah made his own triumphal entry. The crowd had surrounded the first tee atop the hill, six-deep. Angel Cabrera appeared first to muted applause. Harrington was next, and he was greeted warmly, no shortage of Irish descendants in the gallery. And then Tiger, to massive roars, cheers and claps, welcomed like the Promised Redeemer. By now the rain was thumping it down, and those who could, took refuge under their umbrellas. Although Tiger's welcome was warm and very enthusiastic, I couldn't help but feel that some of the New York exuberance was stifled under the charcoal skies. I crouched below some brollies, a small respite from relentless deluge.

'Make it stawp rainin', Tyga,' shouted one local in a thick New York brogue, generating much laughter.

Woods probably could make it stop raining, but he was focused on his assault on his 15th major victory. As the first two stood up, the MetLife blimp had hovered directly overhead, but now it motored away, a gentle whirring in the distance. Tiger took the tee, and in some perverse replay of his drive at the first hole on Sunday at Augusta National, he powered a lavish hook that went about 325 yards and further left than Kim Jong-il.

Viewing was immediately affected by the overnight rains. The slope to the left of the 1st was closed, so wet and slippery that it was dangerous (or fun). It was frustrating to be making compensations for the weather, walking *away* from a threesome that featured the winners of the last four majors. But that was better than careering on our arses down lethal hillsides and rolling about in a river of muck like Augustus Gloop in the Chocolate Factory.

By the time I got down to the bottom of the slope at the 18th I could see Tiger taking his stance, upper body just visible amongst a phalanx of spectators. He made a decent swing and the ball flew towards the green. Minutes later Cabrera hit a chunky shot about 60 yards out of the left rough into the fairway. My poncho and hat were doing a great job, but I was already soaking from my knees down and I continued to enjoy the kind of facial you can't buy on Madison Avenue. Once round the dogleg, about 100 yards from the green, I was unimpressed to see the crossway near the green was also closed, so I was now on the wrong side of the fairway to easily access the 2nd tee, and would instead have to cross at the 17th, head away from the 2nd across one of the internal roads in the state park before starting in the correct direction. It was starting to feel like Mao Tse-tung's Long March.

Epic hike aside, it was business as usual at the 1st and the experience of following Tiger lived up to expectations. Despite driving like a nervous 5- handicapper from the tee, Woods got up and down from the tricky right bunker to secure his par. Cabrera flubbed his way to bogey. Harrington also had a 5, his via a three jiggle. Watching the putts, it was obvious that, despite the rain, the greens were still quick.

If I'd been one of the 80 or so people inside the ropes stalking this threesome, my journey to the 2nd would not have been circuitous, but I got there in time to see Cabrera stripe his tee ball down the middle. While the 1st is a downhill left to right dog leg, the 2nd is a 389-yard elbow, right to left. The hole runs through a small valley, flanked by a ridge on both sides, allowing the fans to look down on the players and, if one is far enough up, to see the green. Although it was early morning, wet, and, in any other circumstances, totally miserable, there were thousands following this game.

The legion of brollies became an issue as the row in front obscured the view of those behind – nothing that a touch of New York chutzpah couldn't cure.

'Brollies down!' a few shouted, even as players eyed up their shots.

'Brollies down!' intoned others, repeating the first warning. As if by magic, brollies were lowered and closed.

'Guy in the purple. BROLLY DOWN.'

As I watch the green being squeegeed, a dufus stands right in front of me, obscuring my view and that of about 20 others. He has to know the spot he's taken is not ideal. He doesn't respond to suggestions from behind that he should move or die, and although it was very innocuous, it now sounds slightly shameful, I reach out, gently place the canopy of his brolly betwixt finger and thumb and give it a very short, firm tug, then immediately release it. Dufus Boy gets the message and moves on.

It's ominous that greens have to be cleared of water so early, and Cabrera really takes his time eyeing his putt up.

'Hit the shot, already,' a fan booms. Not one for patience, clearly.

Ever the perfectionist, Tiger asks for further squeegee work on his line, but nobody shouts, screams or even bats an eyelid. Hit the shot, already. As Woods eyes up his putt, a massive roar erupts from the 3rd green: Justin Leonard has obviously hit it close. Three pars and they move on.

The worst thing about following Tiger can also be the best. I hadn't noticed it at Augusta because he was playing with Phil. Every time Tiger plays a shot, about 70% of the gallery starts moving to get in position for his next, and the other players' shots are easily followed. At the back of the 3rd tee, the walkway consisted of mud and more mud, with a spot of standing water. It was nasty, wet, cold and, in parts, smelly. I peered through the bodies and brollies to see Tiger fizz a long iron onto the green. His shot was in sharp contrast to Cabrera's pushed iron, and some form of utility club from Harrington. Once Tiger struck his tee shot, I went from fourth row to on the ropes. All this movement and noise must be extremely frustrating for the other players, but I wasn't complaining.

Walking down through the trees, I was hoping to get across to the 4th tee, but the steep 70-yard slope up the right side was blocked. On Wednesday, when the weather had been nice, the slope was verging on treacherous and had taken out a couple of victims, so I stand at the bottom of the hill and listen to the players finish up at the 3rd. I have no idea what they score, but assume from the lack of cheers it's a regulation par for the T-Man.

The 4th at Bethpage Black is sublime. For a golf hole that contains and flanks no water, it's the most beautiful on the planet. On first seeing it, it gave me goose pimples. It epitomises the Black; high, wide and handsome. If you were an average guy and you tried to chat the 4th hole up in bar, she'd give you a look of disdain and walk away, glass of Cristal in hand, Manolos tripping across the floor, and still you'd think she was the best thing you'd ever seen. For the average golfer this hole must be the scene of countless cataclysms.

The vastness makes it look 617 yards long against an actual 517, and it sits on four different levels. The players hit from an elevated tee, across a 200-yard dip into the first section of fairway which is about 130 yards long and flanked by a bunker down the left. From the middle of the back tee, it's 293 yards to carry the trap, and Harrington really pumps one up there, 325 yards. For the world-class player the second shot is a long-iron, rescue or fairway wood up to the green on the fourth level, missing out the third. This third level sits above one of the most fantastic bunkers in golf – an 85-yard long, diagonal, variegated sand trap in which you could easily imagine a 24-handicapper spending a long weekend. Similar to the 10th at Augusta National, the large cross bunker is not really in play for the big guns; however, as the championship progresses, anyone missing the fairway and finishing even in the first cut of rough has to take their medicine and pitch out to the front of the second level.

I've played golf courses in Scotland that have about six holes crammed into the space of this one hole at Bethpage. Flanked by trees for the first 150 yards, the trees on the right remain, but meander away. The trees on the left stop, and the hole opens out. From the middle of the fairway, the trees to the right are about 60 yards away, but on the left they're about 160 yards away. It's a vast golfing arena, and each shot will require steady nerve and total commitment.

It's still Tiger away first. As soon as ball contacts club head there's a cry of 'Get in the hole!' and everybody laughs.

This pointless shout is regarded as the golfing equivalent of reciting the Lord's Prayer backwards. It sounds really dumb when you hear it over the TV. But for some reason, this morning I have an epiphany, and I get it. Hearing it for real I understand it is *total* nonsense, a joke. I'm not condoning the behaviour, but I think it has no point except its own absurdity. When someone shouts 'Get in the hole!' on Tiger's second shot, and I'm standing in the middle of a bush, the only way I could guarantee myself a view without impeding the shifting masses, I quite enjoy the novelty value.

It's time for me to try and catch another game, and as I walk back down the hole to cross, two shouts ring out from the crowd around Woods' game.

'Go Phil!'

'Tiger, you suck.'

I leave Woods, Harrington and Cabrera as they march up the hill. I want to see Geoff Ogilvy, Jim Furyk and World No. 3, Paul Casey. They teed off at the 10th hole at 07:55. As I leave the 4th, Ryan Moore, Eric Axley and Ben Crane play up the hole. I watch as Crane plays his second shot. He is one of *the* slowest players on tour, fashions have been known to change quicker. By the time he gets finished today, platform shoes will be back in vogue.

After I left the golf sloth behind, it was a five-minute walk through a wood before I popped out at another hole. The rain was nasty again and it was coming down like soggy marbles. The threesome in front of my target game, Henrik Stenson, Andrew Svoboda and Steve Stricker, were putting out on the 13th green, so I sat in the stand.

At 605 yards, dead-flat and sodden, the 13th was playing super-long. Casey and Co. had laid up about 100 yards out. Paul and Jim both hit lovely shots in to about 12 feet. Then Ogilvy hits his approach right down the throat of the pin, but it lands over it and hops into the rough, nestling down in the fashion so beloved by the USGA. As the players walk up, the rain is shifting and unpleasant. Ogilvy goes behind the green, takes a look at his ball and chooses his most lofted club.

'Never in my life would I do that,' pipes up the guy next to me, his tone telling everyone it's the wrong shot. Ogilvy is lying slightly down, hitting to a fast-running but receptive green and he has about eight feet to play with. He has some of the softest hands in the golfing short game. A three-quarter swing later and a beautiful pop out to two feet. Anyone who knows the Aussie's game is not surprised but still highly appreciative; it's a delight to behold. Furyk and Casey both miss, and it's par all round.

The short 14th hole offers good birdie chances, although with the pin cut middle right and a bunker protecting, the threesome all take their shots to the centre. None holes, but again the putts look very slick, slowly but inevitably meandering holeward. Crossing to the 15th, I spot a small legion of handsome youngsters all dressed in red Puma ponchos. One, a young, attractive brunette, is handing out badges that signal one's love for Puma players. I request one for a souvenir, and although I don't actually love either player, I favour an Ogilvy badge over an Edfors one (sorry, Johan, but I know with a good support system in place and some counselling, you'll get over it).

Picking my way down the muddy right side of the 15th, I cross left, which takes me to Paul Casey's tee shot. He's pulled his drive into the weapons-grade fescue, two feet high, soaking and thick. So thick that not only does Casey want to take relief under penalty, he can't work out his best option. The conventional two-club-length drop is likely to create as many problems as he has already, so he explores options of going back in line with the pin, or pitching backwards.

By now the rain has gone nuclear, and it's coming down like well-cooked sprouts, lashing into Casey as his caddy tries to keep player and equipment dry. I turn and cock my head in an effort to avoid the rain that is thrashing into my face. It's getting mildly ridiculous, and the rain has gone from a wet irritation to a real hindrance to golf and spectating. Just then, air-horns blow across the course. Play is suspended.[1]

I'm one of the lucky ones. I have a ticket that includes access to the Trophy Club, and it's across the 16th fairway, just a 120-yard walk. I'm quickly inside; minutes later it's full and a massive queue forms outside, the tent unable to cater for all the eligible fans at once.

1. It's 10:16: around 2,500 ponchos had been sold and 600 umbrellas had gone by 9 o'clock.

The rain was thumping down, massive pools formed and there were rivers of water everywhere as I looked out the door. It was so wet Chesley B. Sullenberger could have landed a US Airways Airbus on the 15th green. I was convinced there would be no further play.

I grabbed some food and, unlike at The Masters concessions, it was back to reality, as I was mugged, the total bill around $20. I tried to find a place to stand and eat, but there was nowhere to sit, wet bodies everywhere. I located a spot near a TV and hooked into my $9 fish and chips. As well as the problem of over-capacity, there was nowhere for people to place their trays when finished, so folk abandoned them with half-finished drinks and half-eaten burgers, stinking of fat, reeking of cholesterol. No seats and a challenge to keep the food down: I'd paid $50 extra a day for this privilege. I was not impressed, but it could have been worse. Two hundred poor souls were stuck outside waiting in line.

I looked at the TV, straining to hear while watching the news scroll along the bottom of the screen. It was now so wet outside that any restart should see the players go out two-by-two, with Noah as the championship's head referee. As I watched the box and played with my damp, matted hair, I was asked by another fan what the latest was. It turned out that Ben Fontaine was on his own too, so we broke open a couple of Heinekens and got chatting.

Ben was at Bethpage courtesy of French player Thomas Levet, one of the vanquished in the 2002 Open play-off won by Ernie Els at Muirfield. He'd played with Thomas in a pro-am in Biarritz a few years back and they'd kept in touch. Ben's slot with Levet had been secured courtesy of winning France's most improved player – having just taken up golf in 2004, in a single season his handicap tumbled from 54 to 11. I bet he was popular at his club. He now plays off 4, and as an employee of Air France he'd flown Business Class from Paris. Un sacré veinard.

Play was finally cancelled at 1.55; we'd had four beers by then, and were feeling no pain. Again life seemed good. Ben was also staying in Manhattan, so we waded through the mud towards the buses, looking forward to whatever tomorrow would bring. Worst-case scenario, we both had a drinking partner if things got wet.

On the train, one fan told how his day panned out. He'd arrived at the golf and spent about an hour in the merchandising tent, then checked his purchases. He made for the Trophy Club, ordered a panini, and at the same time heard that play was being suspended. When it was finally cancelled, he'd seen no golf. Another saw a single shot. It soon became apparent that their experiences were common. At least I'd been there early, seen some golf and could get back to my hotel mildly satisfied.

After showering and changing, I went to a few bars I'd been to on previous visits. After visiting the Red Lion and the Soho Room, I wandered up to the White Horse Tavern, a bar with major literary credentials. It was here that Dylan Thomas once claimed to have beaten the world whisky-drinking record (18 straight, one after the other), and where he also eventually killed himself, collapsing outside after a session and dying later in the Chelsea Hotel. After my day, I began to appreciate how Dylan felt, although I didn't feel compelled to match his efforts. I wasn't certain what Friday had in store, but one thing was for sure, times were bad if even Tiger couldn't make it stop raining.

US OPEN FRIDAY: FRIDAY'S GOLF IS LOVING AND GIVING

The forecast for Friday was no picnic. Rain was expected and further delays were in the offing. In the morning, the weather segment on the news had described Bethpage as 'wetter than the mistiest day in Ireland'. With only 136 minutes of play on the Thursday, the USGA's backs were immediately up against the wall in terms of completion and, ominously, Mike Davis – tournament director – had already mentioned Monday and Tuesday in a press conference.

Yesterday's rain was just half the battle, previous rains throughout June had saturated The Black. I'd come to the US Open really hoping there would not be a play-off, but already Monday play was looking certain. In fairness, an extra day spent at Bethpage wouldn't be a hardship, as the course was a visual and golfing feast to test the world's greatest players. The consensus among them was almost 100%: the course was very tough, but very fair.

The cancellation emphasised that The Black would be a star of the week. Before heading to Long Island, I had the chance to speak with Rees Jones, the Open Doctor, golf architect responsible for reworking seven US Open courses, six PGA Championship ones, four Ryder Cup tracks, a Walker Cup course, and an original design for the 2001 Walker. If some designers are the 13th hole at Mince Head GC, Rees Jones is surely the 4th at Bethpage Black: comprehensive and inspiring. Few in golf can claim degrees from both Yale and Harvard Design School.

Mr Jones told me that one of the challenges of redesign for big championships is to ensure the courses can also be playable and challenging for members and the public. Stretching courses and adding bunkers must allow great flexibility during and after events. He'd learned from his father – legendary course architect Robert Trent Jones – that courses should be adaptable enough to demand easy or difficult shots, depending on tees and pins, with a good mix of thinking and power required. A lot of copy on The Black focuses on the great work by A.W. Tillinghast in creating his original design, and other articles feature claims by Joe Burbeck's family that he was the original designer: all of this misses the fact that in 2009, the course also has an awful lot of Rees Jones about it. Hale Irwin (US Open champ, '74, '79, '90) once wished Jones had to play the courses he designed. Rees replied, 'I wish I was good enough.'

On Friday morning I jumped on the 06:07 – today's Tiger Express was an ungodly 05:35 – but this time I had someone to tag along with, having met Ben outside Penn Station. Despite Thursday's washout and today's possible rain, the train was twice as busy as yesterday. I reckoned it was going to be so wet that shoes and socks were a waste of time, so resorted to sandals and bare feet.

Once on the course we realised that we'd forgotten to pick up copies of the draw, so had to walk back, having traipsed halfway down the 18th. After five minutes, just near the putting green, a volunteer passed me, carrying a large pile, so I asked if I could grab a couple, but Big Shot would only allow me to take one, even though I asked politely again. So we had to continue all the way back to get another; customer service at its best.

Initially the draw was a bit confusing. Yesterday's play restarted at 07:30, and the second half of Thursday's play would commence at 10:00. As per usual, the draw would then be reversed, and the second round would start at 16:00. This was too much at 07:40 – I already had a sore head, and I'd only had 15 whiskies the night before. There was a long day ahead.

When it comes to groupings, the USGA has a fertile imagination. The 2008 draw gained a lot of publicity for grouping the top three players in the world, Tiger, Phil and Adam Scott, together, leaving the rest of the field to get on with their golf in an ocean of relative calm while a circus followed the marquee group. This year's draw was less obviously contrived, but imagination was to the fore.

The two Romeros played with Jimenez; the two Singhs were out with Choi. Hansen and Hanson played alongside each other. ESPN commentators were given to calling them the Hanson Brothers, although I don't know if they were referring to the pop combo or the two hilarious zoomers in the movie *Slapshot*.

As well as grouping old guys with old guys, and young handsome blokes with Sergio Garcia, there were some less obvious choices. Lucas Glover, D.J. Trahan and Kyle Stanley are alumni of Clemson University in South Carolina; Les Trois Mousquetaires, Levet, Lucquin and Jacquelin were out together; and finally, with a nod to the USGA's other premier national championship, three former US Amateur Champions were in Group 20 – Billy Mayfair (1987), Matt Kuchar (1997) and Ricky Barnes (2002). Just a bit of fun on the USGA's part, although they missed the chance to put Johnson and Johnson with Jensen. That could have caused no end of confusion.

The final group at the first tee on Friday was Matt Nagy, Shawn Stefani and Doug Batty.

'Yeah, who's going to be out watchin' them? Their parents, their brothers and sisters; their cousins, their grandparents. Period.' One guy's generous assessment as I perused the draw.

Right of the first fairway, in front of a row of corporate facilities, was a complete quagmire. It was like Nutella. In places the mud appeared to be around six inches deep. While yesterday was bad, today was horrid – Special Forces wouldn't swim through this; even farmers would take the day off.

'Go Jimbo! Go get 'em, Jimmy!' rang out as Furyk appeared, eyeing up his second shot to the 1st. Ben and I decided to skip round to the 2nd hole, rather than wallow in the mud. At the 2nd hole Jim Furyk hit a shot you rarely see from a pro – struck beautifully, but in the wrong direction. I expected Jim to aim right and hit a draw. Instead he aimed right and hit it straight there. He looked as bemused as I did, checking his stance and alignment.

Again the rain interfered with spectating, as the right-hand side of the 2nd hole had been blocked off, so we headed up the hill towards the 3rd green. Svoboda, Stricker and Stenson were finishing up on the short hole, but before we got there, at least two people slipped and fell on the hill left of the 2nd fairway.

'Man down. Medic!' was one reaction.

By the time we get round to the 3rd I'm covered up to my ankles in thick, smelly mud.

At the 4th, the course and the dampness show their teeth. Both Casey and Ogilvy hit decent drives but missed the fairway to the right, nestling in the rough. Faced with a possible lay up to the third tier, a shot of about 170 yards into a narrow sliver of fairway protected by a long, evil bunker, they pitch out diagonally, leaving nasty thirds of around 200 yards to a pin nestling two tiers above. Missing the fairway at the 4th now means a very tricky combination of shots for par.

As access to the 5th tee is also restricted, we wait at a crossing, trying to spot the players' balls in flight. Furyk, Casey and the three caddies make their way down to the hole, but Ogilvy is not with them. He's ducked away to further moisten Bethpage Black. When he does appear, the crowd is trickling across the fairway and he has to negotiate his way through.

The gentleman in front of me, white-haired, around seventy and sporting a stomach sponsored by Anheuser-Busch, stops in his tracks and turns to Ogilvy. Referring to the Puma sportswear Ogilvy wears, he says, 'Geoff, I'd like to wear that gear but I don't have the nerve.' I can think of quite a few other fans who also shouldn't have the nerve. Geoff smiles, laughs, and carries on his way.

Sheepishly, the lady marshal who'd let us cross says, 'Sorry, Mister Ogilvy.' But the damage is done, she's off Geoff's Christmas card list and won't be spending winter in Australia this year. As the players walk up the fairway, Andrew Svoboda appears in a buggy, driven back to where he'd hit his second shot. He's either lost his ball or, more likely, had such a horrendous lie and nowhere to drop that he's back to his original spot. Again Bethpage was showing its teeth.

There was little sign of the expected rain, and the skies were threatening sunshine. The course looked fine for the players, even though the walkways were a mixture of closed, boggy, slippery and treacherous. The only way to get along the 5th hole, without closing it completely and rerouting the traffic via the 12th, was along its left side, a steep bank dotted with trees. Keeping one's footing was not easy, and one child I saw took a harmless but muddy tumble. All week it becomes common to see backsides and legs smeared in mud.[1]

Watching Ogilvy play the 7th is a joy. At 525 yards, dog-legging at around 280, it's a killer par-4. Ogilvy hits a lovely drive, adjacent to the bunker on the left that starts around 333 out. With around 230 to go, Ogilvy puts his easy, long, tight, flowing swing on it, and his ball blazes like a meteor, true and straight at the flag, pitching right at it and rolling about 10 feet beyond. He completes the perfect execution of the hole by rolling in the putt. His wood into the green had everything you'd expect from one of the world's best players – controlled power, a beautiful flight, and a direction more suited to missile guidance technology.

In total contrast to the crowds watching Tiger yesterday, there's a feeling that we're being treated to a kind of exhibition, albeit with only two birdies so far. It's only 10:20 when Ogilvy makes his birdie, his 16th hole – so it's slightly surreal anyway – but there's a calmness out here,

1. On the train one evening I saw a young couple who had his-and-hers matching skid-marks, if you know what I mean.

miles from the clubhouse. It's as if Casey, Ogilvy and Furyk are playing a bounce game and word has been leaked, a few hundred turning out to see the players ranked third, fifth and tenth in the world.

We had no plans for the rest of the day, so it was coincidence that a spate of good players were starting their first rounds at the 10th. The list reads like a who's who – Duval, Toms, Kim, McIlroy, Goosen, Els and Mickelson. The right side of the tee was roped off, but a marshal was holding a further cordon on this side, as a massive puddle had formed on the track that rang alongside. After watching a game tee off, the marshal moved and, with some of the crowd dispersing, we waded shin-deep through the puddle and positioned ourselves right on the ropes.

The 10:33 game consisted of the Davids Duval and Toms, and Darren Clarke. Duval received a massive welcome. While Bernhard Langer was the fashion stakes loser at Augusta, Clarke assumed this honour at Bethpage, sporting a flat cap that, had it not had a bank's name on the front and a club manufacturer's on the side, would have made him look like a chubby Belfast shipyard-worker heading for a pint. It was a shocker and I suspect that Darren himself knew this, as he'd worn his usual visor in the practice rounds. His caddy was sporting a lovely white version of the flat cap. New York Fashion Week it was not.

Next up is Kim, McIlroy and big-hitting Dustin Johnson. Dustin averages 310 yards per drive, and he's followed by his caddy who plonks down the Taylor-Made US Open commemorative bag. Johnson reaches into the bag and pulls out a Randy Myers Golf Stretching Pole (not to be confused with a randy stretching pole, something else entirely), and conducts a series of calisthenics, exhibiting flexibility that suggests where his power originates. Some modern golfers are seriously supple, and I'm minded of Lucas Glover on TV just weeks before, bending over at the waist and rotating his arms backwards right round to the ten o'clock position. I can hear my sinews scream and my cartilages rupture at the thought.

Next up it's the Hanson Brothers with their hockey sticks, followed by the reason the crowd has now swelled to hundreds, Phil Mickelson. Social dynamo and twice US Open winner Retief Goosen appears first, to almost no reaction and little appreciation. Joe the Plumber would have received more of a tumult. Next up is all round good guy and occasional beer monster, Ernie Els. By the time Mickelson appears, the tee is surrounded, eight deep, and every single person is cheering, clapping, shouting. We all want Phil to succeed.

The various introductions are made within the group of officials, scorers and volunteers. The players introduce themselves, and while it's usually a case of limp handshakes, at best a quick nod, for Mickelson it's a friendly handshake with a very open, 'Hi, Phil', as if he's meeting this young scoreboard girl at his daughters' school. It's not difficult to see why the fans all love him. With my cynic's hat on, it's not difficult also to see why some players don't like him, considering him false and saccharin, but a bit of courtesy goes a long way. By now Tiger has closed with a +4 round of 74, and I'm pretty sure the players know this and relish the chance of stealing a march.

By the time Phil and the South Africans drive, Darren Clarke is coming off the 11th green, walking to the 12th tee, adjacent to the 10th. Some bloke at the top of the bleacher stands up and bellows something. He shouts it again, thousands within earshot.

'Ben, what's that guy shouting?'

'Lose the hat, Darren.'

Two other quality games tee off, among them Stuart Appleby, Mike Weir and Stewart Cink, and by the time the 11:39 game is due, Phil's game has finished the 11th. Earlier there had been a massive roar, and one didn't need the scoreboard to know that it was a second shot close. Mickelson was under par after just two holes.

'Welcome back to New York, Phil,' shouts one keen spectator. Other shouts and cheers follow Phil down the 12th. We wait slightly longer than most at the tee, as Ben and I were keen to see his three fellow countrymen, Levet, Lucquin and Jacquelin. To my right stood M. Lucquin's wife: lovely. Ben followed the guys while I decided to see what it was like to follow Phil.

Holes 10 to 13 are dead flat, so I wasn't building my hopes up. Down the side of 12 was a muddy mess, another unfortunate trail of agricultural fudge that not much could be done about, and hiking up the banks of the Amazon in rainy season would have been easier. By now the sun was out, the mud was a bit smellier and the beer was flowing. The place was mobbed, fans milling around between holes – 12, 5 and 6 all adjacent. It was so busy, the terrain so flat, I couldn't see a thing; it was difficult unless you were on the ropes, or a midget or a giant. At the par-4, over 500 yards, Phil had hit a great second shot in to around 10 feet. It was a chance for Mickelson to get to 2-under after three, so already, on a sunny Friday, there was a keen sense of anticipation. I took a position as close to the ropes as possible, next to four guys, all over six feet tall, wearing orange beards and bright green leprechaun outfits. Phil missed, and as he walked to the next tee, he was followed by continual shouts and words of encouragement. The cheering for Phil never stops. Never.

Towards the 14th tee it was party time again. Most people seemed to be paying little attention to the golf, concentrating on fat cigars, beer and conversation. The corner was jam-packed, about eight deep, and the hill was pixelated with fans, so negotiating one's way to the green meant taking the kind of route a drunk would take through an empty aircraft hangar.

The mix of fans is diverse. As well as leprechauns, I spot two guys in the full Canada ice-hockey kit (minus the skates) following Mike Weir. Baseball caps and team-brand sportswear are everywhere. Probably unique to a New York major are the many I spot wearing the yarmulke, the small round skullcap worn by observant Jewish men. There's surely a joke about being observant and in a sports crowd, but I won't go there. If you sat down and thought of 25 different body types, heights, colourings, creeds, jobs, you'd find them all here and more. It's America in microcosm.

This Open's New Yorkness is also typified by some of the food on offer. As well as the usual fare of hot dogs, burgers, quails eggs and deep-fried pheasant, some concession stands offer Kosher Boxes, catering for the Jewish fans at the event.

I cross the road to the part of the course that holds number 1 and 15 to 18, and it's back to Mudsville. The right of the 15th is the worst spot on the entire course, the boiling mud pools of Rotorua gone cold. It's ten paces wide, nightmarishly soggy, and at least one person's shoe gets stuck and comes off. Nathaniel Hawthorne it was who said, 'Life is made up of marble and mud'. He was half right. After wading through I found 16 had one of its crossings closed. We could only cross at the pathway below the tee, and marshals were limiting spectators to the high side.

It's a bit of a pain to all have to walk round the marshal and, like me, many others can't quite see the logic, especially when this part of the course isn't in play and we're all covered in God's cake-mix from the ankles down: crowd control has gone anal. Hurried by his mates, one guy shouts, 'Okay, okay, once Stalin here lets me cross, I'll be with you.' As I leave Stalin behind me, I can hear the crowds roaring for Mickelson as he takes the 15th tee. I'm heading to 17 to watch him and others come through.

In its US Open preview, *Golf Digest* ran an article on how crucial bunker play would be at Bethpage. On most courses, bunkers do not represent an issue for the world's best, and it seems to be the same here, although the large, deep bunkers at Bethpage really showcase the players' talents. The 17th is a big short hole and, sitting in a large expanse of its own, the green is about 40 paces wide, runs upwards from front to back, has a ridge up the middle, and is surrounded by five nasty, yawning, whiskery traps. Finding the dance-floor is just the start.

The second game I watch is Clarke etc., and immediately I'm treated. Darren misses short and right, then hits a beautiful bunker shot to about three feet. Despite this being an uphill sand-shot of about 20 yards, onto a green that's running somewhere between a Formula One car and the speed of light, this is pure bread-and-butter to the Irishman. In contrast, but just as enjoyable, Duval has smashed his tee-shot into 12 feet and holes for birdie. Just another par-3 for these guys, but for a lot of average golfers it would be an adventure.

'Dave! Double D!'

'Go, David.'

'Never give up!' Like Mickelson, Double D is universally popular. The birdie gets DD to even par through eight holes, and he'd eventually go on to shoot a 67, placing him in a tie for third after the first round. Despite the doomsday scenario presented by the weather forecast, it was actually starting to feel like summer. It was early afternoon, the crowds were in good spirits and the beer was cool and refreshing, with some fans more refreshed than others.

There was a funny moment in the next game, when a guy behind me, standing on the hillside, sneezed loudly and involuntarily as Dustin Johnson addressed his short putt for par. This led to unexpected laughter from many in the crowd, including me. Dustin wasn't laughing when he missed the putt. Then came more entertainment of the golfing kind as Peter Hanson boxed a 40-foot birdie try.

For the last 25 minutes there had been distant interludes of cheering, shouting and clapping, growing ever nearer as Mickelson inevitably made his way to the 17th. While Els finished in a bunker short of the green (he was already plus-4 and out of sorts), Phil's tee ball finished on the green 40 feet away. Goosen had hit first and flushed it into four feet: not bad for a slightly uphill 207-yard approach.

Yet another great bunker shot from Els into a few feet, and then it is Phil's turn. Studying his putt, Mickelson examines the testing humps and hollows, understanding that touch and precision are required if the putt isn't to get away from him. He strokes the ball and it makes its way across the putting surface, rolling towards the hole, the crowd's murmur increasing as it closes in. Phil's ball dives into the hole and the crowd go mental, a golfing rave hearing its favourite dance beat. The eruption can probably be heard in Chicago, a sonic boom of appreciation, fans jumping and whooping, *Caddyshack* on acid.

'How do you like the weather, Phil?' booms one fan as Mickelson pick his ball out the hole. Phil laughs openly, looks into the crowd and acknowledges the quip. Once again I'm caught up in an immense golfing moment, goose-bumps forming along my neck. The adulation continues as Goosen eyes up his tester for bird.

'P – H – I – L, Phil! P – H – I – L, Phil!' chants a lone first-class scholar from Clown College. Mickelson winces, looks up, hands indicating that Coco should stop. Goosen misses. O – U – C – H. Ouch.

I try to follow Phil up 18, but cannot get past the crowds packed like sardines back left of the 17th. So I wait a while for a few other games to pass, chatting to a couple from Canada who were down to follow Mike

Weir and lamenting yesterday's washout. They tell me they will stay for the weekend only if they think the weather will be friendly.

Later I go to the Trophy Club for food, and again there isn't a seat available. The queues are massive and two guys in front of me are bitching and moaning about the whole set up, $50 – a $150 ticket in total – for the privilege of waiting in a 20-minute queue. I resolve never to set foot in the Trophy Club again, avoiding the incandescent rage it seems to foster in me, and head for the first tee.

As I walk out of the tent, Sergio Garcia is playing the 16th, and a fan blares 100 yards across the course, 'Hey, Sergio. Thanks for the no re-gripping.' Back in 2002 he'd been mercilessly ripped by the gallery for continually re-gripping the club before swinging, seemingly stuck in a mental funk, unable to get the club back. He'd eventually flipped and given someone the finger, but this time he's widely supported and encouraged. Today some King of Banality was ripping him for not doing something. Sometimes you just can't win.

I'd arranged to meet Ben at the putting green just before four. I'd hoped to see Scotsman Martin Laird in the first group, but I'd read the draw incorrectly; he was at the 10th, about two miles away. Still, at the appointed hour, the announcer on the first tee marked the start of the next 18-hole circuit and the 109th US Open entered its second round. Finally this championship was getting somewhere as Matt Bettencourt took the tee. With the delay and restart, it had been difficult to follow who was doing what, but Mike Weir had assumed the lead with a blistering 64, Peter Hanson recorded a 66, and 67s had been posted by DD, Todd Hamilton and Ricky Barnes.

As Bettencourt hit his drive, I pondered the 108 previous championships, full of golfing heroes and intense battles, often between a player's own heart and mind. Jack Nicklaus' benchmark 1-iron (the greatest of all time) at Pebble Beach in 1972, Tom Watson's chip at Pebble ten years later. The late Payne Stewart. Curtis Strange going back-to-back in '88 and '89, then never winning again.

I thought also of Ben Hogan, the best US Open player who will probably ever live. Hogan won in 1948, 1950 and 1951, winning three in a row, as 1949 was the year of his recuperation from the horrendous collision with a Greyhound bus that should have killed him and his wife. He was third in 1952 and won again in 1953, the year he won the three majors available to him. He was sixth in '54, and second in both '55 and '56, the former being his inexplicable playoff loss to Jack Fleck. Ben Hogan is a golfing legend and the ultimate US Open one.

It was a lovely late summer afternoon, and a healthy crowd surrounded the 1st tee, the famous sign reminding us, WARNING - THE BLACK COURSE IS AN EXTREMELY DIFFICULT COURSE WHICH WE RECOMMEND ONLY FOR HIGHLY SKILLED GOLFERS. I love the idea of the sign, a warning siren to golfing lightweights, but even an eight-year-old would be scolded for using the same word twice in a sentence.

For the next two hours Ben and I stand behind the tee and soak up the golf and banter, and we're basically treated to a long-driving contest. Straight downhill at the 1st the air is now calm, and if anything helping the players slightly from the left. A carry of around 300 yards will get a ball over the trees at the dogleg and right in front of the green. In the second game Gary Woodland, one of the longest hitters on tour, crashes a drive right over the corner, prompting much hollering and cheering. There's also an incessant stream of gentle barracking as the players take the tee.

Darren Clarke's hat escapes our wrath this time, but his caddy is now sporting a visor. Dave Duval pumps a big ball round the corner, which triggers high-fives all round for the crowd, 'Go Double D!' Next up it's Kim, McIlroy and Dustin Johnson. Kim's known to be a fan of a good night out.

'Let's go, AK.'

'AK, let's get juiced up.'

'No, no, you can't do that, yeah, drink your milk. Milk and cookies.'

Next it's Johnson.

'Yo, DJ! Go Low. What was the number, DJ, you must know what you shot!?' We're all laughing, it's hard not to. It's all harmless, none of the players seems annoyed, many are amused. I automatically and uncharacteristically find myself thinking of things to yell, looking forward to joining the circus.

DJ pumps the biggest drive of all, a towering bomb that totally ignores the hole's conventions and plummets to earth somewhere near the walkway at the front of the green.

'DJ, you got the number!' cries a fan.

Two games later it's Els, Mickelson and Retief, and as the last man walks on to the tee, Ben and I get in on the act. 'Goo-oo-oo-se, Goo-oo-oo-se,' we intone, and on cue a hundred join us. Goosen smirks, which, for him, amounts to singing 'Wild Thing' in sequined swimming trunks covered in custard.

We watched the first half of the draw tee-off, by which time it was the back of six o'clock, and decided it was time to get into Manhattan. I fancied going out again for a few beers, a gentle sampling of the nightlife, but having cleaned up at my hotel I fell asleep on the bed, fridge clunking away and TV telling of the muddy carnage on Long Island.

In his book, *Duel in the Sun*, US golf writer Michael Corcoran compared the typical US Open to the Bataan Death March, a brutal 1942 WWII trek in which some 15,000 died. It involved a 90km march in stinking heat and featured such in-transit entertainment as torture, beheadings, random shootings and beatings. Now we've all had some pretty bad days on the golf course, but I'm struggling to recall any quite that awful. Of course Corcoran was exaggerating, he meant to say Passchendaele, the battle-scarred muddy wasteland of WWI. I died in Hell. They called it Bethpage. I couldn't wait to get back tomorrow for more crowd interaction and comedy.

US OPEN WEEKEND: RAGE AGAINST THE DYING OF THE LIGHT

Saturday

My weekend in Manhattan was meant to be sweetness and light, culture and calm, finding time around the golf to take in bits of the island's countless artistic delights. I even looked forward to a long lie. Instead I hauled my ass out of bed at 05:00, showered, dressed and put on my smelly, damp, mud-smeared sandals and headed for Penn Station. On the way I picked up my usual *New York Times* to read on the train.

Making the headlines today was another storm, this time a political one. The New York State Attorney General, Andrew Cuomo, had come to the rescue of fans who'd seen little or no golf on Thursday. David Fay, CEO of the USGA, had incurred the wrath of New Yorkers while filling up at a gas station, and the AG had acted where Fay hadn't. The *Times* reported how one spectator, Keith Nelson, had arrived at Farmingdale Station, only to find the golf had been rained off. He was told his two $150 Trophy Club tickets were now unusable, and he railed against the USGA that they shouldn't be allowed to get away with it. In contrast, fans attending the final day of the Yankees-Nationals game were given better seats to make up for waiting out a long rain delay. Ticket-holders attending fully cancelled baseball games are given rain checks for another day. In New York, the USGA was Public Enemy No. 1.

By Friday afternoon the word on the fairways was that the USGA had made a U-turn, and that spectators could either claim a Thursday refund *or* attend on Monday, but this was quickly clarified by the USGA. If there was Monday play, Thursday tickets were valid; if there was no Monday play and the golf was resolved on Sunday, 50% refunds were available. It was possible that at least 13,000 people were going to be rather annoyed, that being the number who only held Thursday tickets. I had sympathy for both sides. It seemed harsh there were no refunds, but also that the USGA was now at the mercy of *all* the rain that had fallen in June, not just during the golf tournament.

Despite the unpleasant taste it left, the Thursday refund or Monday play option seemed to be a good compromise. Some heavy politicking had gone on. Cuomo's representatives had stepped in and brokered the 50% or Monday play offer. Of course the logical conclusion for me was that I was actually being offered nothing, I already had my Monday ticket.

I did feel mildly aggrieved, and the press release from the USGA annoyed me even more. It stated that safety and the spectator experience were the priorities, but then said that if there was less than 90 minutes golf on Saturday and Sunday, those spectators could come the following days, therefore making a mockery of the safety and viewing excuse. The 2008 US Open was the most successful of all time. According to one source, just 12 months earlier over 300,000 fans had visited Torrey Pines, most of them paying their way; TV ratings were the highest for six years; merchandising sales alone took $20 million. None of the papers picked up on this comparison, they were too busy looking up their own NY backsides.

Normally Saturday is moving day, the cut has been made, and the week's wheat has been separated from the chaff, but that wasn't going to happen at Bethpage until, well, whenever they got round two completed. No offence to any players in particular, but I wasn't exactly rapt at the idea of watching the likes of Bronson Burgoon or Clark Klaasen battle their way around the Black Leopard. It seemed that heading out to the short 8th would be a good idea, I could watch the golf and rest my feet. They'd spent so much time in water they looked like a sailor's from USS *Indianapolis*. But my plan was torpedoed and I only made it as far as the 2nd tee.

Trudging through the coagulating, foul mud by the right of the 1st fairway, I could only laugh. Would I really be doing this if I wasn't on some kind of mad golfing journey? Travelling to the *Heart of Darkness* would be more fun. Fortunately the USGA were in the process of laying down straw on the muddy walkways, soaking up some of the moisture and providing a bit more traction for the unsteady. It seemed to give the whole place a different smell, a country feel. I was minded of the old UK Subs' song, 'Down on the Farm', when we're told we can't fall in love with a wheat-field and everything smells of horse-shit. Correct.

Round at the 2nd I watch a game tee off, then start for the 8th green about two miles hence, at the far end of the course. The walk will be worth it once I get to sit on my backside for a couple of hours. As I leave the tee, I spot a photographer I recognise from the European Tour School back in the late 90s, Alex Jackson. Although I don't know Alex, he had come up in conversation at a party just a week before, and is possibly someone who can help with my project. There's no one around, so I stop and introduce myself.

Alex is a legend in media circles, mainly due to his unfailing kindness and slight eccentricity: at any one time he usually carries more cameras than exist in all of Tokyo. Fortunately this makes him easy to spot, and he's often the focus of TV cameras around the world. Seve christened him Rambo, another called him the Octopus, his camera tentacles ready to strike at any moment. Following the PGA at Oakland Hills in August 2008, I'd seen him checking in for my flight out of Chicago and thought about collaring him then. We chat away on all things golf and photography as various games pass through, our conversation stopping as he shoots each player teeing off. More than once he's called into action shortly after, a couple of players having snapped their drives left into the boughs of the waiting tree-line only 120 yards away.

Soon we're joined by Jim Chatman from Virginia, a hearty, tanned, balding gent with white hair. Jim's daughter, Rebecca, is an Emmy-winning Senior Producer for NBC, and as well as the golf she also covers the Olympics. He says it's usually 18-hour days for her, but the weather is playing havoc with even that demanding schedule.

Jim's been coming to the US Open since Congressional in 1997, as well as Ryder Cups and FedEx playoffs, wherever NBC has the TV rights. On an early visit to the media centre, he couldn't understand the clamouring for some crazy gothic guy's signature – it was Alice Cooper. At Oakmont, Jim was watching proceedings at one hole, part of a large throng, when a bear came running out the woods. The bear stopped, saw the crowd, got the fright of its life and ran back into the trees.

After chatting a while, I tell Alex I'll come back later to help him with his equipment, especially if the forecasted rain strikes. I had heard cheering and shouting up and beyond the left of the second, Phil Mickelson passing through. I decide to take a walk round to the 15th to see if I can catch a glimpse of him, but my timing is off, and as I saunter along the road between the 1st and 2nd, and the 14th and 15th, Phil is walking back to the 17th tee, just over a fence from me.

The cheering is intense, and as well as the ovation at the tee, the fans packing the stands left and right of the green, and inundating the hill behind between the green and the 18th tee, get on their feet and clap and cheer Phil. Thousands lining every side of the hole greet Phil. He raises his hands and beams, apparently taken aback.

I stand just off the road, leaning on a post, with a good view of Phil's shot, although I can't see his ball on its tee due to the green mesh that forms the backdrop of the tee. He flushes a long iron directly at the flag, homing in on his target. However the ball lands at the front of the green and, although I'm about 250 yards away, I get the distinct impression he's 35 feet shy. As I wait in my spot above the tee box, I feel sure that he'll birdie, despite the length of his putt. My thoughts are interrupted as Fred Funk, Todd Hamilton and Stuart Appleby appear on the tee.

I turn my attention to the faraway Mickelson. He's stalking his putt, assessing it from every angle. Once satisfied, he takes his stance and gets into his pre-shot routine. I can't see any of the ball, but I just know he'll make this. I can see him make his stroke and the ball is on its way towards the hole. Over the next four seconds the noise rises, exploding into a crescendo, and as the ball drops the crowd go wild and everyone near the hole shouts and cheers, rises to their feet and encourages Mickelson onwards and upwards. Goose-bumps cover my body as yet again Phil produces something for the fans to recall. Although it's just a birdie in just his second round, it's a spot of high-decibel excitement in a sea of mud and near-misery.

At this moment I slip into a minor fugue. It's another great play from Mickelson, and it occurs to me that he's given me my four best moments during the majors so far, each one charged with raw energy, emotion, determination and the power to capture the imagination of all who watch. His big ass hook second to the 7th in Augusta National's final round; his towering second into the 15th during that same afternoon; his two determined birdies at the 17th at Bethpage. Each shot has ignited the fans and sent them wild.

It also occurs to me that I am almost at the halfway stage of my journey – the seventh of the 16 regulation major golf days – and that

Mickelson might not be around for the rest. Once the US Open is over, I'll be in the run-in to the finish line at Hazeltine. Watching Phil, it's impossible not to be caught up in the near-hysteria that seems to follow his every move here in New York.

I have a great viewing spot and don't have hundreds and thousands of people jostling to get past me or to fight for a view, so I recline further against the post and watch the golf go by. It's difficult for life to get any better. After Funk it's Cink, Weir and Ames. It's playing long enough that Weir hits a hybrid while Cink blocks his shot, finishing on the far right of the green. A lone spectator claps; the pin is about a two-day mule ride away, on the other side of the green.

It's now midday; crowds are streaming down the hill from the clubhouse, out and across the course. The sky is patchy, the sunshine aching to break through. It's pleasantly warm, but today there's talk of an electrical storm lurking. I'd grabbed an on-course radio, courtesy of my American Express card, and the commentators are filling time, discussing Billy Casper's son's birthday in four days.

'Wow, we'll be in the third round by then.'

I'd bumped into my friend Ben earlier, he was still tracking the French guys, and we arranged to meet up later for a sherbet or two. The skies look threatening and I'm sure there's going to be rain. There's no way I'm not having my Saturday night out in Manhattan, so I am committed to not staying for the duration today.

As I arrive behind the 17th, it's Vijay Singh, Jeev Milkha Singh and K.J. Choi shooting up the stadium hole. Vijay gets a lot of support in the US, fans attracted to his easy stride and long, powerful swing. The fans cheer and clap as the players make their way to the green.

'C'mon Vijay!' shouts one. And seconds later he's at it again.

'C'mon the other Singh!'

Next up it's Poulter, Leonard and Allenby. The lady next to me has a keen eye for the better things in golf. Talking of Poulter, she says, 'He's got nice hair, it's just like Scott's.'

There's roaring and cheering down at the other end of the hole now. Harrington, Cabrera and Tiger are on the 16th green, and Tiger has a birdie putt. I watch the green about 300 yards away, ignoring Justin Leonard. I can tell from the lack of reaction from player and gallery that he's missed, settling for par. Tiger is a staggering 4-over to Ricky Barnes' record breaking 8-under through 36 holes. Lucas Glover is on minus-7, Mike Weir's at 6. This isn't how the fans imagined it. Woods is so far behind he might as well be playing in another tournament.

Woods and his group walk onto the 17th green and the hole is alive with excitement and anticipation. Tiger finds the green, but Cabrera pops it in the back left bunker, and Harrington goes long, into the nasty, tall fescue rough at the back of the green.

'Paddy's in the fescue. You know, that's Shinnecock Indian for "screw up the golfer",' laughs the guy next to me.

The pin is cut sharp left at the back of the green, and Cabrera, an ox with the hands of a cherub, hits the softest, sweetest bunker shot, almost holing it. Most amateurs would have struggled to keep it on the green; it's a beautiful shot and highly appreciated by the crowd. Next it's Harrington, and as he takes his practice swing in the deep, demonic grass, he stops, bends down and picks something out. He's found a yellow ball, and the crowd is in uproar. He looks at it and throws it into the gallery. Ultimately he saves par from his infernal lie.

Next it's Tiger. Coming up to the green, Tiger, in sharp contrast to most, did not smile, did not look up to the fans. He's stony-faced, hunting birdies to avoid a missed cut.

'Step it up, Tiger,' someone shouts. 'Time to make a move, buddy,' comes from another part of the crowd.

Woods does neither, takes par and sulks up the back of the green to the 18th tee. However, 20 minutes later there's an almighty crash of applause as Tiger birdies the last, his 9th, to crawl back to plus-3. Just as his putt drops, the rain spots that have been threatening become more lumpy. It's only mid-afternoon, but I'm convinced it'll soon be bucketing, so I decide to head home via the golf shop.

For years I had been used to the golf shop at the Open Championship in Britain, but the American ones are another story. At the PGA at Oakland Hills, golf retail was taken to a new level for me. The PGA and US Open stores are hypermarkets, and the US Open just edges it as the best.

The store is like main street USA from the early 20th century, old-style electric lamps lining the centre of the tent. It's mobbed, fans filling shopping baskets. I count at least eight different shirt manufacturers, and I've honestly never seen so many caps and hats in the one place. It would take too long to count them, but in a space 25 yards long and 20 yards wide, hats inundate shelves in every imaginable style (except Darren Clarke's). There must be about 250 different hats available.

Everything except a musical pizza-cutter is on sale, but you can buy the US Open toilet seat cover and potty. Well, no, you can't, but it would be apt. As I walk round the shop, plasma screens are showing the golf coverage, commercial breaks included. An advert for Avodart appears and a man of a certain age tells me of his prostate enlargement problem, and how he can't control his bladder flow. I decide against buying the logoed beer mugs, and leave for the bus.

Even though it's only three o'clock, the bus to Farmingdale is full and the train is heaving, standing room only. I get back to my hotel, lie back on the bed and watch the golf. Getting the end to end view on TV makes a big difference, and I start to get an understanding of how it's all panning out at the end of the second round. Ricky Barnes and Lucas Glover's nearest challenger, Mike Weir, is 4 and 3 shots behind respectively, at 4-under. Mickelson is 2-under and Tiger is tied 41st, a distant 3 over par. Maybe Woods should be coming to the pub with me and Ben.

Before heading down to Greenwich Village for a few beers, I take a walk up town to MoMA, the Museum of Modern Art, when I'm caught in an almighty downpour that pounds the streets. Pedestrians everywhere scurry for cover, but it's futile. I'm drenched in seconds and go back to the hotel. By the time I'm out of my shower, the same biblical torrent has enveloped The Black and the golf is suspended, with only 75% of the field having started their third rounds. It's 18:55, and my decision to leave the golf early is vindicated.

Drowning our sorrows later in the Soho Room, Ben and I consume Guinness at the rate and fashion of the fans' heckling – continuously and enjoyably. Although neither of us is used to this apparent nonsense, it's difficult not to get caught up along with thousands of people all trying to have a good time with a few idiots thrown in for good measure. When we'll ever get to the end of this event, neither of us knows, but Sunday is another day.

Sunday

Arriving at Bethpage for 07:30 was a bad idea on two counts. Firstly, a combination of Guinness and getting to bed at 03:00 was not good preparation. The fact that Ben had managed even less sleep did not assuage my feelings of self-pity and loathing. Then we discovered play had been delayed until noon. Great. None of the food stands were open, it was dank and verging on miserable, and I wanted to curl up into the foetal position and sob. I'm no expert on customer service, but this level of catering was as useful as a chocolate range-ball in the Palm Springs sun.

With no internet access and the usual stream of weekend info-mercials on TV, I'm not sure how we were supposed to learn of the delay. Certainly, especially after a few beers the night before, telepathy was not one of my strong points. Staying in bed until 10:00 would have been just the ticket. Annoyed didn't even come close to how I was feeling, and the 109th US Open was starting to look like a badly-run mixed scramble at Deliverance Country Club.

While we were contemplating our options, staring at an empty putting green and a near-empty clubhouse, beyond it an empty golf course, Alex Jackson appeared with another photographer, Mannie Garcia. It was good to just see a friendly face. After the introductions, we headed out on to the course, the guys wanting to shoot the carnage that lay everywhere. Last night's rain had topped up the water table and it resembled Thursday. There were expanses of water and mud-covered spectator walkways, and lonely fans picked their way through these ephemeral marshlands. We hiked down 18, along past 17, across the 1st and up the 2nd, where greens staff were hard at work.

In the left rough at number 2 a fluorescent orange flag marked the location of Phil Mickelson's ball. There was nobody around at this point, and it occurred to me that I could just pocket the marker and help reduce the championship to near-farce: it was getting there anyway, without my help. Of course I'd never do such a thing and we continued, but it was my chance to make Major history for all the wrong reasons.

We crossed from the left side of the 2nd green to the right side, skirting under the ropes and trudging through the rough bordering the green. Feeling and seeing the rough was interesting; it was soft, rubbery and flexible, while also being thick, twisty and strong. Rough like this does not exist in Scotland, and the closest thing to it would have very different qualities – it would be more liable to snap and break, the grass would be less malleable and more inclined to fracture. It struck me that this was more like the synthetic grasses I'd seen, and it wasn't difficult to imagine the Sturm und Drang created by knocking one's ball into it. Rather them than me, that was for sure.

As we walked I chatted with Mannie, asking him what sort of golf he usually shot and if he was a regular at the US Open. It turned out that his day-job is on Capitol Hill, photographing the movers and shakers of the world's most powerful nation. He's probably seen a thing or two. For Mannie the golf provides a stark contrast to Washington, DC, especially on beautiful, spacious golf courses like The Black. He has covered some of the war-torn parts of the globe as well, which puts my moaning about the golf delay right into perspective. He's also a Vietnam vet.[1]

Killing, pain, suffering and death are not words usually associated with golf outside Sergio Garcia's putting stroke. Covering Haiti, Somalia, Bosnia and especially Rwanda, Mannie tells me he's witnessed devastation and the outer limits of humanity's experience. Clearly he's a man who will have everything in focus, literally and figuratively. Working for

---

1. Mannie is also modest. He never told me he was the man who took the photo on which Barack Obama's iconic HOPE poster was based. Nor did he mention his close call with death when shooting the Ramstein Airshow disaster in 1988, and the World Press gold medal he was awarded for his picture that terrible day. See Wikipedia and *www.manniegarcia.com* for more information on a remarkable life.

Golfweek at a wet and miserable Bethpage must be a breeze, and getting down to Florida for The Players every year can't be bad, either.

When life deals you a lemon, make lemonade, and the delay on the Sunday morning turns out to have a silver lining. After meeting Alex and Mannie, Ben and I are able to get into the Media Centre, passing through a number of checkpoints with the various guest tickets Ben has. Once inside we're able to sit down, watch some television and eat proper hangover food and bev – muffins, bagels and sugary drinks.

The centre is busy, full of media-types killing time. Rumours float around of a further delay, even though it isn't raining and the course itself looks playable. It's a mystery why the players aren't out there, especially if the USGA is serious about finishing this event. One feasible conspiracy theory doing the rounds is that the organisers have delayed Sunday on purpose to ensure a Monday finish and a handy way to deal with the previous ticket. For them Monday play is the lesser of two financial evils. It's all getting very Machiavellian.

Another debate centres on 'lift and clean'. Given the conditions, should a player be allowed to take a preferred lie on the fairway, during which he can clean the detritus off his ball? This would be the *modus operandi* during a normal tournament, but in a major it's considered sacrilegious. However, mud balls, as they are known to the players, often take on minds of their own, veering offline like those misshapen comedy golf balls. Having caddied for a pro and watched his ball fly at a tangent into a water hazard at a critical moment, purely because of a lump of mud, I have some sympathy with this argument. Between the Thursday ticket issue, Sunday's delay and the Great Mudball Debate, there are more conspiracy theories flying about than on the subject of Area 51 and JFK put together. At this rate, if Ricky Barnes is in front on the 71st hole, there will be a Martian on a grassy knoll ready to take him down with a headshot.

Having some shelter and warmth is ideal, and time flies. There's also some light relief when Alfie Lau, a Canadian golf scribe, tells us that he was stranded last night. Having left the course after all the shuttles, he had no means of getting to Farmingdale. A volunteer told him he was basically screwed, although he might want to try one of the local policemen. Two minutes later Alfie was in a patrol car, sirens wailing, moving at speed to the station.

Before we know it, midday is approaching and we head out to see the day's play. Although it's Sunday afternoon, it is quite hard to work out what round we're watching.

We get down to the 1st and reacquaint ourselves with the fact that it's the resumption of the third round and there are eight games still to go out – four at the 1st, four at the 10th. By the time we get this championship finished, Iran will have nuclear capability and the Washington Nationals will have won the World Series.[1] Deciding to follow the top game for a few holes, we stand at the tee. Sean O'Hair, Nick Taylor, one of the Hanson Bros., David Duval, Azuma Yano and Mike Weir all tee off before the final group arrives. Ricky Barnes is one ahead, courtesy of a record-breaking first 36 holes of 132. Not bad by the world number 519.

'Go Tigers!' one fan shouts, trumpeting the name of Lucas Glover's Clemson University team. It's *not quite* the cry of support we'd expect at the back of the draw in a US Open. When Barnes appears he's all smiles, looking up at the crowd, hand up, thanking them for the ovation. There's no hint of nerves and he appears to be up for the physical and mental challenge ahead. I'm impressed by his apparent calmness and enjoyment of the spotlight, and he exudes the kind of handsomeness found in a US daytime soap. When he's confident, Barnes has a lot of game, some of it flawed. I'd seen Ricky at close hand before, when I was caddying in a game in front of him during a practice round at the 2003 Scottish Open. I recall that at the 560-yard 13th he cruised a drive and rescue club into the middle of the green. It looked very easy back then, but of late he's faced lean times, struggling with the flat stick.

However, these times are forgotten as he starts his round in the fashion suggested by his exuberance on the tee. He birdies the 2nd hole with

1. Belying their awful display against the Nationals, the Yankees went on to win the 2009 World Series, their first since 2000. They defeated the Philadelphia Phillies, the defending champions.

a putt from 15 feet to move to 2 ahead of Glover. We watch Barnes par the 3rd, and by the time we get up to the green at the 4th, he's waiting for Duval and Fisher to finish on the green. Barnes revisits days of old and knocks his second shot into about 8 feet behind the pin. He has a putt to go minus-11 and to lead by 3, assuming Glover birdies. Barnes rolls his putt in and the crowd lets rip with a massive cheer and a realisation that we're watching something special. Right out of nowhere Cinderella is playing free and attacking golf, showing the world's best a clean pair of heels. Tiger Woods is 14 shots behind.

Barnes and Glover both par the long, hard 5th and at the 6th we stand on the hill just shy of the green. Barnes' caddy, brother Andy, reaches into the bag, picks out two bottles of water and throws them 30 yards towards us, landing them just in front of a blonde and a brunette, Andy's wife and Ricky's girlfriend. Barnes has missed the green but successfully chips and putts, maintaining a lead which is now 4, courtesy of a bogey by Glover.

We make our way up the long 7th as the leading group walk back towards the tee. As we get beyond the dogleg we are near David Duval as he hits his approach. On impact with the club a large spray of water appears and his ball travels about 80% of the expected distance. Bethpage is now so testing that danger lurks even on the middle of the fairway.

During the next 20 minutes Glover's challenge implodes as he doubles the 7th after going way left of the green. We stand close by in the funnel of fans as Lucas chips up the gallery and back towards the flag. This double is then compounded by a poor tee shot at the next that results in a bogey. Barnes now has a 7-shot lead and is cruising. Glover's minor collapse will usually do for most players and I assess that his chances have evaporated. He's likely to continue heading backwards and to have an early tee time in the final round. Goodnight Vienna.

At the 8th green we decide to stop and watch some of the other games and to rest our feet, especially mine. Sunday is not as hot as the other days, and my sandaled feet never dry out. Instead the moisture and friction have rubbed away skin on my feet, and the tops of my big toes look like pink, uncooked sausages. Not very pleasant and mildly painful, and I wonder what sort of environmental pathogens have been introduced into my bloodstream. I used to work for a water board and these kinds of bacteria were kept in a locked freezer. For the time being these microbial agents and aberrant proteins will need to wait on the hill well left of the 8th green and watch the golf.

Standing next to the scoreboard, Ben is frustrated as much as I am entertained by the blue-collar six ball sitting below us. The words bashful and retiring are not in this group's vocabulary, and they have a mixture of mild abuse, encouragement and foolishness for every game. Although it's not usually the done thing at golf tournaments, I find it all rather amusing, but then again I'm not trying to play golf.

Smoking big fat cheap cigars and sporting oil-stained denims, the guys and lone lady look like the types that drive 1992 Chevy Impalas and smoke Marlboro Lights for breakfast. Their idea of a balanced meal is a bucket of chicken nuggets with an even number of pieces. A few neck tattoos wouldn't be out of place. They have an answer for everything, and sport that peculiar brand of arrogance that comes from nothing but the fact that they live in New York. Still, watching and listening is strangely entertaining.

The clouds are greying as we take up our position for the next few hours.

'History. You're making history,' shouts one of them to Barnes.

Three games later it's Anthony Kim, again playing with Rory McIlroy.

'Go Anthony. Go AK. Go Kim, you're my boy. Everyone's been short today from there,' – including Kim a few minutes later. Still, the spectator's not wrong, as player after player fails to get their ball to the hole, despite 80% of tee shots coming to rest within 20 feet of the flag. Time and time again we see it happening, and it highlights the subtlety of the slopes and breaks on the relatively flat greens at The Black.

Occasionally rain showers pass; as we see them sweep over the trees up at the 9th tee, leaves fluttering violently, we stick on our rain tops. We have to wait for 14 games before we see a birdie. I'd called it before it happened – as Vijay Singh stepped up to his downhill 15-footer I said to Ben, 'Vijay's putting is so bad he'll make this.'

When it popped in, the stooges chanted loudly, 'Veeedge, Veeedge, Veeedge, Veeedge, Veedge.' Playing partner, Jean-Francois Lucquin looked over, shook his head and laughed. He'd clearly never heard the likes during a tournament. Neither had I.

Next up was the second-to-last group to finish their third rounds at 9, Tim Clark and Ian Poulter. Poulter was one of the few who actually missed the green, finishing up in a small valley pin-high between the flag and the roughnecks. Just as Poulter hit, a guy in a pair of jeans and red t-shirt staggered up, totally blitzed, and fell onto his back on the grass to our left. He lay there, looking at the sky, mumbling to himself. He was youngish, with a healthy beard and thick-rimmed retro glasses. He reminded me of Mark Oliver Everett, lead singer with the band Eels. Everett's father, Hugh, was the man who came up with the theory of quantum physics that involved parallel worlds, and he'd be proud of the guy on the grass next to us. He'd manage to transport himself from Bethpage to some exoplanet, stardate unknown. He was buckled with drink and I feared a bit of scene. Fortunately he was so hammered he barely knew what was going on. He continued staring and chanting heavenward.

Poulter ambled up to the green before walking down to his ball. Dressed in a salmon shirt and cream, green and salmon checked trousers, he was right in the lead stooge's crosshairs. As IP walked down to his ball, this comedian cocked his head and whinnied in a tone somewhere between Truman Capote and Liza Minnelli, 'San Fran Cisco-o-o-o.' To his credit Poulter did not rise to the bait, did not look up.

After watching the final game hit down to the green, I needed to get to a First Aid station for my feet. As we passed the scorers' enclosure between the 9th and 10th, the Mark Everett doppelgänger was barking madly at Poulter, 'Salmon-coloured shirts fucking rock!' Oh dear. And you could tell from his tone that he wasn't exactly serious.

After I'd had my two big toes cleaned up and bandaged, we wandered back towards the first and, finally, thank God, the start of the last round. As we loaded up on the usual Powerade and hot dogs, a message came over the walkie-talkie, informing staff to not serve anyone who appeared intoxicated. The woman gave me the once-over as I ordered.

'How do I look?' I asked.

'You're fine, honey. You should have seen some of them here last night. Shouting and screaming, heckling Tiger, jumping on the back of official golf buggies, whooping it up and catching rides. It wasn't good, I thought there was going to be trouble.' This was disappointing to hear, but if you feed enough people enough beer, strange things can happen.

Again I was dying to leave early; it would be bliss to sit in my hotel room and watch the last round get under way. But I knew the opening holes would set the scene for Monday, so we stayed, standing down the left side at the 1st, on the dogleg. Quite a crowd had assembled, most of them in good spirits, and we watched Henrik Stenson and J.B. Holmes start the proceedings. As the players came down the hill, I ducked behind us into the portable toilets. Once inside, it wasn't nice. There was mud everywhere, making it impossible to tell mud from, well, you know what. It's even worse when you're wearing sandals and bandages.

At least the golf isn't shit. We are treated to some early class when Stenson pitches it in the jar for a birdie from the right of the green. Tony Kim in the second game also birdies, to shouts of 'USA! USA! USA!', and Edfors in the fourth game also makes a gain. We've only been waiting four days for this championship to catch fire!

By now the caddies have bibs on identifying the players – the turnaround must have been hectic – and we watch Garcia hit a big pull down into the crowd. As decent golfers, Ben and I immediately see Sergio's route to the pin is directly over our heads, but nobody in the crowd moves, and no marshals take charge. Sergio and caddy manage to create a bit of a gap in the mass of spectators, then in a moment of sheer audacity and chutzpah, Garcia just plays, hitting a high draw up the alley of fans, over our heads, and it's all over the pin. We all go wild, dancing like mad. It was showmanship underscored by technical brilliance. Spoiling the anecdote, Garcia then takes five.

Next up it's Tiger, along with Scots-born Michael Sim of Australia. The atmosphere nears fever-pitch, warmed up by the fiery Spaniard, and there's all sorts of shouting going on.

'I love you, Tiger!' screams a girl along to our right, 'I love you!'

'Can I have your pay check for a day?' comes next from some wise guy.

'I love you!' the girl almost pining now.

'Tiger, wait for your partner to play first,' bawls another, as Woods pitches out of the rough to keep proceedings going in the fading light. Tiger signals with an outstretched palm to his left side that the guy needs to shut the **** up. He's right.

'I love you!' It's her again.

'Tiger, she loves you,' bellows someone across the fairway, and the entire gallery collapses in laughter.

A few games later, in the gathering gloom, Stephen Ames' teeth appear, like a jack-o-lantern, next to partner Peter Hanson. Eventually, at 19:40, the final pairing of Glover and Barnes appears on the tee, and it's clear nerves get the better of Ricky. Even from way down the fairway I can see his swing is shorter, a bit quicker. He starts with a very nervy bogey to tie with Glover at 7-under.

I immediately get the impression that Barnes will disappear horribly, and when he pulls his tee shot at the 2nd, he finishes in an abominable lie in the left rough. Glover finds the middle of the fairway. It's approaching eight o'clock and I reckon they can play for another two or three holes, but as they approach their balls, the siren sounds and play is suspended, although the guys can opt to complete the hole.

Lucas and Ricky approach their balls, Glover walking tall and confident, Barnes hunched like a bare-knuckle fighter who's just taken a beating. A twenty-something lanky male pipes up in an intoxicated voice, 'Finish it, Luke, Ricky's nervous.'

He bellows again, 'Finish it, Luke, Ricky's nervous.' Apart from this cretin, it's eerily calm, only a few hundred people following the game so late in the evening. This is really the only malicious thing I've heard shouted, and it's made worse by the timing.

The drunk starts again, 'Ricky needs to go to the clubhouse to think it over.' This cuts across the silence in the middle of the fairway. Barnes' family are right behind the guy, next to the trees, anxiously watching their loved one amidst sporting turmoil. I look around for a marshal or a law enforcement officer, wanting this creep surgically removed from the grounds. Barnes' family remonstrate with the guy and he barks back at them drunkenly, the word 'assholes' ringing in my ears.

This happens in the space of seconds, but I am contemplating taking him to task myself. He's way out of line. My bravado is ultimately checked as he probably doesn't know what's going on, and only bad things can happen if anyone intervenes. The players mark their balls and we all stream back to the clubhouse, thousands from the games ahead swarming around us as we head up the 1st. It was an edgy end to the day, but with thousands attending, there's always going to be a few idiots.

I was sure the players could have continued for a bit longer, but a lot was at stake, so ending in the gloom was no bad decision. The weather for Monday was to be better, so finishing 72 holes looked on. A play-off could prolong things, however. The rain had totally fouled-up my schedule. Instead of picking up a car and driving to Saucon Valley, Pennsylvania – home of the next golf major, the Women's US Open – for two days, I needed to be up at 04:00 to pack, checkout and get to the golf, before returning and moving to another hotel.

US OPEN MONDAY: SOME DAY THIS WAR'S GONNA END

When Lieutenant Colonel Bill Kilgore (Robert Duvall) delivers his 'I love the smell of napalm in the morning' reductionist view of the Vietnam War, carnage all around him, he finishes, 'Someday this war's gonna end', followed by silence. Kilgore gets off his haunches and casually walks away. I was like most of the guys on Kilgore's battle-scarred beach. I dearly wanted the war to end, and to end soon.

It had been a long and strangely enjoyable week at Bethpage, but I was knackered. I wanted the championship to end today, and I did not want to be one of the thousands watching a playoff. This was my idea of the horror! The US Open is the most played-off event on the PGA Tour, with 28 instances of extra time. If we had a rain delay, and play in some way carried forward to Tuesday, there was a possibility that, just as I had not seen the final minutes of The Masters, I would also not see the final holes of The US Open. I couldn't really afford to pay for another flight.

Ben and I did our usual and were on track for an 07:30 arrival, even though play wasn't scheduled to commence until 09:00. We passed Bethpage Cemetery, agreeing there was a good chance Ricky Barnes' golf game would be interred there before the day was out. The night before, he seemed to be unravelling. I hoped I was wrong, but things didn't look good.

Given the seemingly interminable nature of the week, we had discussed a plan of attack the day before and struck upon what seemed like a good way to proceed, making use of a service we hadn't used up to now.

As well as giving away a free radio to cardholders, American Express had a service called CourseCast TV, a hand-held television that could be slung around one's neck, allowing those lucky enough to snaffle one before supplies ran out to watch live television while on the course. With all of the fourth round underway and games on every hole, we could sit on the bleachers all day at the 18th, allowing us to see the 72nd (and please God, please, the final hole of the 109th US Open) being played and the winner crowned.

The bus to the course was always a rich seam of rubbish and one guy was discussing a chat he'd had with friends on the possibilities of the final round, and whether or not Barnes and Glover could hold it together. He didn't see what all the fuss was about, it was just golf.

'And my buddy said, it's not the same, this is the US Open. I don't understand that, what does that mean?'

For some reason the average golfer and even, in my experience, some local circuit pros, cannot objectify their own golf experiences and the pressure they bring. The relative pressure of playing in a Major is akin to the pressure the average golfer would feel trying to win his club championship – you can't just skip up levels and treat all golf events the same, the human brain doesn't work like that. Winning, for example, the St Jude Classic is not like trying to win one of the four Majors. Think about the pressure you feel when you have a chance to win a club medal or even to beat your handicap. If the Majors weren't special and more pressurised, why would you bother coming along to watch?

As we stood in the substantial queue to collect our TVs, there was further ill-informed chat. Discussing the appalling lie that Barnes had ended with on Sunday night, one punter came out with: 'So, what happens, did he leave his ball or does he place it today?'

'Yeah, he'll place it, and he can probably give himself a better lie.'

'Sure, that's what we were all thinking.'

Sorry, there's a word for that: CHEATING. Barnes will place his ball in exactly the same spot and continue from there.

We took our seats in the stands around forty minutes before play was due to start. We had a good view of the putting surface, up to the tee and down to the first, where the bottom half of the field would make their way to their final hole, the 9th.

As we waited, I concluded that one of the scoreboard operators, Rusty, had been having some fun. He'd inserted his name on the board at 1-under – if he could get a tee-time, he'd have a chance of winning. Around 08:30 some of the greens and USGA team appeared and set the hole for the day, right at the front middle, allowing the players to be aggressive with their approach shots. It was going to be a hole that delivered some excitement. They'd moved the tee up too, making it just 364 yards to the middle, and a good risk and reward challenge.

If confirmation was required that this was a unique day in major golf championship history – a Monday, all the games on the course already from a two-tee start – Phil Mickelson appeared, walking down the 1st fairway, heading to the 3rd where he'd recommence. The crowds around 18 and those on foot clapped and cheered. 'Go Phil!' rang out more than once, as did 'Go get 'em, Phil,' the twin mantras of the New York golf fan. Mickelson acknowledged the support, nodding his head and smiling in appreciation. If Phil was to win today it'd be very special. I didn't have a favourite as such, but I'd love to see him pull it off, not least for his wife and kids.

The stand was relatively empty for a last day, especially since we were guaranteed action from the outset. At 09:00 a continuous blast of the air-horn rang out around Bethpage Black, play was under way.

Billy Mayfair and Francesco Molinari were the first to come up the last, their 9th, as I watched Barnes on TV slash a great recovery on to the 2nd green, belying his lie and the nerves of last night. It was a great shot. Watching this combination of golf was the ultimate in dramatic irony.[1] I was going to be aware of how the final hole would play today, but each player would have to find out for himself.

At 354 yards to the hole, the 18th should be rich pickings, but this doesn't appear to be the case. Of the first eight players to pass, a measly three hit the green. Mayfair narrowly misses his birdie. In the next game Gary Woodland finds the fairway but gets too cute with his wedge and leaves it in the rough shy of the apron. In the same game, much to Ben's chagrin, Thomas Levet pulls his tee-shot, tries to play out safe but over-shoots the fairway and finds the rough. With little green to play with, he slashes out to about 30 feet and three stabs for a double. The game after that sees Carl Petterson way right. He takes an age to play his next, takes a drop and eventually bogeys. In contrast his playing partner, Dustin Johnson, has hit a drive so far I'm sure I can smell the cordite from his driver: he's 30 yards from the pin. He fails to birdie, but has shown that the big boys can get seriously close to the green.

Ben Curtis and Vijay Singh, playing together, both birdie from three and twenty feet respectively. After a few more games, Kenny Perry and Tom Lehman make birdies in their different pairings. Birdies are eminently possible, pars the norm, but bogey or worse lurk for the bad shot or decision. The tall fescue by the bunkers could mean carnage.

Later in the afternoon two other bombers create problems for themselves. J.B. Holmes pulls his drive left and finds himself next to a tree with an awkward stance – his second shot is a shank. And Bubba Watson hits further left than Holmes and stymies himself behind a thicket. It would appear that almost anything is possible at the last hole and, as I

---

1. When the audience in a film or TV programme becomes privy to information that a character doesn't know, that's dramatic irony – when we hear the music in *Jaws* we know a shark is on the way, but the swimmers don't realise it yet.

watched the final groups play the last at Augusta National and saw only one birdie and a smattering of pars and bogeys, I again get the feeling that the final hole at Bethpage could be the scene of pivotal action. As if mirroring my thoughts, on TV Johnny Miller sees the writing on the wall. 'This is going to be quite the finish.' If the guy on the bus doesn't now understand what it is to try and win the US Open, he never will.

The action elsewhere is mixed, although there seems to be more dross, resembling the final stages of a club championship where a few 10 handicappers are in the mix, out of their depths and getting ahead of themselves. After a brilliant par at 2, Barnes is on the bogey train but looks as if he's keen to get on the double express. His second shot at the 5th is one of the worst shots I've ever seen from a professional golfer in the top flight, a horrific snipe that the Smothers Brothers would be proud of, quickly pulled into the trees. Glover slipped on his tee shot at the 4th and does a great job even hitting the ball, good fortune following bad when his ball at least finds the bunker short and left. At the 5th, in another bunker, Glover has to take a penalty-drop and bogeys. David Duval also has bad luck, this time pretty horrendous, having started with a treble bogey due to a plugged ball at his first hole, the 3rd. Keeping your head while all those around lose theirs could be the key to triumphing. As bad as it was to watch – and I really did feel for the players – it meant that with about two hundred minutes left, it was not at all clear who was going to win.

I alternated between live action and live TV. When I saw Barnes' shot at the 5th I exclaimed out loud, almost shouting in surprise and disappointment. I immediately realised where I was and fortunately no one was on the green mid-stroke. The TVs are a great idea, but they'll disappear as soon as you can say 'Fred Funk' the moment someone watching one cheers at an inopportune moment and impacts the result of a championship. That would be heinous.

Rocco Mediate and Jean-Francois Lucquin appear at the 18th, walking up to the green. Mediate is a mere three feet away, Lucquin a more generous twenty feet.

'Pick it up, Rocco,' bellows a spectator, everyone laughs.

Getting into the spirit Ben cries, 'Allez JF!' and Lucquin looks up, smiles and acknowledges the encouragement. Audible support is quite infectious at New York sporting events, like Swine Flu.

The trials and tribulations continue. Barnes hacks his way down the 6th, bogeying there and at 7, and at 8 he hits the tree short and right and almost backs into the pond. Surely it can only be a matter of time before he has a total shocker. At Bethpage Cemetery, the shovels are out and they are digging deep. Glover seems to have it together but misses chances at 6 and 7.

And then the stalking horse appears, like Golfing Death come to undo the rest of the field. Tiger birdies the short 14th and is below par for the first time this week. His fist uppercuts the air as his putt drops. He knows he's in with a real chance if he can pick up another couple of birds. Ben and I both hear the roar from afar. Things are getting interesting. I imagine to myself a play-off – Woods, Duval, Mickelson.

Back at the last we are finally into the second half of the draw, the top of the field playing it for what it is, the last hole of regulation play in this 109th US Open Championship. Henrik Stenson posts a total score of plus-1, a tally good enough to have won back in 2006 and 2007, but Winged Foot and Oakmont are two very different courses to soggy, receptive Bethpage Black.

And then, as quickly as he's appeared, Tiger falters. I watch on my TV as he hits what must look like a world-class approach into the 15th, right down the barrel. Except it's long and lands beyond the pin, nestling into the wiry rough around the green. Left with a very tricky pitch, Woods fails to get up and down. Bogey. He's 4 back again, and only has three holes to play: a blow to the solar plexus. Even Rusty was struggling, his name had dropped off the leaderboard.

Thirty minutes later Tiger is given a standing ovation at the last. He thanks and acknowledges the crowd, but only in a had-a-really-bad-day-at-the-office kind of a way. I don't stand up, instead choosing to watch the real action on TV. On completing the hole Woods stalks off, ignoring the cries of the crowd for balls to be lobbed into the stands. Later Woods will cut off a reporter mid-question to highlight his disgust at coming up short, complaining that although he's hit the ball great, he couldn't make a putt. The last time I looked, putting was a part of the game, too.

While Tiger is probably the greatest clutch putter the game has seen, not even he can expect to hole all of the putts all of the time. When things are going his way he's all smiles, and while I have total admiration for his golf and am often in awe of it, he's in danger of becoming golf's greatest champion and sorest loser. You don't have to enjoy losing, but how about some graciousness in defeat? With seven of the top eight places, and 12 of the top 15 from the other side of the draw from Tiger, Woods can feel aggrieved, but that's what happens in golf. Shit happens.[1]

As if energised by Tiger's departure, almost simultaneously Phil Mickelson hits his second at the par-5 13th into five feet. When he holes the putt, cheers ring around the course, from the green and from the thousands listening on radio and watching on TV. The People's Golfer is back in the thick of it.

Ross Fisher makes eagle at the 13th, too. Glover and Phil are at minus-4, Fisher is at minus-3, Barnes and Mahan are at 2-under. Mike Weir remains in the hunt at one below the card. I'd been starting to feel that if Phil couldn't do it, Ross Fisher could be the man, as he'd played excellent golf all day, hitting few wayward shots. Johnny Miller senses this also, and as Fisher converts his eagle, he has me in stitches pointing out that if he wins, 'Ross Fisher, you'll be more famous than Susan Boyle.' She'd become known as SuBo in the British press. Here at Bethpage, RoFi could be the man.

I'm starting to feel tense, even though I'm not bothered who wins, as each candidate has a unique story. Duval and Barnes would be back

---

1. Woods was imperious in the final round of the Memorial. That week he had his best driving display for 10 years. Matt Bettencourt had a disaster, shooting a 75 after being joint leader. Minutes earlier, at Bethpage, Bettencourt had turned, taken off his cap, dropped onto one knee and clapped the crowds, acknowledging the unceasing encouragement that every single player received all week. It would appear that Bettencourt understands what Tiger appears to have forgotten – without crowds on the course and people watching on TV, there would be no tournament or sponsorship money or deification of the world's best player.

from the wilderness. Fisher would be the first English winner since Tony Jacklin in 1970. A Mickelson win would speak for itself on so many levels. Jim and Allen from Clemson would be rooting for Glover, and all of Canada is behind Weir. It was quite the finish.

Then a series of events unfolds that makes it clear the final hole is crucial, and Ben and I will be ringside. Mickelson bogeys 15 and 17. Fisher bogeys 15 while, almost impossibly, Duval birdies it to be right in the thick of it, birdying also 14 and 16. Mahan's approach at 16 lands in the hole (!), is catapulted back to the front of the green and he bogeys: a cruel twist of fate. Glover three-putts 15 but has one of the few birdies at 16. Amazingly, to his credit, Ricky Barnes hangs tough, playing as good a final stretch as anyone. The 18th, that risk-and-reward strip of a mere 354 yards will hold the key.

Glover has a 2-shot lead and has to par 17 to maintain it, the same penultimate hole that Mickelson, Duval, Fisher and Mahan have all bogeyed in the last 30 minutes. If Glover falters, there's a good chance there will be a play-off, and I'll start to feel as if I'm caught in some US Open purgatory, never to escape. Even the TV commentators are nervous. This is it.

The last three games are between the 17th and the final green. Glover is on the short hole in one and has two putts to maintain his lead. Phil Mickelson has smashed his drive at the last and has a pitch up the hill of around 50 yards. Phil plays an aggressive pitch, looking for some spin to bring the ball back down the green to the front pin, but it stops 25 feet above the hole. He'll have a putt to reduce Glover's lead to one and put a whole different complexion on the final hole. As he marches on to the putting surface we're all cheering, shouting, screaming, 'Let's go, Phil! Let's go, Phil!' Every single person is willing Mickelson to drop the putt.

We all sit, watching Phil, the culmination of five days' intense golf. And if he holes it, it'll be the culmination of tens of thousands of golf fans' hopes. Phil and caddy, Bones Mackay, survey the putt from every angle, the crowd hushed between occasional shouts of encouragement. Never has it been so quiet as when Phil addresses the ball. He strokes his putt and I can immediately tell the pace and line are good, it has a chance. The crowd starts to gasp, slowly rising to their feet, but the ball slips past the right side of the cup, so close yet so far. A great effort and Mickelson sinks to his knees. His dream is over. It was a great moment that promised much, and we're all amazed how good it looked, how close he came.

Next it's Duval with something similar to do, and on the same score as Phil. He, too, has pitched up and has a quick putt down the hill that realistically he must hole to deliver himself from golf's no man's land. Duval also receives a rapturous welcome as he comes up to the green. He'd been in the thick of it since his 67 in round one. A deeply shy and modest man, this is Duval's chance to win a second major after years out of the top flight.

DD also hits a superb putt, tracking to the hole, but it misses fractionally. Twice in ten minutes we are left on tenterhooks, and then it's the final pair, Glover and Barnes. Both had parred the 17th so there are two shots between them; a bogey and birdie respectively would see them tied. This is why you come to the US Open, this is what it means and takes to win it – 72 holes and 156 players, and still it comes down to the last putts.

Glover had shown great maturity from the tee, and acted as if he'd been sitting beside me all day: he hit about a 6-iron to take all the trouble out of play, landing around 200 yards out, shy of the bunkers on the right. Barnes was well down and would have a short pitch. By now I'm sort of rooting for Lucas – it'd be nice if the Clemson boys could have a major winner, especially when I'd been keeping in touch with them via email during the week. But it was far from over. Glover had about 162 yards to the pin, so would probably be hitting an 8 or adrenalin-fuelled 9-iron. Putting a good swing on it, he finished well past the pin and just on the fringe. A tricky 35-foot putt awaited him. Barnes played a lovely pitch up beyond the flag, leaving about 20 feet for birdie.

All the rain; all the mud; the early starts; the USGA unable to run a members-guest in Alaska; all these things are forgotten as we watch the players battle with themselves and destiny. Barnes is a different man from last night, relaxed and assured, this could be his moment. But first

Glover trickles his ball down the slope to four feet shy. He'll have a slightly downhill putt from the left to win. If Barnes holes, Glover must make.

Ricky has a putt that feels similar to Phil's and Duval's, and it's the same scenario, he must hole. He and brother Andy eye-up the fast-moving downhill putt, and Barnes takes his position over the ball and strokes it, seemingly nerveless. It tracks towards the hole, appearing destined for the bottom of the cup, but like the other two, it's tantalisingly, cruelly close, but doesn't drop. The US Open trophy is Lucas Glover's. In an unbelievably close finale, three players on the last green could have closed to within a shot, but it wasn't to be: Glover had won.

Ben had to shoot to catch his flight, so we said our farewells and promised to get some golf in Europe soon. I sat back and enjoyed the ceremony, at which Glover was both modest and engagingly funny. A group of his friends had travelled from South Carolina to see him play, and they were all wearing the same T-shirt. When asked about these, Glover responded, 'They have a picture of me on the front, so they can't be that good.' He added, 'Thanks for comin', guys, I'll pay for your gas,' much to the amusement of the crowd and the loud cheering of his buddies.

As well as Lucas and USGA officials at the trophy ceremony, there was one final piece of torture to add to the memories. New York State Governor David A. Paterson couldn't be present due to an ongoing constitutional crisis in the State Senate, so he was represented by Carol Ash, the State Parks Commissioner. I'd never heard Mr Paterson speak publicly, but his voice could never be as grating as Ash's. She droned on as if it was her great aunt's 90th birthday party, in a nasal tone somewhere between a filing cabinet being dragged across marble, and a metal worker slicing through the hull of a ship. If her voice could be packaged up and fired into Deep Space from a ray gun, it would destroy planets.

With my golf in Pennsylvania washed away by the June rains, I spent the Tuesday hobbling around Manhattan, up Fifth Avenue to the Metropolitan Museum and into Central Park. Past the Gate House where Laurence Olivier lost all his precious diamonds in *Marathon Man*.

115

Across to the Upper West Side and the site of John Lennon's slaying by Mark Chapman, a loner obsessed with *The Catcher in the Rye*. As I continued down to Borders bookstore at Columbus Circle, I thought of how that neatly segued into the next Major, to be held in Ayrshire, home of the famous poet, Robert Burns. J.D. Salinger had taken the title for his seminal work on disaffected youth from Burns' poem, 'Coming Thro the Rye'. Coming thro the mud would have been more appropriate for the Major we'd just had.

On my flight home I was fast asleep in no time, knackered, travelling overnight to Scotland. On landing I made straight for my flat, showered, changed, and jumped on a train for a three-hour journey to Aberdeen and a Neil Young concert. After a great gig and return car ride, I got to my bed at 01:00. The next morning I had agreed to take on some work for a few days, and rose at 07:00. Jet-lagged and totally befuddled, I looked about for my golf kit, imagining myself late and thoroughly disorganised. As the haze of sleep and tiredness subsided, I began to understand where I was and what I was doing. I finally realised I was in Scotland, and the 109th US Open was over.

Where the Land Meets the Sea: the Home of Major Golf

The Open Championship

We watched much of The Open, had to get up early to see it live, especially the first two days. I too had mixed emotions. Was pulling for Watson, but Cink turned out to be a most gracious and class champion.

John Sullivan, Woodbury, Minnesota

OPEN WEEK: LONG WALK TO PARADISE

The Open Championship – my third Major and my home Major – is a chance to meet up with golfing friends and foes, and to enjoy a cold beer along the way. It was being played only 100 miles from my flat and I'd arranged to stay with my long-suffering parents for ten days, 14 miles north of that famous strip of land between the Firth of Clyde and that sparkling white hotel, the sentinel that watches over Turnberry's famous Ailsa Course. Staying at my folk's place certainly had its benefits. Apart from square meals and central heating, it also allowed me to avoid the British version of the hospitality industry. Staying at a small hotel in the UK is often an experience akin to short-term incarceration for petty theft in Bangladesh.

My trip started the Saturday before The Open with a day at Prestwick Golf Club. Venue for the first ever major, The Open Championship in 1860, won by Willie Park, Prestwick is a classic, a challenge for every golfer. Much of our play that day was in keeping with Park's winning 174 total for 36 holes, so after a hearty lunch we retired outside for a relaxing beer in the warm sunshine. There was quite a gaggle of others with the same idea, and we spotted a familiar face.

Billy Foster, Lee Westwood's caddy, was in the middle of a charity walk covering the 90 miles from Loch Lomond to Turnberry, lugging a tour bag in aid of Candlelighters Children's Cancer Trust and the Darren Clarke Foundation for breast cancer. Prestwick was one of his watering stops. After some mild banter and chat about his trip so far, we made our donations and wished Billy and his team well, pointing them to the next clubhouse along the shore. It was still a long walk to Turnberry, but Billy had already encountered some of the greatest links golf known to man. Immediately north of Prestwick is Royal Troon, and further on comes the total links experience that Western Gailes represents. A long and challenging track, Western is a primal test.

I popped down to Turnberry on the Sunday evening, and it was great to be back dodging between the hedgerows of my boy-racing days, reliving times with the top down on my old Lotus Elan, AC/DC blaring from the speakers. As I passed through villages smaller than Tiger Woods' en-suite bathroom, it was a clear, bright, sunny evening, boding well for the week's golf.

When I speeded up and over the hill shy of Turnberry, the Firth of Clyde bolted into view, the green of the fields transformed into the dark blue of water and the rock of Ailsa Craig rising from it like some Bond villain's aquatic headquarters. It took my breath away and my juices quickened in anticipation of the week ahead – Major golf was back home, and the first sight for all visitors was the most breathtaking view in the golfing calendar.

I'd come down to give Alex Jackson a hand with his equipment, and after lugging lenses and bodies down the hill from the car park, we wandered onto the Ailsa. The course was superb, with luscious greens, fast-running fairways and rough that belonged to the corn-fields of Nebraska.[1] Missed fairways would equal misery. Strolling in the setting sun and warm

1. In a medal just before the championship, members lost 480 balls between them.

breeze, we heard Tiger had just finished his practice, and crossing numbers 5, 3, 2 and to 18, we spied Sir Nick Faldo and Robert Rock hitting to the final green. I'd last seen Faldo on commentating duty at The Masters. Since then he'd been knighted for services to golf, not public speaking.

On Monday I got up very early in the hope that I'd see Tiger. Mid-summer, the Scottish sun rises around 04:00, ideal for a man who likes to play before badgers get to bed and the streets have been swept. I arrived at 06:15 and some random chap offered the information that Woods had just gone out. As I got to the 2nd green – the 1st at Turnberry runs parallel to the hotel in a southerly direction, and the 2nd comes almost directly back – two minutes later, TW was hitting towards us, most likely wedge or 9-iron, right at the pin but 30 feet shy. Following Tiger for the next 16 holes was to receive an object lesson in the focus and professionalism of a world-class performer.

Photographers initially outnumbered the gallery three-to-one, but with each hole more and more spectators followed Tiger as he stalked his way around the dunes and tall grasses. David Howell, the 2004 Ryder Cupper, described it as the best-conditioned course he'd seen for an Open Championship, and it looked the part. This was music to the R&A's ears. For a year Ayrshire had been awash with rumours that the Ailsa was in terrible shape, an overplayed corporate pasture. Further speculation had it that the hotel refurbishment would never be complete, and Royal Troon was on standby. The hotel was a close-run thing, but Turnberry was clearly ready.

The popular perception of the professional practice round is about three tee shots, a couple of approaches, 27 putts and 400 bunkers shot on every hole, and if you're lucky, 18 holes completed before dusk. In contrast, Woods rarely hit more than one tee ball, the exceptions being when one went severely off beam; he never hit more than one approach, although occasionally had a pitch from closer; and he always spent time on each putting surface, eyeing up his options, second-guessing the pin positions for the rest of the week.

Plotting the greens was uniquely Woods. With green chart in his left hand, he'd putt using his right, a tee placed in his target area, watching the roll of the ball. Hugh Macdonald in *The Herald* reported that Tiger was testing the resistance of the slopes. It's also likely that using one hand aided his feel, letting the putter flow and release, something that becomes increasingly difficult in times of tension: just ask Doug Sanders.

The physical aspects of Tiger's practice were impressive, but the psychological elements impressed me more. He never made eye contact with those watching. He made rare direct eye contact with caddy Steve Williams. Tiger was in a cocoon, playing his own game, plotting his own round, on his own hole. No intrusions. At least six times I was no more than three yards away from Tiger, I could have reached out and knocked his hat off, but there was never a fleeting glance left or right, not the merest indication that I was even in his peripheral vision. He was totally in his zone.

For most, that level of concentration is severely wearing, but you get the feeling it's just another day for Woods. His driving was impressive, not outstanding, but you could tell it was all totally in control, finding fairways as required, using mainly irons and 3-woods. Turnberry was not the place for super-powerful, towering drives. His approaches were always around pin-high. Nothing suggested Tiger was going to be too far away come Sunday.

So much about Tiger is unique. To the outsider, his marshals are like the others, in red jackets and caps, doing their jobs. However three are special marshals for Tiger, who have performed the role for a decade. As Woods left the 18th, heading to the practice green, these marshals strong-armed spectators out the way in a manner that would create a melee on a night out. Those spectators who wanted to watch their hero on the putting green were told it wasn't a viewing gallery and to move on. Tiger both creates his own cocoon and has it maintained by others.

Earlier, at the 13th tee, an unofficial photographer fired a few shots just as Woods commenced his downswing. Woods stopped, a disgusted look scored across his face, and fired some Tourette's at the maverick shootist. He reached for his back and made a few loosening movements – I couldn't tell whether he'd really hurt his back or was trying to make the guy feel bad and discouraging others. As Woods and Williams left the tee, a marshal gave the guy a bollocking.

As the crowds swelled, more spectators fitted the mould I've seen so often at this great championship: the hill-walker out of his comfort zone, in the great outdoors but surrounded by real people. Most walkers I have met seem to be able to bond with bushes, babbling brooks and large hills, but talk to them about anything else and they go into their shell. Heading down the last hole, one spectator next to me was wearing a peaked cap and a headdress. You'd think the guy was trekking in Borneo, or that he was a fugitive from the Laurel and Hardy film *The Flying Deuces*, when our comedy heroes join the French Foreign Legion. And of course he has a backpack on, just in case a tropical storm sweeps in and he has to set up camp for four days.

Tiger left Turnberry after 30 minutes of putting, and it wasn't a courtesy car driven by a faceless blonde for him. Instead Stevie Williams gunned a high-end German saloon into the countryside, headed for the secret lair.[1] The last time Tiger Woods hadn't held a Major championship was 2004. Everything possible would be done to change that in the next six days, much of it top secret, all of it planned with military precision.

It was approaching midday, I'd seen Tiger at close quarters, and it was time to head north. As I walked up the hill to the right of the hotel and to the car park, hundreds cascaded onto the course. It was going to be a pleasantly bright afternoon. I pulled out down the hill to the south end of Turnberry and turned north, going slowly up the road between hotel and course. As I motored past, a tall, handsome, strongly-built young man cantering along the verge caught my attention. It was Martin Kaymer, the 24-year-old German star who'd won the last two European Tour events – the French and Scottish Opens – and in the process bagged over £1 million. And here he was, looking fresh as a daisy, following his daily fitness routine. Here was the answer to Scotland's current golfing malaise. There is no silver bullet, no secret formula. Just sheer talent isn't the answer. Hard work, dedication, focus and total commitment are a

---

1. Anyone renting a house to the great man is contractually sworn to secrecy: I'd hate to think of the consequences for anyone who divulged his whereabouts.

good start. I smiled, put my foot down, and headed for home – I needed a rest, a cup of tea and a digestive biscuit. After all, old boy, this is The Open.

I also headed down to Turnberry on the remaining practice days, and spent time ambling about and talking to people I bumped into. On the Tuesday I went with a pro friend of mine, Edward Thomson, who works under the tutelage of Bob Torrance. Of course this week Bob would be busy with Padraig Harrington; very busy, judging by Harrington's lamentable form and inability to hit a barn door from ten feet. The defending champion even discounted his own chances. Eddie and I frittered away the day engaged in bullshit and golf chat, behaving like most other men at golf tournaments.

I did manage to get into an argument with one marshal who wouldn't let us cross at 16 because players were putting on the green (100 yards away). The trouble was, players were also walking down to their drives, soon to hit in.

'Can we cross?'

'No, the guys are putting.'

'Yeah, but the game behind is coming to their drives, and will be hitting up soon.'

'Yes, I know.'

'You know? I walked past here four minutes ago and the crossing wasn't open. When will we ever be able to cross? According to your logic it's never going to happen.'

He just looked at me and said nothing, dumbstruck because I was asking him to think. This was just the first of many shocking examples of stewarding at the event.

On the Wednesday I thought I'd pop out for a couple of hours with my camera, and ended up staying for about six. The sun was out again, and on every second hole I seemed to bump into a marshal I knew. At each Open, holes are allocated to a local club and marshalled by their volunteers. Fortunately I managed to avoid any arguments this time.

I wanted to get some gifts for my PGA trip in a few weeks. Compared to the US Majors, The Open shop is a disappointment, like comparing a supermarket to your local store. The tent must be about one-sixth the size of the US Open and the PGA ones, but Britain has never been known as the epicentre of retail innovation.

Although the US tents have almost everything you could think of, they don't offer a cornucopia of golfing copy. One corner of The Open tent is occupied by Rhod McEwan and his collection of out-of-print books, along with some new ones. I find *Massacre at Winged Foot* by Dick Schaap, a blow-by-blow account of the legendarily difficult and farcical 1974 US Open won by Hale Irwin. The greens were so quick that Jack Nicklaus putted his ball off the 1st, his 25-foot putt travelling 50 feet, the surfaces slicker than marble. It was also the scene of an early Tom Watson collapse, a final round 79 which he soon laid to rest by winning the 1975 Open at Carnoustie. That US Open at Winged Foot is iconic, but for none of the right reasons.

The other book that catches my eye is the famed Herbert Warren Wind's *The Story of American Golf: Its Champions and Its Championships*. Wind is one of the greatest golf writers of all time and this history of stateside golf is a classic. I decided not to buy either, or many of the others I leafed through, and instead went for something a bit different, a signed copy of a golf novel by Dan Jenkins, *Dead Solid Perfect*. Jenkins has had me in tears of laughter, so I was hoping it was £30 well spent. With hard fairways, penal rough and the likelihood of some wind, dead, solid, and perfect were going to be the winner's main food groups this week.

OPEN THURSDAY: SLEEPING WARRIOR

The first day of The Open in Scotland dawned to a fiery sun and was relatively cloudless, quite unlike Thursday in New York. Another contrast, I had to make Sarah, my brother's girlfriend, her breakfast before the off. A first and last for my Major adventure, but I think she enjoyed her Coco Pops.

I'd been fortunate to meet Ben at Bethpage, but today was my first championship day at a Major when I'd actually planned to go with others, namely my brother Alan, Sarah and her son, Nick. Nick is over 6 feet tall and acts like a 15-year-old most of the time, just as I do. He is 15, I'm pushing 40. They'd arrived at the house around teatime the night before, promising to bring dinner. Wandering round one of the supermarkets in Ayr, they'd seen Masters champ Angel Cabrera and his entourage buying some mince. They'd followed him for a while, contemplating asking for an autograph, or a good recipe.

Having boarded the Tiger Express in NYC, today I was in the Tiger Motorcade, a long line of cars heading to the south Ayrshire coast. Having seen Tiger at Augusta National and Bethpage, I was keen to see the Tiger Effect in action in Scotland, the supposed land of the discerning golf fan. The first time I'd seen Tiger was the 1995 Open at St Andrews, the days of his prodigious drives and uncontrollably long wedges. I thought then he was a flash in the pan.

That year, 1995, had been on my mind earlier in the week. Living in Aberdeen at that time, I hitched a ride on a helicopter, flying to the Home of Golf in 40 minutes. We not only avoided the traffic, but enjoyed some hospitality in the field where we landed, red wine and cheese an ideal boost after an early start. The golf was quite good, too. I would have fancied doing the chopper thing again, hopping from Prestwick Airport to Turnberry in a matter of minutes – but the £650 per person price-tag was ample discouragement.

Avoiding the main car route, the A77, and cutting cross country, we completed the drive to the course in a gentle 25 minutes. The bigger route was arteriosclerotic, would have taken at least twice as long, and although traffic continually moved, it was slower than Ben Crane with a herniated disc.

A further 20 minutes was spent getting through the pay gate and scanning. I can't talk for the other majors, but The Open used to have pay gates all over the place. In the world of post-9/11 paranoia, propaganda and, from the R&A's perspective, common sense, security was in place to ensure no one smuggled in weapons, explosives or an adult in a school uniform liable for full ticket price. This was also the first year The Open adopted a 'no re-entry policy'. But soon we were through security and scrambling over the walkway above the road, down and across to the course.

The game waiting to be announced for 08:31 featured poster-boy Camilo Villegas, Sean O'Hair and a Japanese player, Yuta Ikeda. Ikeda's win in the 2009 Japan PGA Championship won him an exemption to Turnberry. The Open Players' Guide stated he was selected in 2006 as the Most Variable Player. I hoped this was a translation issue. Anyhow, Yuta's inclusion in this game explained why, of the 16 photographers at the first tee, 15 were from the Land of the Rising Sun, all with very variable equipment.

In the next game there was another Japanese player, Azuma Yano, whom I had seen at Bethpage. Yano was at Turnberry courtesy of his second-place finish in the niftily-titled Gate Way to The Open Mizuno Yomiuri Classic. One more sponsor and it would be a haiku. It was a treat to see that Darren Clarke, playing with Yano, had abandoned the daft cap he wore at Bethpage.

The crowd continued to swell as Woods' time of 09:09 approached. The viewing here is not great, as the 1st is largely a flat hole, and one side of the tee is consumed by the starter's hut and a thicket of gorse. Tiger appeared just after 9:00 and almost smiled as the crowd clapped and cheered him. Standing at the rope separating him from the crowds, I could see that as he walked up the alley towards us, Woods appeared to be talking to himself, as if intoning a mantra, psyching himself up.

Like all the players we had seen, Tiger, Lee Westwood and Ryo Ishikawa hit longish irons down the fairway, taking the first trap at 224 yards out of play. Good, cold, sensible, modern golf-course management – and totally boring.

The Open is the Major that has the longest playing day: the first game goes out at 06:30 and the final game finishes around 21:00. Over two-and-a-half hours before Tiger, Paul Broadhurst had opened proceedings by shanking a 5-iron off the first, hitting a lady spectator square on the chin and dislodging her false teeth in the process. Just kidding, he safely found the fairway with a hybrid 3-iron and the 138th Open Championship was under way.

In an effort to see how futile an activity it was, I followed Tiger for a few holes. A friend from Edinburgh, Grant, down for a spot of corporate hostility, joined me as we tussled with the crowds. We didn't bother going down the 1st, knowing that by heading for a hill to the right of the 3rd we'd be in position for the 2nd green and approach, the 3rd hole, and handily placed, too, for the 4th and 5th. The weather had been pleasant – somewhat changeable, but relatively good for Scotland. Over the hills south of Girvan, about 20 miles away, the skies were dark and angry and wet. Although I had enjoyed Bethpage, I really didn't want to spend another Major getting drenched.

Walking down to the third, we watched Graeme McDowell hit a beautiful mid-iron into the tricky 5th. He boxed his 15-footer and assumed the lead at minus-3. By this time Tiger had parred number 1 and we were in position to watch him coax a short-iron into about 15 feet at the 2nd. Westwood and Ishikawa were both inside Woods and all made birdies, Westwood repeating his opening hole; two holes, four birdies already. Welcome to Scotland.

At the 3rd – we're standing about 180 yards from the tee, on the right – Tiger hits a vicious hook, his first shot of the day with a driver, which lands at the base of a TV camera tower. I'm starting to believe I have special powers. Every time I have gone out of my way to watch Woods, his first use of the big stick has resulted in an appalling hook better suited to a weekend golfer who's had too many strong coffees.

Fortuitously, Tiger gets a nice drop and hits a medium iron out of the downtrodden hay towards the green. This could be the start of some sort of slash-a-thon, or continued good luck for The World's Best Player (aka The World's Worst Driver of Ball When Least Expected). Already Tiger's game is in total contrast to his Monday practice session.

By the 5th tee, watching the 3rd green – the short 4th comes back up on our right – I point out to Grant a guy in the crowd with a curious sense of style. His hair is jet-black and combed forward, with a skunk-like streak running across and back from his forehead. All of which is complemented by the pallid complexion of the terminally ill. Imagine if The Cure's Robert Smith had fallen out of the ugly tree. Bizarrely,

I've actually played golf against the guy on two occasions. During one match, a fellow team member of his told me they'd recently played at Gullane, a genteel club near Edinburgh. While they were waiting in the clubhouse for their food, the club steward approached and said, 'Excuse me, Sir, there are no hats allowed in the clubhouse.'

'It's my hair,' he replied. If I were him, I'd be making an appointment at my local salon. Or vet.

Westwood had his own streak going, and birdied the 3rd, too. He was cooking with gas. The gas ran out when he hit a poor tee shot to the 4th and made bogey. At that same hole I noted Tiger's close protectors in their marshals' kit, nattily accessorised by Nike of Oregon. Unlike all the other marshals bedecked in red, Tiger's three were watching everything but the golf, scanning the fans, marshals, photographers, other media-types and horizon for threats to their principal. Although the other marshals are volunteers and most do a great job, too many spend too much of their time watching the golf. It was no surprise that Tiger's men were real professionals.

Tiger fizzed his trademark stinger off the 5th tee, the ball shooting past us at a hell of a clip, and we followed up the hole. When we had gone as far as the green on the left side, there was no access above to the 6th, so we walked back with countless others to cross. Grant headed to his hospitality and I decided to wander towards the 16th. I walked down the right side of the long 17th, crossed towards the tented village and continued across what is usually the 18th tee of the Kintyre Course. From here I looked 250 yards west, over towards the blue sea and the bluer sky, both of which framed the players on the 7th tee. I watched as Tiger swung, his body language telling me he'd gone right. I knew that stroke was the second use of his heavy artillery: another bad shot, the flight right a reaction to the hook at the 3rd. The more the wind got up or changed, the more Woods could be forced into using his driver. Things could turn interesting.

Having been a member and played Turnberry numerous times, this was the one Major course I did not feel compelled to circumnavigate endlessly to work out the best routes and vantage points. I felt I knew most of them. Back in 1994 the 16th had been a mundane, arrow-straight 410-yard par-4 with a burn in the front. It required a decent drive and iron shot – often a very short one – into the green, where even the middle was never too far away. Now it was a very different proposition. The 16th showed the effect of the Ailsa's 247 additional yards and 23 new bunkers.

The original fairway is now the right rough, and the line of the hole cuts about 30 degrees left of that, with the fairway on an adverse camber to the direction of the hole – always difficult to hit, never popular with players, and that's without any wind or pressure. To add insult to injury, there are two fairway bunkers ready to catch an errant tee shot. The routing of the hole; the camber of the fairway; the fairway bunkers; the burn; the green that slopes back-to-front, protected by humps – Hunter S. Thompson would call this a King Hell Bastard of a golf hole, and he wouldn't be wrong.

When I finally got to the 16th and sat down, I realised what I'd forgotten since I'd last spent any considerable time down at Turnberry: it was a natural golfing paradise. I last played the course on a very cold, windy and grey December morning. With the combination of the weather, a few hours' sleep, a wretched hangover, the fatigue that goes with it and some bad golf, you don't have a great experience, nor do you recognise what's around you. That day it was definitely head-down, let's get on with this: it was hell. Today it was heaven, the sun beating down, Scottish summer at its best.

The stand behind the 16th looked north-west, back up the hole and out onto the Firth of Clyde, across to the Isle of Arran, the outline of the island's peaks forming the shape of the Sleeping Warrior. The sky was a bright, light blue, peppered with wispy clouds, and the white and yellow lighthouse stood resplendent on the edge of the course, a beacon today for quality golf, not maritime peril. Beyond the lighthouse and the 8th hole to my left, the water was like a mill-pond, any shimmering of waves imperceptible in the glare of the sun. Even in a good year of weather, you can count on one hand the number of days like this in the west of Scotland.

Back across the water on Arran, its highest peak, Goat Fell, sat behind the Holy Isle. I felt a Zen-like calm. Not since standing at the very different 16th at Augusta National, soaking up the serenity of the pond and the majesty of the trees all around, had I felt this air of tranquillity and peace on the golf course. Silently, far in the distance, a hydrofoil began its journey from Troon to Ireland, and beyond it a large ferry glided silently, effortlessly, across the water. Closer, in a spot of opportune advertising, a catamaran tacked up and down the shore, its large sail advertising a well-known German clothing brand. It was hard to believe that while so much was going on, all could remain so peaceful and therapeutic. At one point, a large white jumbo jet with a dark blue tail fin floated noiselessly across the sky, a technological behemoth in sharp contrast to nature's glory below. I'd lived the first 24 years of my life in this area, but was still struck by its beauty.

Meanwhile the golf was like a ten-car pile-up. The R&A had chosen a sucker pin, 6 yards from the right of the green, a hump protecting it, and the burn front and right a recipe for watery disaster to which even Tiger Woods would later succumb. And missing the green to the right also meant a horrific chip after one's penalty drop. The pin was so tightly cut that the players' idea of an aggressive shot, even with the likes of a 9-iron, was 12 feet left of the hole. Richard Finch missed the green and found the water – he hit an excellent post-water pitch but even that was 18 feet beyond the pin. He holed the putt for a great bogey while Mark O 'Meara followed him in for a birdie. A birdie at this hole was going to be a variable commodity.

In the next game, normal service had resumed for David Duval. Last year DD had done well at Birkdale before crashing to a third round 83, and while he'd vied for first place at Bethpage, he was currently 3-over. One of his playing partners, Nick Dougherty, scored a lovely birdie, while the other, Adam Scott, showed the disaster this hole could become after a couple of bad shots or decisions. Scotty drove it into the bunker down the right at 280, played out, then left his pitch of 90 yards shy of the flat part of the green and it span into the burn. He then virtually stiffed his chip and had a single putt double-bogey. In the following game, Greg Norman made double, as did Kenny Perry, while Oliver Wilson parred. After I'd watched a total of 12 players, those who didn't make par had managed three double-bogeys, one bogey and three birdies. And those who missed birdie chances all missed on the low side of the hole. This hole would have a lot to offer on Sunday, and I was glad I didn't have to play it.

Annoyingly some spectators had a habit of standing up to see, and then of course the people behind them couldn't, leading to a reverse domino effect. At Bethpage such offenders were usually greeted with a polite but firm cry of 'Sit down!' or 'Seats!', and they would sit down. Not here, and instead the polite British fans would suffer in silence as a group of dingbats got in their way. It really grinds my gears, but how do you have an argument with 15 chumps dressed as if they are on a hiking holiday in Wales? I, too, suffered in silence.

As I left the stand and walked up the right of the fairway, Sergio Garcia was making a real hash of the hole. Impressively, his playing partners, the 59-year-old Tom Watson and 16-year-old Amateur Champion, Italian Matteo Manassero, were 4-under and 1-under respectively. Garcia was minus-2, but soon not to be. On the ropes I was only feet away from him as he eyed up a tricky shot out of the rough. He slashed, made decent contact, but hit it left into the hay beside the green. This was the start of his troubles. He then hit his third, a pitch from the side of the green that ran to the right and poured into the burn.

As my luck would have it, Sergio then came back up the fairway – keeping the place his ball entered the hazard between him and the flag – to play his fifth. As I crossed the walkway I was about 20 yards behind as he hit a crisp pitch right at the pin. Bouncing and skidding, it almost went in the hole for a mere bogey; however even a double was a great result after three poor shots in a row. It was another double-bogey to add to my collection.

I wandered over to the 7th, where Chris Wood, Boo Weekley and Rod Pampling were making their way up the fairway. There weren't too many people around and I'm guessing it was nice for Weekley not to be continually assailed by shouts of 'Boooo', although there was the occasional cry. On first playing The Open, at Carnoustie in 2007 – his first experience of links golf and Scotland – he remarked that it was still target golf, the targets were just different. If all the golfers in the field were like Boo, the competition would be quicker, funnier and less uptight. He had been reiterating his desire to retire in the next few years. Earning millions of dollars each season would allow him to put his clubs away and live happily ever after with his Bowie knife, rifle and fishing rod. He's a breath of fresh air.

It was after midday and I was due to meet my brother, a pro, at the PGA hospitality area for lunch. It's a nice tent where PGA professionals from around the world can take friends and family to sit, relax, eat and watch the golf on TV. I'd been in the facility a number of times over the years, not least at Hoylake in 2006, when a middling PGA Tour player walked in, stole a sandwich, made no effort to pay, and waltzed straight out, as the young lady on the till did a double-take, not quite sure of what she'd seen. I'd never liked the player and always thought he was an ass: I didn't change my views.

Eventually I spotted my brother at our meeting place, but just as I got to him I spotted another familiar face, a near-namesake of mine. Kenneth Reed, attending his 41st straight Open. He used to be the official artist for the R&A and USGA. Having met Ken at Ponteland Golf Club a couple of years before, I went up and reintroduced myself: he couldn't remember my name.

After lunch we agreed we'd watch Padraig Harrington, the defending champion and holder of the Claret Jug for two years, teeing-off. Harrington had played some shocking golf this year and his accountancy degree was coming in handy for totting up his scores. We arrived a couple of games before the Champ and on the tee was Ian Poulter. What is he wearing?

Apart from a bright red Cobra visor and white Footjoy shirt, the rest of his outfit is a cataclysm, a sartorial tragedy. He's wearing a Union Jack waistcoat and red and mauve tartan trousers. He looks like a tin of Scottish shortbread about to be buried with full military honours. And he probably doesn't care that in the current political climate, wearing a

Union Jack in Scotland is asking for it: he should just have turned up in the England football strip with a smouldering copy of the Braveheart DVD in his hand. I expect to see him at the PGA dressed as Osama Bin Laden.

While I ponder Poulter's get-up, and as if things aren't surreal enough, a girl behind me is having what I know will be the most bizarre conversation I overhear at the Majors. She's telling her male companion the tale of a guy who, at speed, fell off his jet ski, hit the water buttocks-first and died of anal injection, water entering his passage and causing a lot of damage. It's fair to say this takes my mind away from the golf and into places it doesn't want to go, so I quickly regroup.

From the putting green, Jim Furyk, Geoff Ogilvy and Padraig Harrington have a smooth passage to the tee. Each is met with great cheers and applause, not least Harrington. Momentarily I lapse into Bethpage mode and shout, 'Go get 'em, Jimbo,' drawing a suspicious glance from my brother. Padraig hits a nice shot down the first and his challenge is under way.

Following the defending champion are Stuart Appleby, Davis Love III and Paul Lawrie. I stay purely to watch the players introduce themselves. When Lawrie won The Open in 1999 at Carnoustie, Love was quoted as saying Carnoustie 'got the champion it deserved'. Lawrie is on the tee first and when Love comes over to shake his hand, that's all it is, a shake of the hand, no eye contact, no hello. No love lost there, then.

However, no fighting breaks out, Love finds the middle of the fairway with a nice 4-iron, and I head north, agreeing to meet my brother later for a lift home. In the next hour, instead of seeing some fighting between Davis 'Tough' Love and Paul 'Hands of Granite' Lawrie, I encounter someone who's been knocked out and another with a recently broken leg. It's a dangerous business, The Open.

I walk along to the 5th, and down below, on the green, Anthony Kim is putting and the scoreboard has him at 5-over. That must be a mistake, I think. Only later do I find out that Kim had a 9 at the 2nd. Turning between the 6th and 17th, as I approach the large hill that forms the right bank of the 6th green, there's a gentleman flat on his back, blood pouring from his head and quite a crowd gathering. I know the ball wasn't from the 6th, and at the 17th there are three balls in the fairway, the nearest about 25 yards from this guy's head.

As I arrive, so do the paramedics, and fortunately the chap is conscious, although not exactly feeling great. As he sits up, the game at 17 appears – Bryce Molder, Richie Ramsay and Jaco Ahlers. There's enough of a mess that perhaps Ramsay could be looking for a drop for 'casual blood', but it's actually Molder who has hit the spectator, and his ball is on the far side of the fairway, a good 40 yards from where it landed – the gentleman's forehead. Molder looks visibly shaken when Ramsay tells him he's the one who has done the damage, especially once he realises his ball is the furthest away.

Molder's caddy fishes into their bag, and Bryce signs a ball and a glove, hands it to the gentleman and says, 'If I'm holding the Claret Jug on Sunday, you're drinking with me.' This is unlikely, as Molder has only one professional victory to his name, the Miccosukee Championship, which sounds more like a Japanese sex contest than it does a golf tournament.

Leaving the carnage behind me I walk up to the 15th and plant myself there, watching the play on the very tricky par-3, another hole downwind with a sucker pin placement, front right. No matter where the wind is for the rest of the week, 15 and 16 are going to be very tricky, and par won't be a bad score on both. I watch a few games pass through, a mix of near-nobodies and Sir Nick Faldo.

Soren Kenjerson, Lyle, Mike Weir and Ross Fisher all follow. A marshal appears, asking if there's an issue with the exit to the left of the stand. One spectator is demanding that we use the entrance walkway, not the exit. As I look round and down, I notice there are two issues – the exit from this stand at 15 only allows one to head down the hill to the 8th, followed by a long walk round to the 15th tee before one can then head anywhere else. That is a nonsense. The other issue is that a lady has fallen on the slippery hill and broken her leg. She's being stretchered away. If this isn't enough, when I was at the 16th on Tuesday, a man in the stand had a coronary and expired on his seat. At this rate The Open should be shut down on health and safety grounds. I think it's time for me to go, and as I gingerly make my way down the slope, I almost end up on my arse. The grass is matted, dry but shiny, and lethal.

By the time I've walked down the 8th and back up to the 15th tee it's 16:30, and Ernie Els, Lucas Glover and Martin Kaymer are playing the short hole. The two Teutons are long, Kaymer through the back and Els on the fringe. Glover finds the right-hand bank and there follows quite a deliberation. Els is 1-under, Kaymer the same over and Glover is having a bad day, already at plus-2 and in a bit of a spot now. Lucas' lie is so bad he appears to have nowhere to drop, as any relief under penalty in the rough will be more of the same. Rather than return to the tee, he elects to go back as far as possible, keeping the ball position between him and the pin. He drops his ball about 80 yards away, in the middle of the eighth fairway, and proceeds to put his ball back in almost the same place. Almost. He gets a decent lie, pitches up and holes for a double-bogey 5.

It's been a great day for golf and carnage. Jimenez and old Tom Watson lit the course up with 64 and 65 respectively, followed by the unlikely Kuboya and Curtis making up the top four. Elsewhere Anthony Kim feels like he's been hit by a ball and finishes with a 73 – four birdies, a double and a quintuple bogey. I catch up with my brother and in 30 minutes we've taken the country road and are back home, with plenty of time to watch the rest of the golf on TV.

Later I make it out for a couple of beers with Alan Tait and Allan Thomson, two local golfing notables. Tait is commentating for BBC Radio Scotland at Turnberry, and in 1986 he completed a unique treble: Scottish, European and World Boys champion. In the run-up to that winning spree, he'd written to Bernhard Langer and asked for some advice – on golf, not fashion – and received a two-page handwritten letter and signed photo. A great gesture, especially as Langer was Masters champion at the time. Over our beers we talk meanderingly, touching on the golf and some of the personalities involved, and Thomson gives us some of his insights. As a player who's won the Scottish Amateur once, lost in the final twice, and is its most medalled player, he's no slouch.

We get round to Thomson's opening shot in The Open at Royal Troon, 1982. Drawn with Bruce Lietzke,[1] then an eight-time PGA Tour victor and Ryder Cupper, Allan was nervous on the 1st tee, and snapped a drive into the stands at 18. He laughs about it now. On asking his caddy how it looked, the caddy replied, 'Pretty good. I didn't know you could hit a golf ball without a backswing.'

Standing up on that first tee, with thousands watching, was mind-numbing for a player like Allan. For the seasoned pros it's just another day at the office, and Tom Watson has had a good few days there. Can he keep it up?

OPEN FRIDAY: THERE IS NO SUCH UNCERTAINTY AS A SURE THING

It's a function of the British press that increasingly The Open Championship has a side story, tittle-tattle ticking over in the background, giving rise to column-inches and air-time. A few years ago it was the voluble Gary Player harping on about drugs in golf. Always one to open his mouth and let his stomach rumble, sometimes he'd be better off eating biltong and keeping his thoughts to himself. Certainly without drug-testing we'll never know if there are any offenders, but the fact that Player blabbed on about Creatine – which is not banned – didn't encourage me to give any credence to what he said.

This year the big side-story was cheating. The very mention of the word in golfing circles is a no-no, a complete taboo: don't go there.

The cheating storm was over comments Sandy Lyle had made about Colin Montgomerie's 2005 drop in the Indonesian Open. Lyle called it a 'form of cheating'. This was a drop Monty himself said he was

---

1. Lietzke was known for not practising. At the end of the 1984 season he told his new caddy he wouldn't play at all until the next tournament, 15 weeks later. The caddy didn't believe him, so stuck a banana under Bruce's headcover. Four months later, Lietzke pulled off his headcover on the 1st tee and discovered a foul fungal mess. The headcover and bag stank, both had to be replaced.

'disappointed' about when shown TV footage, and subsequently he donated his winnings to charity while denying any intentional wrongdoing. At the time, John Hopkins in *The Times* reported that 98% of European Tour professionals were unhappy about the drop. Soren Kjeldsen and Gary Evans made complaints to the Tour. You can make up your own mind by looking for the before and after footage on the internet.

The press jumped on Lyle's comments like wild dogs on a leg of lamb, and the whole thing blew out of proportion, with people running frantically around under the cover of golf's reputation for probity and gentlemanly behaviour trying to limit any damage. Cheating does happen, both as a one-off and systematically. Some people will flout the rules to gain an advantage. It's human nature. Most people who are members of a club will know of someone who has the reputation of a cheat. Some people won't play with that person, or if they do, will turn a blind eye for fear of causing a scene or being on the wrong end of a counter-accusation. The PGA Tour and European Tour are also clubs, with many different members.

Professional golfers in the know have very clear and strong opinions about those who cheat or are deemed to be cheats. The golf-ball is treated like some holy object that must not be tainted or profaned, that must be respected at all times. Any golfing insiders I spoke to at Turnberry had a particular view on cheating based on their knowledge of the very real demands of playing golf, a world-class competitive sport, for a living. Others, especially among the general public, will not entertain a discussion on cheats and cheating. We should all perhaps recognise that golf is played by fallible human beings, while saluting the fact that, like no other sport, it demands the highest principles from all who play, and 99% of golfers are honest and fair. But sadly, if you have a discussion with any golf insider about cheating, the same four or so names arise time and again.

In some strange strain of synchronicity, a friend of mine, Michael MacDougall, was refereeing Sandy Lyle's game on the Friday – Game 4, 07:03 – but there was no way I was heading down to see Sandy tee-off.

Michael was one of the many invited referees from around the world who help the R&A run The Open, and all the Majors have a similar system. He'd joined the Professional Golfers' Association after completing a degree in history and politics at Glasgow University, and now occasionally finds himself rubbing shoulders with the world's greatest players. At the PGA at Oakland Hills he'd been roundly booed by the crowd when he had to blow the horn to signal a weather delay, just as Phil Mickelson was about to putt for an eagle. Phil picked up his ball and walked off. On Thursday at Turnberry he'd refereed Kuboya's game, so was on the cutting edge of events, the Japanese having shot 65. I'd find out later what today would bring.

After the US, I was keen to take things easier at Turnberry, especially since one's home Major should be about relaxing, meandering, catching up with friends old and new and bumping into people you haven't seen for years. Like the crowds at the 12th and 16th at Augusta National who enjoyed chatting and drinking, and the fans at the 14th and 17th at Bethpage who had partaken of numerous ales, I planned a social afternoon on the Friday.

Once on the Ailsa I'd tarried somewhat, dithering, continually bumping into people I knew. I chatted to Derek, a sometime golfing partner from Western Gailes. He was a guest of one of his suppliers but there had been a cock-up. As a number of people I met would explain, their hospitality was originally to be housed by the 1st, but had been moved outside the event's boundary. Usually no big deal, but with the no-readmission policy this year, patrons could *not* come and go. As Derek explained, they had their breakfast and then decanted, heading to the golf for the rest of the day. Someone had paid £4,500 for a dozen bacon rolls. I hope they tasted nice.

By the time I got to the 16th, Michael – bedecked in the referee anorak, a style more suited to train spotting – and the Sandy Lyle game were coming down the fairway, or, in Alvaro Quiros' case, were almost in the burn. The big-hitting Spaniard had smashed a 400-yard drive. He hit a lovely lob wedge with a bit of check and duly holed a 10-foot putt for birdie. Nice. Alvaro's caddy was Alistair McLean, who'd caddied for Monty in Jakarta in 2005. Sandy must have loved that.

The player making up the three-ball was Steve Marino, destined to be the joint leader with Tom Watson, so it was good to see him at close range. Marino was a relative unknown to the British public, but I'd been following his progress for a number of years, mainly as he's continually tipped to win, and usually at odds of 80 to 1. He once shot a 59 during a Nationwide Tour event and went on to win by 10 strokes. He can golf his ball.

Marino is down the right side of 17 and hits about a 4-iron into 15 feet. I am virtually in front of Steve as he hits his shot and am surprised to see his hands are behind the ball at address. It is the same with his driver, and the club-head is in front of his left foot too. Not conventional. Marino walks up to Michael and they share a laugh, Marino making fun of his caddy for being useless and not seeing the ball finish – Michael confirms it's close to the hole.

Hoping to get a spot at the final hole, I head across to the tee, paying no attention to the putts, assuming a couple of birdies at worst. When the players appear, I look for the boy carrying the scoreboard. He must be somewhere behind the players and officials. Eventually I spot him, at the right-hand corner of the dogleg, 265 yards from the tee. He's clearly forgotten that his role is to keep spectators informed, not to find the optimal route round the 18 holes. There and then I vow that, as long as I am alive, I will hunt that boy down and beat him like a one-legged stepchild.

My annoyance is intensified when a lady and her husband stand next to me as the players wait for the game in front to clear. In a voice audible only to her, her husband, me and the Bionic Woman, she whispers, 'Boo, leave our Colin alone!', a direct reference to Sandy's 'form of cheating' comments. Trouble is, Lyle would need an ear-trumpet the size of Canada, or a hearing-aid with its own satellite listening station to hear her. What's the point, I think.

'Don't tell me, tell him,' I say to her, and she shoots me a look of horror. I'd never have thought it, but it seems I prefer the New York approach – SHOUT DIRECTLY AT HIM.

I snap out of my malicious fugue as the players hit their tee-shots down the final hole. Quiros, who will miss the cut anyway, hits a mega-high, soaring, powerful fade that starts in line with the scoreboards at the 18th green and fades back towards the fairway. He has started it a good 40 yards left of the others and it comes to rest at the right-hand bunker, not far from the green: a blow of 370 yards.

In true Scottish form, while it's relatively warm and pleasant, for a Scotsman at least, the wind is up today, blowing west-south-westerly around 20 miles per hour, making the outward holes especially testing through the first 11, followed by some respite with the wind at the players' backs. Small sea-horse waves lap the shore. Weatherwise it's an average day in Scotland, and dealing with the wind on a regular basis is a fact of golfing life. It's just a shame it knocks your swing and rhythm out bit by bit until it's wrecked, like a car that hasn't been serviced for a while.

Meeting up with my brother Alan, Sarah and Nick, Al tells me they were out watching Monty play the 14th when, on the large screen in the catering area right of that green, Sandy Lyle's face popped up to talk about the controversy. Monty carded a bogey at 14, so perhaps he saw Big Sandy looking at him across the golf course, like some Orwellian nightmare.

After lunch we wanted to see Tom Watson start his second round. This TW had dominated the headlines in the morning papers, many of them focusing on his age, 59. The way they went on, you'd think Tom was virtually dead. Bruce Springsteen is 59 and no one's talking about him singing *Born in the USA* from a walk-in bath. As we arrived at the first tee, Kenny Perry, Oliver Wilson and Greg Norman were preparing. Norman had been unable to rekindle last year's magic and was sitting at plus-7. This was a shame, as Greg has such presence. As much as I love golf and admire many of today's top golfers, I'd rather watch Greg Norman or Seve shoot 85 than I would see some shoot 65. Sure, the scorecard doesn't have any pictures, but some golfers are as dull and quotidian as the Arabic numerals they post.

Every player we watched at the 1st simply hit a tee shot and allowed it to ride the wind, right-to-left, most hitting a club that ensured they came up short of the first bunker. Later on Friday afternoon Tiger would hit a 7-iron. Tom Watson was the only guy who hit a hold-up fade, his left-to-right ball flying straight as an arrow. We didn't realise it at the time, but this was an Old Master recreating the brushstrokes of a bygone age.

I made for the far reaches of the course, and as I walked past the 15th green, Kenichi Kuboya was coming off. He was now 3-under and had been jumping on and off the bogey wagon for a couple of hours. At one point he'd been minus-7. From the 15th in his first round and the fourth hole in his second, he'd been a championship-best 7-under, and 7-under through those eight holes. The Ailsa was giving up birdies and bogeys in equal measure.

Arriving at the 9th, I stood three-quarters up the hole. Everyone remembers the lighthouse at Turnberry; just as it warns sailors of impending doom, it encourages golfers from around the world to visit the Ayrshire coast. Although one of the most photographed holes in major golf, it's surely one of the worst – a blind tee-shot, a hogs-back fairway, and a partially blind approach. But for the sea lapping the rocks and the beautiful lighthouse, built in 1873, this hole would have been bombed back into the Stone Age long ago.

However, today it is lovely, the wind gusting off the sea as predicted, and for the moment the white and yellow lighthouse is framed by the sun against a grey sky. To the south and the north-west, black, ominous clouds are dumping rain, but at the moment we're fine, and the wind doesn't look as if it will bring the wet weather. Coming up the 9th is the group ahead of Tom Watson's, featuring Henrik Stenson, Steve Stricker and, 'Who's that?' asks the guy next to me of his pal.

'Oh, it's Wen-Chong Liang.'

I notice that Liang's caddy is toting a Hiro Honma bag, the planet's most expensive clubs; nothing but the best for the man from China.

Next it is Watson, Garcia and Manassero, the two pros at 1-under and the young stallion toiling a tad at plus-3, but still going amazingly for a 16-year-old amateur. All have missed the fairway right, the Italian less so, and he's first to play. I notice that the dark black clouds over the 11th are getting darker and closer. In the distance I can see a brightly-dressed

Nick Dougherty, and it looks as if the eye of a storm sits behind him, out at sea, waiting patiently. While Garcia bogeys, the players at the opposite ends of The Open age spectrum, one born in 1993, the other in 1949, both make excellent birdies courtesy of efficient approach shots and nice putts. Watson is doing nicely and will soon have the wind at his back, and he hits a lovely driver down the middle at 10.

By the time the players get down to their drives, the front has closed in and started lashing. Intense, Bethpage-type rain, and people are getting soaked rapidly. As the forecast was for intermittent showers I don't have an umbrella, so it's on with the hat and waterproof jacket, and the players do the same, adding waterproof trousers for good measure. Fortunately many of the crowd have brollies, and as we are all facing the west, watching the 10th, a virtual canopy is created and I am able to stay reasonably dry thereafter. I've mainly come out here to see Watson in action, and he doesn't disappoint. His glorious tee-shot is followed by a superbly struck mid-iron through the wind and driving rain into about 15 feet: despite the weather conditions, it never wavered. He fails to make his putt but delivers at the next, a 2 at the par-3 11th.

Fifteen minutes later the rain ceases, and, unusually in Scotland, it's warm enough that I am already drying. Often a summer's day in Scotland, when combined with wind and rain, can feel very wintry. Mark Twain is rumoured to have said the coldest winter he ever spent was a summer in San Francisco – he should have tried Scotland. Unlike the Masters and the US Open, where inclement weather was almost guaranteed to be accompanied by heat, I'd brought to Ayrshire everything from a woolly hat to a pair of sandals. If you like your golf to be guaranteed sunshine, go to Palm Springs or Arizona. It is not permitted in the other Majors, but you can bring bags into The Open, so fans can plan for all eventualities.

The players hit lovely drives down the tight and demanding 12th, but the pin is another very tricky, almost silly, placement, like the 11th, cut just over a knob. This results in a par for Watson and Garcia, but Manassero manages a superb birdie, holing from 18 feet. Garcia nods and gives the young man the thumbs-up. Manassero is now 1-over and looking good for the cut. Doing so on his own would automatically give him the Silver Medal for low amateur, just four weeks after he became the youngest winner of the Amateur Championship.

I was starting to get thirsty. Not thirsty *per se*, but more in need of a drink at the thought that my friends had been in the beer tent since early afternoon while I had been getting soaked in all the wrong ways. The golf had been good, watching the new and old guard, but now alcohol was required.

I followed the players down the 13th and noticed Andy North, watching the golf as if a spectator. Currently a golf analyst for ESPN, North may only have won three times on the PGA Tour, but two victories were in the US Open: 1978 at Cherry Hills, and 1985 at Oakland Hills. North was chatting to a blonde lady in a Tom Watson Design golf cap. It was Tom's wife, Hilary.

'You must need ten milligrams of something?' said North, joking about the stresses of watching a 59-year-old loved-one contend for a major title.

'You got anything?' she quipped. How times change. Hilary used to be a different Mrs Watson, instead married to Denis Watson, now a Champions Tour player originally from Zimbabwe. In 1985, Denis waited more than the permitted ten seconds for a hanging ball to drop into the hole and was penalised two strokes. Eventually he finished one shot back of the winner – it was the US Open, and Andy North won it. Then, Hilary needed more than ten milligrams.

It was about 16:45 when I went straight from the 13th green to the Open Arms, an outdoor pub in the tented village. Unlike the beer-vending facilities at the other majors, there's a large standing area within the tent, and a larger sitting one outside. The words outdoor and pub, coupled with sunshine, tend to be music to my ears. In fact, were it not for something I once saw in Amsterdam, 'Erotic Discount Centre', 'outdoor pub' would be my favourite phrase.

I joined the guys and all were having a good time, split between the Bollinger Tent and the alfresco boozer. It was time to hook in. I started in Bollinger, another element of the Majors unique to The Open. It's been 40 years since the first Bollinger Tent in 1969 at Royal Lytham and

St Annes. Anthony Leschallas, then MD of Mentzendorff, the agents for Bollinger champagne in the UK, and Andrew Hughes-Onslow had sold the idea to Keith Mackenzie, Secretary of the R&A. That year only 50 bottles were consumed, but after a wet St Andrews in 1970, a sunny Birkdale the next year saw sales take off, and Bollinger never looked back. In 40 years, around 120,000 bottles of champagne have been consumed and £3,000,000 spent by spectators.

Over the years major business decisions have been made in the tent. An EGM of the One-Armed Golfing Society was once held there, and The Grand Match, Walker Cuppers v Ryder Cuppers, was conceived in the Bollinger Tent.[1] I'm not sure if anything else has ever been conceived in the tent, but at Royal Troon in 2004 an old golfing friend of mine proposed to his fiancée there. Sadly it didn't work out and they're still happily married. The prices range from modest half-bottles at £29 to a magnum at £168.

After a couple of glasses I nipped to the toilet and on the way back, bizarrely, given yesterday and Kenneth Reed, I bumped into Kenneth Reid. Kenny and I used to work at the same bank in Edinburgh, and while I'm from Ayr, Kenny's from Maybole, a few miles from Turnberry. We'd shared a few beers and played some golf over the years. I once got a job because they interviewed me, thinking it was him. There were a few embarrassed faces the first day I walked in. Kenny persuaded me to join him and his mate Peter, and we sat and drank lager for a few hours.

As festivities proceeded, we were quite a mixed bunch. We included Andrew Howie, whose brother-in-law, Jonathan Lomas, had led The Open at Turnberry in 1994, eventually finishing tied 11th. Also in the throng was Paul, a house guest of good friend Murray. Paul had come to stay with Murray and his wife Aisling after he'd tried to book a basic hotel in Ayr for a couple of nights: £375 per night. I'd also heard of a lady in Maidens, a nearby village the size of Donald Trump's golf bag, who had a twin room in a bungalow and wanted £900 per bed for the week. Prices like these are grand larceny, and if you could find the right deal in Georgia, The Masters starts to compare favourably.

1. Despite the credit crunch, 2009 saw more bottles sold than 1994 at Turnberry.

By coincidence, as well as nearly being taken to the cleaners at The Open, he'd been taken to the cleaners at the US Open. Paul had been at Bethpage. He and his brother had gone to a practice day at the Black and had a great time, but they also had tickets for the Thursday, saw hardly any golf and were unable to use that ticket on any other day. We compared notes on the NY fans. We agreed: nuts, but great fun.

One in the group told me how he and a friend had been able to sneak in to Turnberry. Getting off the bus just outside Maidens, they'd walked west towards the course, braving their way though prickly gorse, nettles and fences before popping out of a hedge, comedy style, by the left of the 12th tee. This was problematic, as they'd ended up at a point to which only players and officials had access. A dim-witted marshal told them they couldn't stand there. He'd failed to realise that to get there initially, they'd have had to cross the field of play, which wouldn't have been allowed. Almost crapping themselves, they ducked back into the undergrowth but weren't giving up.

Elsewhere within the perimeter of the estate, but not on the grounds of the course, they eyed up the tall mesh fences. A security guard spotted them and walked over. They froze, apprehensive of the forthcoming discussion.

'Are you guys looking to sneak in?'

They stood in silence, not sure where to look, considering making a run for it.

'If you are, there's no way you can get over the fence. You're much better to squeeze under it, at the space between the ground and the end of the blocks holding the fence up.'

Bingo, they were in. Now they were enjoying the golf on the large screen in front of the pub, shooting the breeze and watching Tiger make good his exit as they made their entrance. Woods was having a terrible time, all over the place, and his driving seemed to have gone into systemic shutdown.

Between chatting, I'd occasionally look up at the large screen – a great feature – in the centre of the tented village, and check out some of the golf. Progressively things got hazier, but at one point I could see Tiger so far right of the 10th that his tee shot would have been heading for Sweden. Watching him look for his ball was surreal, as he was surrounded by fans who seemed to follow him mindlessly, rather than actually helping. For once I felt sorry for Tiger. A lost ball and a complete shambles a few holes later, and he was out of it. I knew the feeling.

It took us ages to get a taxi back up the road – one guy waited for three hours and still no lift – and we ended up in a bar in Ayr, babbling rubbish and enjoying the blow out. It was my first and last major Major drinking session, and it'd taken me ten competitive rounds to get there. In comparison, my night out in Manhattan had been a gentle stroll.

OPEN SATURDAY: NOT FOR MOVING DAY

Tiger wouldn't be feeling too chipper, and neither was I, but at least I'd enjoyed my Friday afternoon. While he was hacking his way around the turn at Turnberry, Tiger was the last of our cares. He'd have been better off playing Pub Golf, every hole's score determined by the number of swigs it takes to consume an allotted drink, although from the eighth to the 13th his scores of 5-5-6-3-5-6 would have led to some barracking. It's a safe bet that the world's greatest sportsman doesn't go for thoroughly irresponsible drinking in a big way, although with two double-bogey 6s in four holes, you wouldn't know it.

I felt mildly guilty that while the great man was missing the cut for the first time in The Open, I was in the pub. I regarded it as his first real missed cut in a Major. He'd failed to make the last 36 holes at the US Open at Winged Foot in 2006, but that was only six weeks after his father, Earl, had passed away, and Tiger hadn't played competitively since the Masters ten weeks before. As if to emphasise that was more misnomer than missed cut, Tiger was second on his next outing, then won eight in a row. That was history. Tiger was probably already home and Turnberry had two rounds of championship golf to look forward to. Meanwhile, I had a hangover to combat.

As the BBC provides wall-to-wall coverage, it's almost impossible not to catch some golf on TV. Getting up five hours later than on any day at Bethpage, by the time I'd performed my ablutions and was ready for the off, golf was on the box. As a lover of the sport I often get quite teary watching a well-constructed montage that recalls great events in the past. To some classical music, the BBC ran two back-to-back, firstly Tom Watson and then Calcavecchia, showing great moments from their halcyon days.

Too often we take for granted the winning of these great championships. The ball-control and overcoming of nerves are beyond our ken. James Bryant Conant, the president of Harvard University credited with making the famous seat of learning world-class, once said, 'Each honest calling, each walk of life, has its own elite, its own aristocracy based on excellence of performance.' 36 holes and ten hours of golf separated someone from that elite.

Play was well under way by the time I arrived, although the leaders were not out for another three hours. The wind was stronger and gustier, the degree of difficulty up a notch or two. I wandered down to the short 4th to spend some time there. By the time I got to the 5th tee, adjacent to the 4th green, the 10:45 pairing of Oliver Wilson and Paul Broadhurst were on the tee. The wind was blowing hard off the sea.

Wilson struck a nice ball that went fairly well right, diving in behind one of the heavily grassed dunes, destination unknown. Next up was Broadhurst, who, during a few years in the doldrums, had played in a EuroPro event with my brother. Broady hit his drive down the same line as Wilson's and watched it drift right, destination also unknown. He reloaded, hitting a provisional, and it went further right. No indications came from the marshals; take three, another provisional hit even further right. At this point Paul gave up and walked on, presumably on the basis that he'd find one of them. He eventually made bogey 5, so must have found his first. Much was in store if players were not on song.

I walked down to the tee for a few minutes to see if Alex Jackson needed anything. About to play were two Swedes, Richard S Johnson and Freddie Jacobson, the latter being a contemporary of my brother's. When Al and Freddie were in their early years of men's amateur golf,

Al twice shot course record 66s. On both occasions, within a couple of hours, Jacobsen shot 65 and snatched the records. *Lycklig oäkting.*

As I watched the guys tee-off unspectacularly, I noticed a face that looked familiar, someone I'm pretty sure I recognised from the Masters. As sure as I was, there's always that fear of being wrong, of looking like a total dick. Turned out I was correct, Maurice had been at Augusta National and I recognised him from the flight out of Paris.

We chatted for a while and Maurice told me he was a regular at The Open, coming every year. His trip to Augusta had been his second, and like me he'd also been in Georgia in 2007. A member at his club, Dunscar, in Bolton, had been one of the beneficiaries of the opening of the Patron list to the practice lottery list in 1999, and on occasions when the guy didn't attend, he generously made tickets available to others. I'll wager not too many golfers in the Bolton area are Masters Patrons: another small twist in the tale of the hardest ticket in sport.

Like a lot of Scottish and English people, Maurice was rooting for a local win from the likes of Ross Fisher and Lee Westwood, or for Tom Watson to keep it going. We wished each other well and went our separate ways. In my case I was heading back to the 1st to see John Daly tee off.

En route I met Ritchie Blair. His man Richard Sterne was playing with Daly, and it was quite a contrast. Back at the Masters I'd been chatting with Ritchie about the caddying experience while John Daly had been selling his golfwear and drinking accessories from a parking lot. Just three months later, Daly was in the 12th last game on the Saturday of a Major and was only five shots back. With the wind up, anything was possible – maybe even another Daly major win?

Again Daly was sporting his Loudmouth golf pants, the sartorial equivalent of vomit. I couldn't work out if I felt sick or dizzy, or both. Mercifully not sporting the equivalent miniskirt, today his girlfriend was in a small number called Oakmont Houndstooth, fashioned after the trews that Johnny Miller wore when shooting his legendary 63 to win the US Open at Oakmont in 1973.

While watching Daly and Sterne go about their business, Anna Cladakis was a pleasant distraction. As a former promotional director for Hooters, the restaurant chain that uses certain female attributes as a marketing vehicle, she clearly understands the power of her long trim legs and embonpoint. Many of the male members of the gallery were focused on her, rather than the golf.

The level of chat of those following this game was certainly different. As he was going about making that bogey, one fan remarked, 'Let's watch Daly make a c*** of this out the bunker'. Imagining the Open crowd to be golfing sophisticates in tweed and brogues is just as erroneous as thinking the Masters crowd is full of elegant and monied silver surfers. In total contrast to Ms Cladakis, Richard Sterne's fiancée, following her beau outside the ropes, went totally unnoticed, dressed very casually but very smartly, small Marc Jacobs handbag slung over her shoulder.

I was hoping for both his and Ritchie's sake that Sterne would post around 68 and be right in the frame. Up the second his drive was right, not in a good lie. I didn't see his approach shot, so was surprised that Sterne ended up left, almost next to me at the ropes. His second had turned over in the hay. After ten seconds of deliberation, he struck a beautifully clipped third, out of the rough, arrow-straight into 12 feet. On TV this would have seemed innocuous. His firm hands through the ball and quality of strike, all looking so easy, belied the fact that a medium handicapper would have struggled to hit the green. It was a simple but world-class shot. Unfortunately he missed the putt. He'd go on to shot 75.

Down the 3rd, Long John pushed his tee shot slightly into the rough, then hit a fairly shocking approach that ballooned and tailed right, coming to rest a good 30 yards from the pin, well short. He then chipped in, to quite a fanfare from the crowd. John almost laughed as he turned towards the 4th tee. It would be his only birdie of the day as he marched to a 72. I decided to sit in the stand at the 4th green.

While there is a fine view from the stand – the sea and sands of south Ayrshire spread out on our right and down the coast to Girvan – it's not a great place to be watching the golf. The pin is cut too severely, and the best shot I see, hit almost perfectly by Branden Grace, lands pin-high and continues for another 15 feet. Almost every other shot either fails to make the putting surface or runs right to the back of the green, the slope carrying the ball away.

But as I sit back and enjoy the relaxing breeze, I reflect that things could have been worse. According to legend, around the 1500s, a clan of cannibals roamed these parts, reputedly killing thousands. Forty-eight strong and headed by Sawney Bean, a Scottish cross between Jeffrey Dahmer and Captain Caveman, they lived just south of Girvan. Years later Bean's daughter was said to have planted the Hairy Tree in Girvan, and later she was hanged from its boughs, implicated in the clan's incest. The whereabouts of the tree is unknown, but it's said that if you stand under it, you can hear the sound of a swinging corpse.

Two games after Grace, it's Sergio Garcia and Jeff Overton, and the Spaniard provides some interest. Having missed the green short, Sergio pitches, trying to use the slope front and left of the pin, but his ball comes to rest halfway down it. It's another 15 minutes before he plays his next. The firmness and speed of the greens, combined with a freshening breeze, mean that his ball appears to be moving, and you're not allowed to hit a ball unless it's at rest. Overton is called over for a look, the caddy has a peek, a referee is called, the Secretary General of the United Nations is sent a text message, a ceasefire is held in downtown Basra, and the USA's defence readiness status goes to DEFCON 2; the whole world comes to a standstill as Garcia waits. Any longer and the sun will begin to cool. Eventually the ball is deemed to be stationary and Garcia putts and misses, settling for a bogey.

As I leave the stand two games later, a fan passes me in a T-shirt that reads, KEN BROWN IS MY DAD. I love Ken, but not that much. Watching Martin Kaymer and Matthew Goggin for a few holes, I walk down the left of the 5th and Goggin pops into the players' portable toilet. As he reappears, an Irish bloke next to me says to Goggs, 'Number one or number two?' Goggin ignores him, but I sort of laugh, it's straight out the US Open book of spectating. What's not in the book, is when the crossing is opened, instead of going across it, this Irish bloke just follows the players down the fairway, walking about 15 paces behind Goggin for 30 yards, before cutting over and under the ropes. Not a single marshal does or says anything, and I can't believe it. I've seen marshals with pints in their hands, crossings closed when they should be open and vice versa. This is poor stewarding. I saw a patron do something similar at Augusta when play had finished, and a security guard chased him down, almost as he was across, frogmarched him back to the start of the cross-walk and made him do it properly.

I follow the game, outside the ropes, until the 7th, where the young German hits his long second at the par-5 to about three feet. Easy eagle. I then peel off, making for the catering between the 14th and the 9th, intending to grab food and watch some of the golf on the large screen before latching onto the leaders. When I arrive, there's immediately an issue: instead of the golf there's a movie on the large screen, either because of a technical issue or someone's up to nonsense. I can't make out what film it is, but I know I'm not interested.

After ten minutes the golf appears, to much cheering and clapping from the gathered punters. Just as I notice that Bryce Molder has finished his third round on level, I spot a guy with some stitches right in the middle of his head, the very same noggin hit by Molder two days previously. I speak to him and he assures me he's fine. The damage now looks superficial and not much more than a nasty scratch. With his man at even, he might end up having a very good week.

Five o'clock approaches by the time the leaders reach me, the wind is whipping and nobody is making a move, apart from Steve Marino who's gone backwards. I watch as Retief Goosen and Jimenez play 9, followed by Ross Fisher, Calcavecchia and then the final pairing, Marino and Tom Watson. Watson is a perennial favourite in Scotland, a beloved son of the links. He's at 5-under, one ahead of RoFi, but his three putts at 9 could suggest a chink is appearing. A string of players are lining up at minus 2 – Goggin, Calc, Steve Marino and Lee John Westwood. It's an open book for tomorrow, but I'm favouring a Watson or an English win, although there's a long way to go. Within six shots of the lead there are 28 players.

I follow Fisher and Calc for a few holes. I barely pay any attention to what they are doing, as I first bump into someone I know from the

Augusta National Gatehouse.

Tiger Woods hits a lavish pull-hook from the first tee on Masters Sunday. *Getty Images Sport*

Ritchie Blair looks on as Richard Sterne escapes from a bunker at no. 2. *Getty Images Sport*

Holing this play-off chip would have won Kenny Perry The Masters. Above Perry's head, in a dark slipover, is Chuck Giorgi, and to his right, Ken Olsen. The two Minnesotans I spoke to at the entry gate on the final day appeared in *Sports Illustrated* courtesy of this shot. *Getty Images Sport*

Angel Cabrera celebrates his triumph in the famous green jacket. *Getty Images Sport*

Members of the grounds crew work on the flooded first green as Lee Westwood and his caddie, Billie Foster, look on during the third round of the US Open. *Getty Images Sport*

Lucas Glover and Ricky Barnes walk into the amphitheatre that is Bethpage Black's 17th green. *Getty Images Sport*

On his way to an eagle, Ricky Barnes tees off at The Black's vast and magnificent 4th hole. *Getty Images Sport*

Phil Mickelson in action from sand on Sunday at Bethpage Black. *Getty Images Sport*

Danger awaits as Lucas Glover plays his tee shot on the 18th, preparing to take the spoils at the US Open. *Getty Images Sport*

With Ailsa Craig looming in the background, Tiger makes notes on the run of the 11th green during his practice round for The Open.

Golfers tee off below Turnberry Lighthouse, one of the most iconic images in golf.
Getty Images Sport

Tom Watson, surely at Turnberry just for the ride, puts the finishing touches to his practice round.

The crowd erupts as Stewart Cink holes a birdie putt on the 18th green during the final round of The Open Championship at Turnberry. *Getty Images Sport*

What might have been… Tom Watson shows his class, as ever, congratulating Stewart Cink on beating him to the Claret Jug. *Getty Images Sport*

The sun's up at Hazeltine's 8th hole before the start of the PGA Championship.

Tiger is up early, and what a sweet way to start the day.

Three Major winners, Glover, Cabrera and Cink, on the first tee with the PGA Trophy.

Kaboom! Alvaro Quiros detonates a wood to the 606-yard 11th at Hazeltine.

Vijay Singh, playing with Tiger, picks his ball out after an eagle at the 7th hole.

The author enjoys the glorious views of the 16th at Hazeltine.

Scottish Golf Union, and then two friends who have become separated from their group and don't know how they are going to get home. At the 13th I spot Al Tait with the Fisher game, doing his radio commentary. He's sporting a nice pair of black shorts and knee-length black socks, all he needs is a moustache and handkerchief on his head and he'd be Gumby from *Monty Python*. Walking along with the rope between us, Al enthuses about being out here with the guys in the thick of it, a small part of the guts of a major, sensing the pressure and emotion that goes with the heat of battle.

Watson seems to be cruising, oblivious to his age. Up at 15 I stand just shy of the green, waiting for the players to hit to the par-3. A young Welsh lad turns to me, randomly, and says in the broad accent of the valleys, 'Have you seen any birdies today? We've been here all day and haven't seen a single bloody one. Took us two days to get here and still we're waiting.'

I tell them not only did I see Daly's chip in, I've seen an eagle, and in an instant they change tone and start to enthuse about their visit to Turnberry. Despite the dearth of birdies, where else in the world would you go to the middle of nowhere to watch a global sporting event, they say. Bob and Matthew had come up with a group of friends, driving from Caerphilly and stopping for the night in Preston. They've had a few scoops and are good entertainment. The night before, they tell me, they'd queued to get into a busy pub in Girvan, along with Anthony Kim, who'd gone unnoticed in the sea of visitors, waiting for 30 minutes, just another face in the crowd. The lads had spotted him in the pub and had pictures taken. He was just a young guy out for a couple of drinks.

I bid them farewell. Now Watson has bogeyed and is slipping a bit. I try to track the final game down 16, but the cross-walk to the tee has not been opened and I'm stuck. It takes ages to get past, and already Watson has found the green in two, about 25 feet above the cup. I continue along the 17th and hear a massive cheer: Watson has boxed his tricky, slippery effort to go to 3-under. Rather than wilt, the old boy is coming back strong.

151

I'm at the top of the hill between 17 and 6, and Tom smacks a 320-yard drive down the birdieable par-5. By the time he plays his second, I'm down on the ropes, 20 yards from him. He puts on his trademark brisk, long but tight swing – the same work of art he applied to his final iron in 1977, golfing simplicity – and clocks his ball into 25 feet. We all cheer and shout, urging him to keep going deep; Tom two-putts for birdie, 4-under. Thousands are now following this game and the stands at the 18th green are solid, the hero of yesteryear on his way.

It's impossible to get close to the green; the grandstands and shape of the hole mean the nearest standing room is 50 yards away. I hop onto the stand at the 1st tee, as the 18th pin is cut forward and left enough that I'll have a view. It's a beautiful summer evening, warm, the sky is blue and there's that piercing, pure, crystal-sharp light you find in Scotland. Shadows are thrown across the course, deep lush green mixed with the gold of the rough and the black shadows, a rich canvas of golfing chiaroscuro.

As well as the beautiful scenery, the reception Watson receives is magnificent, a standing ovation on a Saturday night, every single person cheering, clapping, shouting, urging him on, on their feet in homage. Steve Marino might as well be invisible.

'Come on, Tom!'

'Keep it going, Tom!'

The crowd is high on emotion, desperately hoping that the Son of 1977 can repeat tomorrow. While Watson cannot repeat his massive birdie putt of Friday, he walks off the green saluting the crowd, thanking them for their support. He's 18 holes away from history.

Even I want Watson to win, though I've harboured a silly grudge against him for 27 years. As I walked across the 7th fairway at Royal Troon in 1982, I asked Tom for an autograph during a practice round. He looked at me directly and said 'no', his trademark grin-cum-grimace written across his face. Of course now I realise he was concentrating on his job, but in 1982 I was only 12 and didn't quite see it that way.

Thousands of fans stream from the course, and I soak up the sights and the glorious weather. I haven't lived in these parts for 15 years, and it's 20 since I was a member at Turnberry. The sea looks angry, the breeze chopping it, but the day is otherwise beautiful. We all think of tomorrow and what it may bring. Following tradition, as the sun begins to set at my back, a lone bagpiper walks along the gleaming front of the hotel, the windows glinting and the sound of the pipes welcoming guests to dinner. To a Scotsman like me, the sounds of the bagpipes are invigorating and emotional: they represent the best of times and the worst of times. For Watson, tomorrow, what will the piper play – a lament or a reel?

OPEN SUNDAY: THE BEST-LAID PLANS OF MICE AND MEN...

Part of me felt it was going to be too good to be true for Tom Watson to lift the claret jug, too much to ask of one of golf's elder statesmen. But that didn't mean I didn't want it to happen, and not just for the sake of my book. But if Tom Watson couldn't pull it off, I was hoping for a home victory in the shape of Lee Westwood or Ross Fisher, provided Fisher didn't skive off early to witness the arrival of his firstborn. Westwood had been knocking at the door and Fisher's rise to prominence at Bethpage and Turnberry was extraordinary, as he'd only played in his first major in 2007 (The Open at Carnoustie, where he missed the cut). The denouement to the 138th Open promised much.

There are many beautiful coast roads in the world, but as far as I know, only one features a spectacular castle, another ruined castle, the remnants of a volcano, and an optical illusion. Rather than cut over the hills, on Sunday I decided to belt down the coast road from Ayr, past the sleepy fishing village of Dunure and beyond to Turnberry. The road is a journey back to simpler times.

Although there were rain clouds floating about, I got the roof down and took my chances. The first few miles of the A719 Dunure road run along the foot of the Carrick Hills, the Firth of Clyde down and to the right. Climbing up and then down past Dunure, with its ruined fifteenth-century castle, the road then climbs for the next five miles through a series of long straights punctuated with demanding bends. The old Lotus hummed away, reacting sweetly to the need for the speed and occasional sudden braking, as Metallica injected some adrenalin into proceedings. Out over the water, between the beach and the Isle of Arran, a cloud was showering its contents into the bay, the sun piercing it to form a bastard rainbow whose hazy colours floated like some magic talisman or message from the Golfing Gods.

At the highest point, Croy Bay opens out below, Culzean Castle sitting proud and secluded on its southern edge. Culzean – pronounced cull-ane, the 'z' a modern version of a Middle Scots letter shaped like '3', the yogh – dates back to the last decade of the eighteenth century and is a popular local and tourist destination. Fans of the original *Wicker Man* film will recognise it as the home of Christopher Lee's character, Lord Summerisle.

A few corners later and it's the famous Electric Brae, a short stretch of road that appears, because of the hillside and surrounding landscape, to be going downhill, but actually runs upwards. At all times of year one encounters cars slowly rolling upward with the engine idling. This morning there are no such cars, and I fire down (or up) the hill and make my turn for the final stretch down into Maidens and Turnberry.

As I climb the short, sharp hill at the Turnberry end of Maidens, I pass Fanny Sunesson fighting her way up it on a bicycle. Shortly after, I'm adjacent to The Open car parks and the traffic starts to back up. Snapping out of my Fanny-on-a-bike train of thought, I'm struck emotionally by the lyrics on the Metallica song now playing, 'The Unforgiven III'

'How could he know
This new dawn's light
Would change his life forever?
Set sail to sea
But pulled off course
By the light of golden treasure.'

It really hit home what Tom Watson could pull off today by winning. He'd break or equal numerous records – tie Harry Vardon's record six wins in The Open; become the oldest man to win a major; claim the trophy after the biggest gap since previous victory, 26 years . . . and the list goes on. Or would Tom be pulled off course, and would someone else's life change forever? Time would tell.

On entering the course I bumped into the only professional golfer in the world who's guaranteed to get his hands on a major trophy every single year. I asked him if he was up for the challenge – how did he approach it, lots of gins and tonic or none? For 32 years Garry Harvey's late father, Alex,[1] had engraved the Claret Jug. Garry, the pro at Bearsden Driving Range, had taken up the role on his father's retirement in 2005. I imagine he often wakes up in a cold sweat during the night, his nightmare ending as Gonzalo Fernández-Castaño sinks a 50-foot putt on the final green to pip Adam Scott and Paul Casey. I wish him a steady hand and easy spelling for later.

I was in a quandary about how to attack the day. The Masters and the US Open had dictated themselves. The Open was different. I knew the stands would fill up quickly, that any toilet break would lose me any seat I had, followed by a long and possibly futile wait for another. I meandered between spectating points, trying to work out what to do. Should I follow the leaders, or sit in the stand and take my chances?

Pondering, I sat at the 1st hole and watched a few games tee off. Nick Watney and Mark Calcavecchia were first up, their tee time 11:00. Calc hit a most interesting shot – a pull hook with a hybrid that, from my vantage point, appeared to sail over a fence and out-of-bounds. He looked quizzically around, grabbed another ball, dropped it and effortlessly punched a provisional down the middle. His first ball turned out to be fine, and he made bogey 5.

Miguel Angel Jimenez was next, a perennial favourite in Scotland due to his laidback style and masses of ginger hair (he has no business being Spanish). One gets the impression Miguel could chug away on his Partagas cigar while covered in honey and a swarm of bees, and he wouldn't

1. At one time Alex Harvey was invited to do the engraving for the Masters Tournament, and offered his accommodation for the trip. As he wasn't a fan of long-haul travel, he graciously declined.

be fazed. In fact he'd probably make friends with all the bees and invite them down to Malaga for an evening of tapas and lashings of Rioja. True to his image, he walked up the corridor from the putting green to the 1st puffing away like The Flying Scotsman, signing autographs and high-fiving the crowd. Great guy. If only we could understand a single word he says in his TV interviews.

Next up it was, like some new Anglo-Germanic pop combo, pretty boys Nick Dougherty and Martin Kaymer, Take That meets Kraftwerk. As they tee off, the bloke next to me is sporting one of the Nevada Bob caps that have been around all week, black with a large orange section on the front for you to write your own slogan: 'Tiger who?' it reads.

The leaders weren't starting for two hours, so I went for some food. Annoyingly there always seems to be a queue here that never goes anywhere in a hurry, the exact opposite of the US. The Open operates a mix of logoed and independent eating facilities, run by organisations that travel the country providing food at various events. One crowd's next stop was the Tatton Garden Flower Show near Manchester. You'd think they'd come up with a better system than queuing, queuing, queuing, then queuing some more until you have a psychotic episode. After this experience you are then served food that survivors of an earthquake in south-east Asia would refuse. Actually, that's not entirely fair, over the week the fish and chips and various burgers I have consumed have been quite tasty.

Yesterday at one of the outlets, the special was chips and curry. When I eventually arrived at the front of the queue – progress being interrupted by the girl serving me receiving numerous text messages from Sean, which she just had to tell her colleague about – a number of things were obvious. There was a literally gross misuse of the word 'special'; and it wasn't actually chips and curry, but chips in curry, chips in the sauce, bubbling away in front of me. I was glad I'd chosen the haddock and chips. A Scot, Adam Smith, may have charted the way for Western capitalism in *The Wealth of Nations*, but I can only assume his editor expunged the chapters on how to organise efficient queues and effective presentation of food.

Today isn't much better. The queue is actually two queues. Nobody, except the employees, knows this. We stand in line to order and pay, and are then given a receipt and directed to the other queue where our hearty repast will be served. Every single person joining the second queue is less than impressed, and I don't blame them. If I'd known, I'd have gone to another stall with a more efficient regime. Consolation: the Aberdeen Angus burger was very nice, and at £6.00 I don't feel as if I've been fleeced. Fed and watered, I head back to the golf course.

I'm still in a tizzy. My big concern is that, with birdies generally hard to come by, and the wind similar to the previous two days, someone could come out the pack, steal the Jug and I'll miss it all. I don't mind missing it, as long as I do so on the basis that I've made a good decision. Maybe I should drive home and watch it all on TV?

At 13:30 I watch Angel Cabrera hit a low fizzing tee-shot at the 1st. I follow that game up to the green and sit in the stand for the remaining games.

There's a funny feeling to the final round. Of the last six players, Furyk, Goosen, Westwood, Fisher, and Goggin are all chasing, while Tom Watson had first led from his third hole at about 08:45 on Thursday. And he'd been thereabouts ever since. Being in the cauldron of major competition for so long would make a victory for him today even more remarkable. Rarely, if ever, can someone have been in the mix for so long in a Major.

Some in the press pack were concerned that a 59-year-old winner would reflect badly on modern golf, as if Hillary Clinton was going to be crowned Miss Universe. I had some sympathy for this view, as modern players have followed Tiger's lead and brought athleticism to the game. Watson was and is a great player, but he's not Lance Armstrong.

In the penultimate game, Westwood just missed for birdie and Ross Fisher got off to the best possible start, curling in a tasty 11-footer. RoFi was once again in the mix, just weeks after Bethpage. Behind, Watson was in a perfect position for his second, but tugged it into the greenside bunker. I left the stand and got down on the ropes behind Tom, and along with countless others across the world implored him to get up and down. The bunker shot and missed putt were not bad, but nor were they wholly convincing. The jury was out.

By the time I was crossing the 2nd fairway to the 3rd, Watson and Goggin having driven, there was a massive boom up at the second green. Fisher had birdied again and was now in the lead. Minutes later, Alan Tait from BBC Radio told me it was a most remarkable chip-in. The Golfing Gods were watching over Fisher. The adrenalin started to flow – game on. The early punches had been thrown in this enthralling bout.

Down the 3rd, Fish failed to birdie, reduced to par like a mere mortal. As I watched the action at the green, I noticed Lee Westwood roll his ball to a small boy in the crowd, a lady almost snatching it from the child.[1] At the 4th, RoFi hit a poor tee shot that cost him a bogey. As he took 4, I watched Retief Goosen hit a superb 3-wood that faded off the left-hand bunker into the middle of the fairway at number 5. Controlled power. Delicious.

I then had to wait what seemed like an age to get from the 5th tee to the fairway, the crossing point blocked by two buggies with TV equipment, filming the action. It was frustrating to be in the right place at the right time, and not to be able to get anywhere in a hurry. By the time I got down, Goosen was over his ball, ready to pull the trigger on his second. To my surprise, he hit a shot worthy of a 9-handicapper feeling the pressure, a low, squirty neck that only had one possible resting place, the right-hand bunker. These guys are good, but they are also human. Uncontrolled power. Horrible.

Up at the 5th green I waited for Fisher and Westwood, and watched in the distance as disaster unfolded, as if from a ship in a harbour watching an ancient city burn to the ground. RoFi's star had turned into a supernova, exploding into a trillion pieces. I could see Ross was in the rubbish down the right, and could also see him have a hack, not move

---

1. Later I found out it was Dave and Lewis, whom I'd bumped into on Thursday. A lady almost got the ball but fumbled it, and a marshal gave it to the rightful recipient, Lewis. What is it with adults at sporting events? They wouldn't beat up a child who got to the sweeties first, would they?

it very far, and then turn over a horror story of a next shot. With all the deliberation thereafter, it was obvious a drop was in the offing. And before he got to the green, and almost made a tremendous 7 (if there is such a thing), most of the crowd knew that Fisher was figuratively packing his bags and heading for home. The impending birth of his and wife Joanne's first child was no longer an issue (no pun intended), she could drop the sprog whenever she fancied and the history books of golf would remain intact. He'd gone from RoFi to NoFi in 20 minutes.

Westwood also made bogey after driving down the right, and in the next game Watson and Goggin managed pars, but after two bogeys each in their first few holes, the lead was now 2-under and a raft of players were in contention. I knew this was going to happen! Had Fisher continued on his merry way I would have followed the players to the far end of the course, but I was now back in Indecision Land.

I took a seat at the 1st tee stand, and got a view of the last green. Just as I approached it, a tremendous roar shattered the air from about a mile away, Lee Westwood had eagled the 7th, and combined with his birdie at the 6th, he was now the leader at 4-under. Aye, well done Kenny. I knew immediately I'd made the wrong decision, especially when I remembered the battle at Augusta, and sitting at the final hole of Bethpage, watching those putts that could have forced a different result. I needed to be in the thick of it, feeding off some of the adrenalin generated by the players. I saw Luke Donald on level par and Ernie Els closing with a bogey, his second in the last three, to finish plus-1. Justin Leonard also finished on that total, having doubled the 16th. Around par was not going to be far away, especially down the stretch. Only one previous Major winner was in the mix, and he was nearly a pensioner.

The atmosphere was flatter than Luxembourg, all the action was further out. The only spot of excitement was the rocket scientist sitting to my right, a brusque northern Englishman bemoaning the fact that one couldn't reserve seats. He couldn't believe that if he wanted to go to the toilet or grab something to eat, he'd have to give up his seat. I sat at the 1st for about 20 minutes and not once did he stop bitching and moaning, even taking the marshal to task, as if he'd set the rules.

159

He even complained that the composite stand behind the 18th – usually populated by R&A members, guests and others who'd paid for the privilege – was quiet. I was tempted to tell him that nothing in life was fair, plus that he was a f******g idiot and should either shut up or go home and watch the golf on TV. Fortunately I did neither, and left the stand. I needed to be where the action was. To his credit, he quipped as I left, 'Will I keep your seat for you?' I laughed and declined. At least he was an arsehole with a sense of humour.

I'd try to catch the leaders and challengers around the 14th, but immediately I was in the thick of it. Coming up 17 was the young pro and, judging by his hairstyle, hedgehog impersonator, Chris Wood, who'd finished fifth last year as an amateur. Once again he was in the position of a lifetime. He'd eagled 7, birdied 8 and 10, bogeyed 13 and 14, but had rallied with a great birdie 2 at 15. On the hill right of the 17th green, I watched as his second landed short, but he pitched up to around 10 feet and holed for a birdie, showing no nerves. The two ladies standing beside me almost had kittens at this point, and judging by hair and skin tone, one might be Wood's mother. They were beside themselves with excitement and made their way down the last. He was at minus-2, and at the current rate of scoring, I might just have seen the winner. Energised to be back in the thick of the action, I walked swiftly north-west, desperate to get to the leaders.

Thousands are streaming towards 18, some to catch the final two holes, others to watch it play out on TV. The crowds get progressively larger as I walk up the side of the 16th, going against the grain. There's a real sense of excitement that Tom Watson is going to be crowned, although he, Westwood and Goggin are at 3-under. Cink and Wood are one shot back. With some of the trickiest holes to come, and with a good birdie or eagle chance at 17, it's anyone's.

Having fought my way through the fans and rounded the bottleneck at the 15th and 16th tee, I come very quickly to the 14th green. I stand next to a stentorian gentleman who's extremely annoying and extremely useful in equal measure. He provides a running commentary that can probably be heard in Ireland, describing every shot we see. Part of me wants to clobber him, or at least tell him to shut up, *we can see what's happening*, but as he also has a radio, he provides a running commentary on what's going on elsewhere. Good boy.

The 14th green is ringed with spectators, the stand packed. The sides of the fairway are teeming and I can see an army of people following Westwood and Fisher to the 13th green. It's been ten years since Paul Lawrie won at Carnoustie and we'd love another British winner. As I arrive at the 14th, Cink misses a 6-foot putt for par and I reckon he's toast, there are too many other good players out there.

As Furyk and Goosen putt out on 14 there's a big roar behind me. Cink has birdied the awkward 15th and is back to minus-2. Maybe he's not out of it. I look back down the fairway, in the middle of which Westwood stands, cogitating over his approach to the hardest hole of the day. Par will be good here. Behind him, in the distance, Watson and Goggin make their way to the 13th green. The crowd with them looks like the Ninth Crusade.

Lee comes up way short of the green at 14, and amazingly chooses to putt, rather than pitch, from 30 yards. To his credit he knocks it almost stiff, a definite par. Fisher comes out of the right-hand bunker to about a foot, and acknowledges the crowd as he taps in. It has been a rollercoaster day for him, but publicly, at least, he's showing good spirits. There's a nervous tension as Westwood eyes up his putt, but he smoothly strokes it into the middle and we roar encouragement. He, Watson and Goggin continue to lead on 3-under.

I follow Westwood down the 16th, realising that I can also get in position for Watson. I appear to be in a win-win position, as either looks likely to triumph. Once I get round the 15th bottleneck again, crossing against the directions from the marshal and squeezing through, I practically run to see Westwood finish just off the back of the green in two. It's not an impossible shot he's left, but a fast slope awaits behind the hole to gather the ball into the burn. Tricky. There's a quiet hush around the green, hundreds continuing to stream down with Watson's game. Westwood hits a mediocre chip that errs on the side of caution, and when his putt tantalisingly kisses the edge of the hole, he's back to minus-1 after his bogey at 15.

I don't hang about and make straight for the hill to the side of the 17th green. I stand on a grassy knoll, along with about 50 others, and we all stare back down the fairway, watching as Westwood contemplates his second from the left rough. He obliterates an iron that runs up onto the green, coming to rest about 18 feet from the pin. We jump up and down. 'Come on, Lee,' hundreds shout as the Englishman walks up to the green. If he holes this he'll be one ahead, jumping with an eagle back to minus-3.

In the meantime Watson has parred 16 and is coming down 17, too. There's an eerie silence as we contemplate Westwood's putt. He strokes it purely. It has to break, must fall in, but like his putt on 16 it manages, unbelievably, to find its way around the hole, finishing behind it. I feel for him as he clasps his nose between finger and thumb, incredulous at the miss. Cink is minus-2 in the clubhouse, Watson and Westwood are minus-2 and on the course. It's now a three-horse race.

Tom hits a superb approach shot into the par-5, his ball running past the flag and ending just on the fringe at the back. Armies of fans are watching, praying that Tom will get down in two and have the lead. He knocks his ball to about 18 inches and it seems certain, so I scamper from my knoll round to another about 80 yards away, just at the corner of the dogleg on the last hole. As I arrive Westwood is contemplating a fairway bunker shot that is both crucial and dangerous. He's now one behind the lead, Watson on minus-3.

After much musing over club selection, Lee settles in behind the ball and executes one of the best bunker shots of all time down the stretch in a major. He flushes his ball out of the deep trap 180 yards from the green and somehow, inexplicably, finds the putting surface. The fans at the last go wild, it could be the shot of the championship. Amazing skill, nerve and courage, and Westwood receives a standing ovation as he walks onto the final green.

As Westwood deliberated, Tom Watson waited on the tee, anticipating some crowd noise, not wanting to be put off. I was slightly worried. This was shades of Colin Montgomerie at Congressional in the 1997 US Open when he waited and waited for quiet. Eventually Tom flushed his shot down the middle and he'd have three shots from around 180 yards to win his sixth Open. Westwood had spoiled his epic sand shot with a three putt that he'd live to regret. Joining hundreds of others up on the hill, spectators swarmed towards the final hole, mobbing the stands and taking every possible vantage point. As Goggin eyed up his second, a section of the crowd was shouting, 'Tommy! Tommy! Tommy!', and soon it was Watson's turn.

I was almost directly behind Tom, with a clear view of player and target. The tension was palpable. Surely at no other time in any sport could so many in a single crowd be rooting for the same outcome. I was imagining all sort of terrible things: a duff, a shank, a fresh air-shot. The pressure was unbearable, and I was just in the crowd. What emotions must have been going through Watson's mind?

As so often this week and in his entire career, Tom hit a beautiful iron, and in the heat of battle his tempo, balance, direction and quality of strike seemed perfect. I watched the ball soar into the air, clearly seeing its flight and distance, and I felt in those few seconds that it was over. His ball would land mid-green, check, and he'd have no worse than 18 feet and two putts to win.

Perhaps if I'd sat at 18 all day, as I did at the US Open, I'd have known better. We watched Watson's ball roll and roll and roll until it disappeared over the back of the green. Silence was mixed with consternation on our wee hill 230 yards from the ball's resting place. I knew any up-and-down from through the back was not guaranteed.

And so the dream unravelled. The Scottish golfing public went from Mardi Gras to state funeral in a few easy minutes. The hand of history seemed to take over and destiny turned Stewart Cink's way. Watson 3-putted – we watched his first race past – and it was a play-off. The anticipation of the crowd turned from hopeful to nervous. It would be a 4-hole play-off: 5 then 6, then the 17th and 18th holes. Thereafter, if still tied, it would be sudden death.

I walked a few yards over to a hill that gave me a view of the entire 5th and 6th holes. It wasn't far from the 17th and gave me easy access to the 18th.

The play-off started hopefully as Watson found the middle of the fairway, ahead of Cink. Only a few people were up at the tee, but thousands and thousands inhabited the triangle between the first three play-off greens, and many, many more had stayed at the last. Standing to my left I'd noticed Christian Iooss, director of photography at *Golf Digest* and son of the legendary *Sports Illustrated* photographer, Walter Iooss Jnr. In front of us, with hundreds of others, were Stewart Cink's wife and their two boys. I couldn't imagine what they might be going through.

Both Cink and Watson bunkered their approaches to the 5th, and Cink was the man who saved par, a lead of one, three to go. Watson then hit a shocking tee shot at the long par-3 6th, going right of the large mound and effectively ending up in the rough at 17. I watched from afar as he hit a pressure-defying shot back into the setting sun, from where he holed for par, staying one behind. And then it was over, the life of Watson's game smothered like his tee shot at the 17th, and as Stewart Cink birdied the final two holes, Tom's game fell apart. He'd run out of gas.

As Watson slashed his way up 17 and hit a poor drive up 18 I was, after all, going to be able to see the final hole of this Open. Fans left the grandstand at the last, an eerie chatter and dark silence signalling the end of a dream. I easily found a seat, and discovered a mild farce was under way. Over the PA system, an upper-middle-class voice described the events of the playoff, but the gentleman in question seemed to think that Watson's opponent was Stewart Zinc.

And Zinc holes for birdie at the 17th. Zinc's found the fairway. Zinc's done this, Zinc's done that. I was embarrassed for him, and when he eventually stopped waffling, the crowd cheered and clapped, their double torture over. All I could think of was Simon Zinc-Trumpet-Harris, an Old Etonian married to a very attractive table lamp according to *Monty Python*'s Upper Class Twit of the Year Show.

Too much zinc causes ataxia and lethargy: so is this what happened to Watson? Dispelling some of the gloom from the crowd, Zinc hit a great shot close to the pin at the last and we cheered and clapped, applauding a great end to an emotional day. Stewart Cink was going to be a very worthy winner.

It's a shame for Cink that The Open at Turnberry could be remembered for what Tom Watson didn't do, but Cink was a worthy champion, scoring birdies at four of his last eight holes and holing a crucial 15-footer at the 72nd. Watson ran out of steam, his energy zapped by his misfortune at the final hole of regulation play. At least Garry Harvey would be mildly happy, he could start engraving after the final drives.

The Ailsa provided a great test, great scenery and a legendary championship. I hope Stewart Cink moves forward and wins another major, leaving behind the clinical depression that swept Scotland on his victory. After the prize-giving, I and countless others mournfully begin our journeys home, wrapped up in what might have been, punch-drunk on raw emotion.

I fire up the old British sports car. It's younger than Tom Watson, but just as likely to break down on the final stretch. I avoid the A77 once more, a funeral cortege backed up for miles, and shoot past the golf course and hotel. The euphoria I felt at watching Tiger and Phil at the Masters is in direct counterpoint to the numbing sense of loss and depression I feel today. The CD player is on random, and once again Metallica bursts from the speakers like a faraway medium.

I hurtle along the coast road, burning past the slow-moving tourists and golf fans, wind in my hair. I'm high on the hill, the Scottish sun incandescent and angry to my left. The song on the CD shifts from its melodic beginning to its savage midsection: Hetfield, Ulrich, Hammet and Trujillo echoing the feelings of millions with 'The Day That Never Comes'.

> *'Keep praying*
> *Just keep waiting*
> *Waiting for the one*
> *The day that never comes'*

Stewart Zinc, Open Champion. Well done.

Ten Thousand Golf Balls, Ten Thousand Lakes
The PGA Championship

Yang's daring shot on 18 equalled any 'go for it' challenge I have witnessed. He simply wanted the win and made it happen. This is a great day for the game and the field.

Art Benton, Atlanta, Georgia

THE PGA: A MAJOR START TO THE END OF THE MAJORS

'Excuse me, Mr Player, can I shake your hand?'

'Hello, how are you?'

'Fine, thank you. It's not every day one sees a golfing legend waiting for his golf clubs.'

'Have you just flown in from Scotland?'

'Yes, just in today.'

'And are you playing some golf?'

'No, I'm heading up to the PGA. You?'

'Good for you. I'm here to play in a few tournaments. You know, my grandfather was from Glasgow.'

'Far be it for me to suggest that would be where you got some of your golfing talent.'

'It was. He ate a lot of haggis and neeps. Enjoy your trip.'

And so it was that the first person I spoke to after immigration at Chicago O'Hare was Gary Player, twice a PGA Championship winner and one of only five men[1] to have done the career Grand Slam. The winner of nine Majors was waiting for his clubs at the outsize luggage section. You can't write this stuff. It seemed like a good omen for the final leg of my journey. One of the events Player was headed for was the final Major of the Seniors' year, the JELD-WEN Tradition. Curious that a golf tournament should be sponsored by a character from *Star Wars*.

Before heading up to the PGA, I was spending the weekend in Chicago, a beautiful city which feels like a laid-back, less frenetic version of Manhattan. Manhattan Lite. With cool breezes from Lake Michigan, the heat in the city usually has less of an edge, and it's a great place to stroll around. The city was largely rebuilt after the devastating Great Chicago Fire of 1871, and architects from around the world flocked to the shores of the lake, eager to stamp their mark on the new cityscape, and Chicago was reborn as the home of the skyscraper.

On Saturday I walked from my hotel down to the home of the Chicago Bears, Soldier Field, to watch training for the upcoming American Football season. At only $10, a ticket to the Family Day was a bargain slice of Americana, and the recently rebuilt Soldier Field was impressive, marrying traditional columns with a modern stadium construction around the top.

With grown men running at each other, slamming together and throwing things, it was just like any typical Saturday night out in Glasgow. In 1927 the original Soldier Field had been the venue for a battle of a different kind, the legendary Gene Tunney-Jack Dempsey 'Battle of the Long Count' heavyweight championship fight, when 103,000 boxing fans saw defending champ Tunney benefit from 13 seconds on the canvas and a second chance to defeat his challenger. Tunney knocked Dempsey down in the next round and went on to win a unanimous decision. The fight was the first $2 million gate in sport, but in contrast the Bears' practice was watched by just under half the stadium capacity of 61,500.

The big draw, during a series of training plays, was the Bears' new quarterback, Jay Cutler, who'd previously been at the Denver Broncos. Almost all the crowd were bedecked in navy blue and orange kit, and

1. Gary Player, Ben Hogan, Tiger Woods, Gene Sarazen and Jack Nicklaus.

at least I'd had the foresight to put on a navy polo shirt in an effort to blend in. Rock music played incessantly from the stadium speakers as the crowd clapped and cheered impressive receptions and interceptions, and groaned at incomplete plays. A bonus at the top of the north-facing stand was a great view of downtown Chicago, across to the planetarium, up through Grant Park – where the Lollapalooza music fest was into its second day – and onwards to the skyscrapers.

I planned to do more sightseeing and walking on Sunday, and possibly a boat tour covering the architectural sights, but a severe case of fatigue got the better of me. Suffering from jet lag on Saturday afternoon, I was destined for my hotel room quite early, but accidentally went into a number of pubs, mixing it with sports fans and Lollapalooza goers. As a result, Sunday was a total washout that involved going for lunch, trying not to pass out in the 100-degree heat and heading back to O'Hare.

Once through security I received a text, reminding me that Tiger and Paddy Harrington were going at it in Firestone. It appeared that the Irishman was not only out of the doldrums, but in the ascendancy. Of course, by the time I had located a television in an airport eatery, Harrington had put a carrot in the nose of the snowman: eight at the 16th. Game over.

Woods had won back-to-back, and next up it was the PGA. As I ate my lunch, I got chatting to the gent at the table next to me. Although an African-American, he was just as annoyed as I was that despite Paddy's great fight, his collapse had resulted in a predictable win. He was a golf fan, and wanted to see the winners' circle include more than Tiger Woods. He left to catch his flight, and as I went to pay my bill, I found he'd already paid it: a random act of kindness from a total stranger. I hunted him down at the gate for his flight to Portland, Oregon, where he was to meet his buddies for a few days' golf, and thanked him very much. Thanks again, John.

Our plane left its stand on time, but due to inclement weather between Chicago and Mexico there was a traffic jam waiting to take off. I'd never seen anything like it, and with a second-wave hangover kicking in, I was feeling very ropey. It was an hour before we were in the air. Still, I was excited to be heading for Minnesota, as it wasn't your typical US state, if there is such a thing. More than half of the five million residents are of German or Scandinavian (mostly Norwegian) ancestry. This was immediately obvious on the plane. The reading selection was a bit more exciting than *Bridget Jones* and *Juggs Monthly*. The young lady sitting next to me was reading *Giants in the Earth*, by someone called O.E. Rølvaag. I had never heard of it or, I assumed, him, but I was fairly sure it'd be some earthy tale of good Scandinavian folk.[1] And the young guy to her right was reading *Stern*, the German weekly news magazine infamous for being duped into publishing the fake diaries of Adolf Hitler in 1983.

My thoughts turned to the 'championshipness' of the PGA. Glory's Last Shot is the final chance of the season to pick up a Major, and given that the next one is the following season's Masters, the PGA Champion gets to enjoy being the 'last Major winner' longer than the others. The PGA suffers at the hands of many a writer as it doesn't appear to have the glamour or prestige of the other three Majors, and it's not always known for being played on the best courses. It also has the tag of producing some ropey winners, but I beg to differ from that assessment.

Although you can often make numbers do what you want them to, like some quirky Indian numerologist who says you must have five guys named Mohar in your Bollywood movie or forever be unlucky, I am of the opinion that it's not as bad a championship as people like to make out.

For a start, you'd struggle to find anyone who'd give a PGA win back in return for something else, like more prize money or a victory in another strong field like The Players. Both Arnold Palmer and Tom Watson didn't win a PGA and failed to complete the career Grand Slam. Do you think Arnie and Tom would surrender a Masters Green Jacket or an Open medal for a PGA win, so as to join the pantheon of career slammers? In a New York minute they would. I'd pay their airfares to go and collect the damn title.

1. *Giants in the Earth* is the first in a trilogy by Rølvaag that charts the life of early Norwegian settlers in Dakota Territory, part of which was Minnesota.

I'm willing to bet that in his mind, because he's only interested in accumulating majors and trumping Jack Nicklaus' tally of 18 professional Majors, Tiger Woods sees each and every Major as absolutely equal in stature and kudos. Yes, he wants to win all his events and be regarded as a golfing master of all trades, but it all boils down to Major wins for him. He wouldn't care if the PGA was played midwinter in Buttplug, Colorado, with orange balls and snowmobiles.

We should celebrate the PGA because in so many ways it's the most unusual of golf's Majors. It's the only modern Major to have been played in the winter. And that was because it was also the only Major to have been played to avoid a lawsuit. It was the first Major to be won by someone using a metal driver – Lee Trevino, Shoal Creek, 1984. It's the only Major to have been contested in the matchplay format (from 1916 to 1957). For many, this is the purest form of golf. If you look at some winners over those years – Jim Barnes; Walter Hagen; Gene Sarazen; Leo Diegel; Tommy Armour; Denny Shute; Byron Nelson; Sam Snead; Ben Hogan – there aren't too many goofballs.

The PGA's Achilles heel is deemed to be the quality of its winners. Looking back from 2008 to the year of my birth, 1969, the four Majors have produced the following numbers of players who have won only that single Major victory – the Masters has 10; US Open 11; Open 10; PGA 13. But if we expand the category to include 'single Major specialists', players who won only one of the four titles once *or more*, but no other major, we have: Masters 13; US Open 16; Open 11; PGA 14. These figures and others could merit a book on their own, but I think they show that on many levels the quality of the PGA and its victors is really no better or worse than the other three. Walter Hagen once said, 'any player can win a US Open, but it takes a helluva player to win two'. And Cary Middlecoff said of the same championship, 'Nobody wins the Open. It wins you'. The same could be said for all the Majors.

Our eventual landing at the Lindbergh Terminal of Minneapolis-St Paul International Airport was fine. Steve, my host for the week, was good enough to pick me up, saving me a $75 taxi ride to Chaska. It was good to see him again and we shot the breeze as we headed to his home. The PGA was alive with possibilities, most of them centred on Tiger.

PGA WEEK: TIGER STALKS THE PLAINS

One of the many great things I'd experienced in the golfing year was the friendliness of most people I'd met. My journey to the PGA was in some way a journey back to the start of my year, as I was meeting up and staying with people whom I had met at The Masters. The offer to stay at Steve's house was a massive gesture, typical of American hospitality.

Steve had made the offer when I was justifying my aloneness at Augusta, and he immediately invited me to stay with his wife and two daughters. Faced with such kindness I was taken aback, embarrassed by such generosity, but I assured him I would love to take him up on his offer and we could swap emails after The Masters. I also planned to meet up with Ken and Chuck, the two Minnesotans I had chatted with as we waited for the gates to open on Masters Sunday.

Steve was keen to show me some local golf courses and had arranged some tee times. I had taken my clubs across the Atlantic four times for the other two US Majors, and had played the sum total of nine holes. At Ansley in Atlanta my golf was atrocious for at least five of the nine, not helped by the fact I had just stepped off a plane. Although the weather had conspired against me in April and June, a great feature of golf travel is that you can take your sticks and play a whole variety of courses. Most other sports don't offer the chance of a unique playing arena every time.

On the Monday and Wednesday of PGA week we played at Chaska Town (where I was tickled that the Course Superintendent was called Mark Moers) and at a new Tom Lehman design, Troy Burne, just over the state border in Wisconsin. Chaska Town was the course used in conjunction with Hazeltine when the latter hosted the US Amateur in 2006. It was a lovely course with a nice blend of open holes and wooded holes, some with water and some without. My golf was mixed, but as we played the short 6th, I noticed a helicopter doing some low-level flying nearby. Fancying it was a transfer chopper from the PGA I asked Steve if this was the case. He just chuckled, and told me it was spraying for mosquitoes over the marshland. Usually the area is thick with these airborne horrors, but as the weather had been relatively mild for Minnesota, and there had been little rain, this year there weren't many around. A few days later, Steve's uncle, John Sullivan, told me that he wouldn't say the mosquitoes get big, but in a neighbouring county one was arrested for raping a chicken.

I'd never seen anything like the chopper's manoeuvres, and for a number of holes was very impressed with an aerobatic display that was more akin to *Chickenhawk* in Vietnam than it was to the waters of the Midwest. At one point the helicopter came very low out of the sun, over the treetops and looked, to me, as if it was going to smash into the clubhouse roof. Then it banked, turned and headed back on itself; a free air-show with my green fee.

Another first was in store at Tom Lehman's course. As we parked and changed into our golf gear, two Bald Eagles circled above the hillside behind us, waiting patiently for their prey. Troy Burne was a good track and we all had our moments: at least the sun was shining.

In the run-up to the championship start on Thursday, as well as becoming familiar with some of the local airborne inhabitants, I had the chance to reacquaint myself with the mammal who has stalked grassland around the world for over a decade, devouring prey at will, usually showing no mercy. Tiger was in town, and as I'd followed his early morning practice at Turnberry, I fancied I'd do the same again.

As soon as Tiger had missed the cut at Turnberry I felt he was a good bet for the PGA – that which does not kill him usually makes him stronger. This was emphasised by his wins in the previous fortnight. Victory in the Buick Open had given Woods a unique place in golfing history: he'd won each of his warm-up tournaments a fortnight before the year's Majors – Bay Hill, the Memorial, AT&T and finally the Buick. One writer labelled it the Premature Grand Slam, although I prefer to call it the Warm-up Slam. In winning the Bridgestone Invitational at Firestone between the Buick and the PGA, Tiger had further stoked the fires of certainty. He was the red-hot favourite to pick up the last Major of the year. Tiger not winning? Yeah, like Bernie Madoff gets parole and spends the rest of his 150-year sentence bathing in asses' milk and eating truffles. It wasn't going to happen.

Between our games at Chaska Town and Troy Burne, I'd been down early on the Tuesday to see Tiger practise. You'll have gathered by now that I'm more of an admirer of what he does and how he does it, rather than a big Tiger Fan, but watching him practise is like golfing crystal meth; addictive and hyperstimulating, although fortunately the parallels stop here, and don't include increased libido. Part of you wants nothing to do with getting up at 05:00 to watch another human being play golf, but you recognise this is something unique and should be watched. I was ready to crank up another dose of the T-Man.

The Tiger Woods I saw this time was in total contrast to the one at Turnberry. He was smiling, laughing and joking, and he wasn't playing on his own. On the 1st tee he and Ernie Els were having a good laugh, shooting the breeze for at least five minutes, like two guys recounting the drunken transgressions of the previous night. At The Open, Tiger had cut a solitary, almost sullen figure on the course, seemingly obsessed with every hump and hollow, every swale and slope. In contrast, at Hazeltine a few weeks later you could sense it was a very different Woods. He already had one hand on the trophy.

Els was out behind Tiger, along with Richard Sterne. It must have been a pleasure for the two South Africans, as Tiger carried hundreds, then thousands, around the course. Leaving the solipsism of Turnberry behind, Woods teed it up with his two playing partners, good friend and regular practice buddy, Bubba Watson, and young gun Nick Watney, who *must* be the secret lovechild of Jim Carrey.

I got down to the course just after 06:10, and asked a security guard if Tiger had gone out, even though the practice ground and course were thick with early morning mist. He answered that he hadn't seen him, as if he neither knew nor cared who Tiger Woods was, going a step further by adding, 'it isn't as if it's Obama'. I knew that much, and thanked him for his socio-political insight. At that very moment Woods appeared on the bridge from clubhouse to range, and I watched him limber up, hitting balls in between back massages from caddy Steve Williams.

I followed Tiger, Bubba and Carrey Jnr. for a few holes, and they picked up spectators like an avalanche picks up snow. Watching Tiger practise at The Open, there had been a few hundred, maybe a thousand, watching by the end of the round. At Hazeltine there were already more people than that by the 3rd hole. Early on, Hank Haney, Tiger's coach, joined the entourage. Haney and Tiger chatted, usually looking serious, sometimes smiling and laughing, pointing here and there, motioning this way and that. It was all business, in a relaxed yet focused fashion. Tiger didn't appear to be trying anything in particular, and having won two weeks in a row, his game had to be pretty solid. I got the impression Haney was just showing face, on hand if his client needed anything, a tweak or a word here or there.

By the 3rd green, the crowds were already too much for me – my fourth Major, and *only* a Tuesday morning practice round. It was reported that on Monday around 20,000 fans had watched Tiger. The great man said it was unbelievable, he'd never seen anything like it. I took it as my cue to leave, as I was keen to familiarise myself with Hazeltine. Later that day, the final hole was reputed to be surrounded nine-deep with spectators. With all those fans, and his recent stellar play, who could possibly stop Tiger?

PGA THURSDAY: BIG COURSE ON THE PRAIRIE

After I had left Tiger on Tuesday morning, with thousands of Minnesotans, who rarely get a chance to see him in action, swarming to get a clear view, I'd meandered around the course. My plan of attack for the Thursday was based on what I considered to be the best parts of the course for seeing the play.

Initially I had been concerned about how difficult viewing would be. Tiger's game had been followed so intently by a massive crowd it seemed like a job of work to get any sort of view at all, let alone a decent one. Also, the 9th and 18th greens were at the top of a hill and I could tell immediately that unless I was sitting on a bleacher, or dangling from the Goodyear blimp, getting a view of the finish at the end of the week would be nearly impossible. But I'd worry about that when I got to it.

Fortunately, my initial impressions did not last and I found lots of great viewing spots. Hazeltine is an easy course to get around, a bit like Augusta National, where the layout is not linear. And unlike both Bethpage and Turnberry, it didn't take a walk to get out into the body of the course, followed by a trek back. For example, walking roughly west from the first, you came to 9, 18, 10 and 16 within ten minutes. Walking down the 1st and continuing north, you skirted past 8, 2, 7, 11, 12, 15 and 14, all within 20 minutes. The main spectator gates were east of the range, almost adjacent to the first, so within minutes you could be on the course. Little time was wasted getting somewhere before you saw the action.

Again like Augusta, great holes coincided with great vantage points. As someone who has played most of his formative golf on links courses, the lure of a lake or large, still pond is too much for me. Both the 10th and the 16th were beautiful golf holes. The former afforded a birdie chance, where carelessness would be punished, and the latter was similar, but a sterner test. Johnny Miller once said that the 16th was the hardest par-4 he'd ever seen. I wouldn't go that far, but two things were certainly required to play it this week, especially down the stretch – balls of steel.

As one of my fellow spectators down the 10th fairway acknowledged to his buddies, parts of the PGA draw were packed with quality, a feast of golfing delicacies to whet the appetite of even the most sated fan. Looking at the starting times on paper, the choice of what to do on Thursday was a no-brainer. Tiger was starting at the 10th. On the opposite side of the clubhouse from the first tee, it's a 425-yard dogleg par-4 that dips sharply right to left around the 300-yard mark, down to Lake Hazeltine and a green that is protected back and left by the water. Standing on the dogleg affords a great view of the tee shot and the second down the hill.

As this was my last Major of the year, I was not going to miss the first shot of the championship. It was dark when I left the house, but already warm and a bit muggy, a guaranteed day for T-shirt and shorts. First up was Clemson alumnus D.J. Trahan, playing alongside Keith Dicciani (one of the twenty PGA pros in the field, comprising the top twenty finishers in the 2009 PGA Professional National Championship) and Briny Baird, a player many think is the best on tour yet to have a win. Trahan hit a towering drive, and he would assume the immediate lead with a birdie. Dicciani had other concerns on his mind. His father-in-law-to-be, Craig Thomas, was also in the field, and Keith had told him that if Thomas beat him this week, he wouldn't have to pay for the wedding.[1] Ouch.

In a nice touch, the Rodman Wanamaker Trophy – the heaviest in sport at 27lbs – was on a plinth on the tee, glinting in the morning sun as the players began the 91st PGA Championship. I watched the start with mixed emotions, looking forward to a great week of golf, but aware that it signalled the beginning of the end of my travels.

Thomas was in the third game out at the 1st, but I headed straight round to the 10th. There had been a sizeable crowd at the 1st for the 07:15 starting time, but round the corner it was busier. Naively I had expected the right side to be moderately populated, thinking that I had exclusive rights to a great viewing spot. Given the crowd that had followed Tiger's final practice session, I should have known it would be mobbed.

As I arrived, native Minnesotan Cameron Beckman was off to the worst possible start. Via a nasty stance in a fairway bunker and then the lake, he racked up a triple bogey 7, rather blunting the spike of interest the local Star Tribune newspaper had talked about in recent days. For most players, a triple at the first hole is as good as a fast taxi to the airport. And you've already mentally taken your shoes off at security and live in fear of hearing those rubber gloves being snapped on.

The games following Wreckman read like a *Who's Who* of global golf talent. Ross Fisher; Henrik Stenson and Kenny Perry; Sabbatini and

1. Both players missed the cut, but Thomas shot 151 to Dicciani's 152. Looks like Keith had an expensive week at Hazeltine National Golf Club.

Sergio; Justin Rose, Hunter Mahan and Villegas; Padraig, Rich Beem and T. Woods; Fred Couples, Lee Westwood, Alvaro Quiros, Mike Weir, Boo Weekley and Zach Johnson. Standing there was like being back at Augusta. A gentle, rising heat, lovely weather and the world's best parading for one's entertainment. I soaked it up and watched.

Despite the 10th pin being tucked left, over a protective bunker and about six steps from Lake Hazeltine, Fisher's 140-yard second shot was lasered right at the stick, coming to rest about 10 feet beyond. First iron shot of the day and he's gone right at it. This is surely one of the nicer benefits of improved golf technology: more forgiving irons allow the best players to take on challenging shots from the get go. No messing here. He then missed the putt.

Two games later Jim Furyk and Rory McIlroy were playing with Martin Kaymer. Furyk hit from the fairway bunker in to about 12 feet, and McIlroy almost holed his second, tapping in for a birdie. Furyk also birdied, an unlikely sandy escape. Rory went on to birdie 14 and 15 to take the lead at 3 under par. After Camilo Villegas also almost holed out from the fairway and tapped in for bird, it seemed like the perfect start to a perfect day's golf.

Every player was encouraged by the warm, enthusiastic Minnesotan golf fans, many having driven for hours to see the day's golf. Even PGA Professional Champion Mike Small's caddy got a massive ovation for his diligent raking of a bunker.

With the tee around 310 yards away, most players were hitting fairway woods towards me on the corner, then playing around a wedge, the slope taking about two clubs off. I was tucked under the canopy of a tree and this, combined with a gentle breeze from the lake, was cooling and comfortable.

The crowd had cheered madly at the approaches that went close, while also being appreciative of other good, but conservative, plays. Now it was time for The Man.

Tiger was out with Rich Beem, the 2002 champ at Hazeltine, and Padraig Harrington, defending champion and man he beat just days before at Firestone. The crowd began to chatter nervously as Woods appeared on the tee, his light-blue shirt and dark trousers framed by the green trees and crowd behind. Unmistakably Tiger. He was ready to pull the trigger.

Recalling the weather at the Masters, the clear blue Chaska skies and piercing light allowed for a crystal clear view of each ball leaving the club head. Harrington found the middle of the fairway. Beem found the right side. In hushed reverence, the eight-deep crowd anticipated Tiger's first blow, his last chance at a Major in 2009. The ball exploded off the club, starting low and fizzing right, turning back towards the fairway; the stinger. The crowd whooped and hollered as his ball came to rest just in the rough on the right side, a good line to the left pin position.

A swarm of photographers and other media-types funnelled down inside the ropes, the usual cast of hundreds who follow the best golfer on the planet, led a merry dance by their pied piper with the magical swoosh on his chest. Minutes later Woods would touch the hole for birdie but fail to make, and Harrington would miss a golden chance from five feet. The battle had been joined, and Woods et al creamed off three-quarters of the crowd and took them away down the 10th and along the 11th, soldiers on a golfing crusade. I was staying put. There would be plenty of time to watch Tiger on Friday, and my current spot was just too good to give up.

The few of us remaining watched Alvaro Quiros pumping a ridiculously long tee shot, either born of hitting the wrong club, or a course-management strategy best described by two words: gay and abandon. He was all the way down the hill and slightly blocked out by the boughs of a tree that was not in play for anyone else. As I listened on the radio, the commentators said he was looking at a safe play in to around 35 feet. Of course he pitched it mid-green and had it spinning left into about eight feet. The commentators' rapture with this result was the start of a week-long love affair with Quiros and his prodigious length.

Next up was Boo Weekley. He stiffed it. Well, it was a kick in, until he missed from a matter of inches. I love Boo and his approach to the game, playing golf because he can. But today his attire left something to be desired, putting him in real danger of winning my Sartorial Disaster

Award at the PGA. Wearing a camouflage top for duck-hunting that bordered on cheap and nasty leopard print, he looked like a 1980s glamour model who'd let it all go horribly wrong.

By now it was after nine o'clock and I'd been up for four hours; breakfast was required. As I walked to get some nosh, I listened on the radio as Woods' game played the 606-yard 11th hole. As they putted out, a ball ran on to the green.

'Well, a ball's just come onto the green in two shots. In the game behind are Lee Westwood, Alvaro Quiros and Fred Couples. Quiros would be suspect number one. While we called Freddie, "Boom Boom", I think we'll just call Quiros, "Kaboom." He's won every year on the European Tour for the last few years. He's mega-rich, handsome, and has 2% body fat. He hits every drive over 315 yards. I really don't like this guy. Sure, he's nice to woman and children, but there must be something wrong with him.'

Up at breakfast I bumped into Canadian golf scribe Alfie Lau, whom I'd met at Bethpage. I asked him if he'd been following Tiger.

'Were you at Torrey Pines last year for the US Open? No. Man, it was nuts, 25-deep along the first hole and the same at just about every other one. You had all the people who usually follow Tiger out there. Then you had the fans' favourite, Phil Mickelson, and all the people he trails round. And then you had Adam Scott, and all the babes were following him. I mean, it was the Perfect Storm.' I took his point.

As at the US Open, the two-tee start at the PGA sees the first half of the field play in the morning. An interval then allows them to get past the 1st and 10th holes, and then the second wave tees off.

I headed down to the shores of Lake Hazeltine to watch some action at the signature hole, the 16th, a demanding par-4 that runs alongside the lake, with an additional water hazard down the left side, the green on a corner of the lake near the 10th, water to the right and behind. In short, disaster lurks everywhere. If you stand by the fairway, the landing area seems quite generous. Standing on the tee, it looks about the size of a scarf, and there tends to be a breeze off the left or right, towards one hazard or another. The thought of playing this hole in a medal round is enough to make the average golfer weep.

Stupidly, again, I had underestimated the Minnesotan fans' keenness for golf, and found that the stand by the green was full and a healthy queue had already formed. I walked to the hill next to the middle of the fairway and found that, by moving left and right on the hill, I could see firstly the tee-shots, and then the approach shots to the green. Just as I arrived, a loud roar greeted Tiger's birdie at the 15th. He was now 2 under par and in the chasing pack.

Woods hit another stinger, his ball disappearing against the now battleship-grey skyline as if heading towards the middle of lake, only to reappear on the right side of the fairway, running towards the middle. The hillside was mobbed with fans, lining the side of the curved fairway in the shape of a massive polychromatic Dreamtime boomerang. They cheered and clapped as the Great One approached. Harrington and Woods chatted as they strolled up the hole and crossed the Payne Stewart Bridge, a commemorative plaque acknowledging the life and death of the three-time Major winner who'd taken out the 1991 US Open at Hazeltine. It would soon be a decade since he passed away on that fateful flight from Orlando to Dallas. Five others also died that day, 25 October 1999, 16 weeks after Payne had won his second US Open at Pinehurst No. 2.

I once had the privilege of watching Payne Stewart in action during a friendly game, while he was the reigning US Open champion, fresh from his Hazeltine victory. On a blustery and chilly day he played Prestwick as around a hundred people followed, word having leaked out. He chatted, joked and played consummate golf, rarely missing a fairway or a green. Infuriatingly he made it all look very, very easy. Had he not met a premature death, he would surely have won more majors.

Framed by lake, Harrington knocked it close and made birdie. Beem holed a decent length putt for bird, but Woods appeared to hit a slightly chunky approach, which came up short of the pin and spun back. Par. Already, however, on the longest course in Major history, a number of players had gone sub-par. I wasn't massively surprised, as I'd seen a ridiculous number of shots hit down the throat of some tight pins. Attack seemed to be the order of the day.

As I took some notes of the setting and the players passing, a fellow spectator asked me if I kept a record of all the games, what the players hit etc. I doubted that anyone could be that sad, although I was aware that America is full of baseball fanatics who love to score games themselves and build a collection of stats. Michael Lewis' excellent book, *Moneyball*, charts how the Oakland Athletics baseball team turned these ardent fans' knowledge into a winning formula for Major League Baseball. If only that was possible in golf.

I told him that I didn't, but rather I was writing a book on the four Majors.

'You gotta lotta snow?' he said.

What did snow have anything to do with golf in mid-August?

'Excuse me?'

'You gotta lotta snow?'

Ah, I've got to let you know. No problems. I gave him my card and shot off towards the clubhouse in my skidoo.

At midday I was due to rendezvous with Ken and Chuck, the two Minnesotans I had met waiting for the gates to open on Masters Sunday. At noon two familiar faces appeared, along with some of their buddies, and we retired to a nearby refreshment stall for a cleansing ale. The guys had arrived around 10:00 and spent most of their time milling around, taking in some practice, some putting and some tee shots at number one. Unsurprisingly, on a hot afternoon, the beer went down very well at $5.50 a pop. The food and beverage experiences at the US Open and PGA are similar, with some small variations on prices and selection, although it is evident that while the USGA is in bed with Coca-Cola, the PGA favours Pepsi's brands. One big difference, since this was not New York, there wasn't much call for the Kosher option.

One beer was the order of the day, although I'm sure that another nine would barely have slaked my thirst. As we all remarked, one thing the PGA didn't have at Hazeltine – which could be found at both The

Open and the US Open – was a large screen on which to watch the action. I could easily have stood that afternoon drinking JumboBeers in front of a JumboTron. And given that the big screens are a popular feature at the Ryder Cup, it seemed strange the PGA of America hadn't installed at least one here.

The guys from St Paul went on their way, but not before Chuck revealed that he was actually an award-winning writer. He hadn't mentioned this when we spoke at The Masters. He'd won a competition sponsored by US Steel – when he was eight.

I turned my attention to the putting green as the big guns in the second half of the draw prepared for their rounds. Immediately it was clear who'd won the Sartorial Disaster Award. Standing next to Ian Poulter was the likable Shingo Katayama. Although sporting his usual cowboy hat and light slacks, he was wearing a luminescent orange top. He looked like a traffic cone, and could no doubt be seen from the outer reaches of Space. I strongly suspected his shirt was interfering with images transmitted from the Hubble Telescope. I felt slightly sick, and half expected both him and Poulter to vapourise, their fashions cancelling each other out.

I hung around the first tee watching the likes of Anthony Kim, Ryo Ishikawa, Geoff Ogilvy and Vijay Singh tee off, all of whom were followed at 13:35 by the winners of the year's Majors thus far. It was nice to see Cabrera, Glover and Zinc playing together, all on the first tee alongside the PGA trophy.

'Go get the second one, Cink,' a fan shouts as he makes his way to the tee. There's a lot of support for all three, but especially the two Americans. Some of this dissipates when Cink doubles the first. He would soon add two more sixes; plus 5 through five holes. Pretty dire for The Open champ.

Trapped in the space between the 2nd green, 3rd tee and the 3rd fairway, I am forced to stay back and watch Phil Mickelson play out the 2nd hole alongside Paul Azinger and David Toms. Phil has knocked it in close but misses the putt, followed by loud groans from the gallery. As he walks between green and tee, Phil hands a young girl one of his golf balls, and she's delighted. Aged around nine, she and her sister now have a ball each, the other from a similar gesture courtesy of Sergio Garcia earlier. Neither player will come close to winning the tournament, but they win the hearts and minds of the fans.

As I'm catching up with the Major winners, it's about three deep at the 3rd green and I cannot see what's going on. But Glover misses his birdie putt; I know that much from the reaction of the gallery. Play then backs up a while and the Major guys have a bit of a wait on the 4th tee.

I can't be bothered to share their wait, so I stroll down to the adjacent 7th, a 572-yard par-5 with a long, narrow green flanked by bunkers, a slope on one side and water on the other.

As usual Bubba Watson appears to have made a mockery of the long hole. Playing three games in front of Cink et al, with what looks like a 6-iron, he hits a towering shot into 8 feet; then misses the putt. At this point it has started to cloud over and it's looking like rain. Not ideal, as I have no form of rainwear with me, and getting wet quickly isn't going to be any fun. I go down to the 7th green and it's ringed with fans standing on the hill to the right, more left of the pond, and others in a bleacher behind the green.

Trying to take some form of shelter by the stand, I watch a few games come through, featuring such luminaries as Els, Stricker, Singh, the three Major winners and Mickelson. The rain never gets serious but it's sufficiently annoying that I decide to pop into the Wanamaker Club for a look around. Stepping inside brings back some nasty memories, as it's clearly run by the same company that put together the Trophy Club at the US Open. Bar the change of logo and menus, it's exactly the same facility. Fortunately, unlike the Thursday at Bethpage, it isn't oversubscribed with wet, miserable bodies with nowhere to sit. In contrast, while it's busy, there are plenty of seats and it has a relaxed air. Maybe I did the USGA a disservice, as there's lots of room, but perhaps if it began tipping it down it would soon be jammed with the sodden masses.

It was now heading for late afternoon and the day's leader board had substantially taken shape, not least with Woods and Harrington at the top. They must be getting sick of the sight of each other. I decided to grab a bite to eat and kill some time, as I'd arranged an appointment with someone later that afternoon, in an effort to gain further insight into the way the championship worked. I cheekily spent an hour or more watching the golf on TV in the Wanamaker. However, annoyingly, I was badly let down by a boneheaded PA, someone who clearly didn't want to contact her boss – despite the appointment – and who seemed fixated on the idea that I was from the Golf Channel, ignoring my protestations to the contrary. A nice lady I'm sure, but feeble-minded: I hope she reads this.[1] I was pretty pissed off, as I had not thought it worth venturing out on to the course because I'd have had to come straight back 45 minutes later, and I'd gone to the trouble of turning up 15 minutes early.

Tighter than a camel's arse in a sandstorm after my ludicrous but difficult conversation, I decided to head up to the bleacher at the 18th and watch play close for the evening. It had clearly been a long day for everyone. The guys on the radio were describing Els as Stricker played, and vice versa; they were dressed similarly. Of course only people at the right hole and paying attention would have noticed this error: one of the perks of radio broadcasting. It was a bit of light relief, and my desire to head down to the Mall of America with a panoply of automatic weaponry soon passed.

It was a lovely evening with warm clear sunshine, at the end of what had been a superb day's golf. One player nobody was getting confused about – Tiger. He'd done the job and put himself in pole position. Three rounds to go.

PGA FRIDAY: GLORY'S EXTRA SHOT?

Following a press conference on Thursday by the International Olympic Committee (IOC), one newspaper story on Friday was that golf was

1. At the time of writing I am not, never have been, and most likely never will be, with the Golf Channel. Unfortunately. Looking at my notes from the encounter, I see typing them word for word would be defamatory and unjustifiable, so I have paraphrased them.

being shortlisted, with rugby sevens, for inclusion in the 2016 Summer Olympics. Tiger's response: 'I'd love to play for the rugby team.'

One newspaper described the Olympics as golf's fifth major. I do understand the reasons why the powers that be want to have golf included in this global sports-fest, but I don't agree. It should be enough of a warning sign that rugby sevens is a bastardised, popular form of an existing sport, and that on the same day that it was shortlisted with golf for 2016, women's boxing was approved for London 2012. Golf seems an odd bedfellow for these two derivatives of major sports. And have some of the administrators within golf and the IOC really considered whether golf is appropriate for inclusion, especially in light of certain golf clubs and organisations being men only? I think golf may have made a rod for its own back.

Okay, golf was previously included in the 1904 Olympics, but that harks back to pre-Masters and pre-PGA days, when amateurs in golf were still steeped in Corinthian spirit, and The Amateur and US Amateur were considered Majors. The rationale for inclusion in 2016 is to widen the global appeal of golf. Does anyone really think that worldwide televising of Olympic golf will spirit thousands of sets of golf clubs and hundreds of golf course projects into sub-Saharan Africa, South America or spread golf like a wildfire across South-east Asia? As one who has attended all of the majors in a single year, and other events over the years, I can testify that 99% of the ethnic-minority faces one sees are either in catering or security, not on the course watching or playing. If we can't promote golf to all levels of society within an essentially stable and wealthy western world, what chance of doing it elsewhere?

At the Olympics in Beijing in 2008, 87 countries won medals. Two-hundred-and-four different national committees sent teams. Under the terms of the IGF proposal, golf's idea of inclusion is 30 countries, most of whom will be drawn from the usual suspects.

Tiger was quoted in a press conference earlier in the week as saying, 'I think it would be great for golf... especially some of the other smaller countries... a great way for them to compete and play and get the exposure some of these countries aren't getting.' Nobody drew Tiger on what countries specifically he had in mind, and nobody mentioned the specific criteria of the IGF proposal to him. I'm all for promoting golf around the world, and widening the appeal of many of the values that the game holds dear, but golf belongs in the OIympics like I belong at Tiger Woods' dinner table.

Any angst I felt over the Olympic conundrum soon subsided on another balmy early morning hike to the golf course, via Chaska High School and over Highway 212. Staring down at the modest concrete road underfoot, it was hard for me to believe it ran for over another nine hundred miles to Yellowstone National Park. The searing heat, although it was just before eight o'clock, explained why the road was made of concrete, allowing give in the heat of summer and the intense cold of the Minnesotan winter; exploding, melting or frozen tarmac roads are no fun. The road's continued extension is also testament to the growth of the Twin Cities area.

Minneapolis and St Paul first entered my consciousness when, years back, the quality of life there was deemed the best in the USA. Highways and schools spring up regularly to service the requirements of a burgeoning region, but still doors remain unlocked. Neighbours take shortcuts through each other's yards, and eye contact and a welcoming hello are the norm. People here are just plain friendly, and expect the same back. Chaska was assessed by CNN to be the eighth best place to live in the US. On my way home from the golf on Thursday evening, a couple walking their dog asked me if I'd had a good day, and we stood and spoke for 15 minutes. Try doing that in Edinburgh. Although at home we live much more closely together and in a city regarded as friendly, speaking to a neighbour twice in the same calendar year usually results in harassment charges and three weeks of Chinese water torture by the local secret police.

As I approached the course, flanked by banners right and left showing former winners, a number of gentlemen stood with loudhailers, providing instructions. The first guy suggested that if we had weapons, we should get straight back on the bus (Chaska High School was the free, public bus drop-off location) ride it back to our car, and leave the weapon there. This was one instruction not required at Turnberry.

Further up the pathway, the next gentleman had a more theatrical manner.

'On the course you will not have your cell phones or your camera phones. It will be as if you are living in the 1980s. However, do not fret, you will be able to check them in and re-acquire them at the end of the day.'

At the security gates, one volunteer who was helping to hand out Junior Tickets – children under 15 got in free with a ticket-holding adult – apologised for the weather. There was not a cloud in the piercing blue sky and it was already about 80 degrees. Another dream day on the prairies of Minnesota; a day Tiger could really stamp his authority on the championship.

I headed up to the Practice Range to see what was happening. I'd follow Tiger, but he wasn't out until 13:45, so I had to fill my morning and early afternoon. Not normally a massive issue, but a combination of walking around for six days, plus the heat, had left my feet in a real mess. Every time I stopped and started, it took a while for the pain to disappear behind the nascent sores and blisters. Eventually my blisters had blisters. Today's viewing had to be based on the following: morning, limited walking; afternoon, Tiger stalking.

As well as numerous players smashing shells down the range, another Major first was lurking at the rear. At the three US Majors both county and state police were in clear evidence. At Bethpage, plainclothes officers – plain blue shirt, chinos, sidearm, and an ID badge that read 'POLICE' – were also, paradoxically, somewhat obvious. However, the PGA was the first place where Federal Agents had been in clear view. ATF (Alcohol, Tobacco and Firearms) operatives were standing to the rear of the range, ATF and K-9 emblems on their shirts explaining why they had a black Labrador with them.

I can only presume that the three gentlemen and their dog were golf fans, as the untrained eye could detect no gun-running, plastic explosives, or Marlboro Men hitting balls. I did see Vince Cellini of the Golf

Channel dragging an AK-47 across the putting green on Monday, but I presumed it was licensed.

By the time I had watched some range action, grabbed some breakfast and got on to the course, the third from last morning group was heading out. The sparkling blue eyes of Ben's mate, Thomas Levet, were glinting in the morning sun, and alongside him were PGA pro Steve Schneiter and Y.E. Yang. Out on the back nine Vijay Singh was going nicely, so I decided to see what he was up to.

Vijay had shot 69 and immediately went to minus-4 with a birdie at the 10th on Friday, putting him one shot back of Tiger. He bogeyed the testing 12th, and as I arrived at the 15th he was just missing a birdie chance to get back to 4-under. Walking to the 16th I spotted the man I knew to be Vijay's fitness coach. It's not unfair to say that he was built like an old bank safe. He'd pumped some iron.

Not quite sure what to expect, I engaged Gabe (Gabriel Lopez) in conversation to get some insight into his role on the course. No offence to Vijay, but I couldn't imagine it'd be much fun following the same guy at all his golf tournaments (although I could see how it'd beat the hell out of sitting at a desk in front of a PC).

Belying his Incredible Hulk build, Gabe was incredibly helpful and forthcoming. He told me that, with a tee-off time that morning just after 08:00, Vijay had been up early and into the gym. At 04:30. He'd spent an hour in the gym doing weights and various other exercises. An hour was the minimum standard session, and sometimes it would run for longer.

As well as training programmes, Gabe works on an integrated approach with Vijay. They look at overall diet, as well as how best to stay hydrated and what to eat on the golf course. Factors like weather and terrain are considered. Gabe follows Vijay for each round, including practice, providing moral support and keeping an eye on particular moves or swings that Vijay makes, including elements they have discussed or worked on.

After the round, Singh and Lopez will debrief each other on how it felt from their different perspectives. Gabe will input what he noticed and sensed, including keeping an eye on hip turn, balance and weight transfer, and Vijay will do something similar. Where Formula One cars use computer diagnostics to detect faults, issues, and areas for optimisation, Vijay Singh has Lopez at his side, watching his every move.

Thanking Gabe for his time, I headed for the short 17th hole, a 182-yard par-3 across a small valley, with the left side of the green falling away to a water hazard, the right side flanked by two bunkers. In some ways this hole is similar to the 16th at Augusta, as from front-right to mid-back-left a ridge runs through the green, forcing the players either to shoot for the target or accept a difficult putt that is unlikely to yield a birdie. The water is not generally in play, especially as the bank down to it is thick, with rough of the sort that is penalty enough.

I stood on the hill, halfway up the left side of the hole, under a tree, enjoying a cool breeze and shade. I watch as Singh makes par, and then another player who is going along nicely at minus-3, Ian Poulter, takes the tee. By now there's a good wind blowing across this hole, it's more than a zephyr and wouldn't feel out of place on a Scottish or Irish links. Poulter backs off his shot a couple of times, debating with himself the task at hand. When he does play, his ball lands on the slope down left of the green and rolls down the hill, almost beyond the hazard line and into the water. Poults plays an exquisite lob from this precarious position to a matter of feet, but sadly he misses the putt.

It's just beyond mid-morning, it's only Friday, and already roars are ringing out around the course. This was not something I was aware of at either Bethpage or Turnberry, although these sporadic explosions of joy are a feature of the Augusta National script. The Midwestern fans are flocking to the prairie land of Minnesota, and support focuses on one key ingredient of this week's PGA – good golf.

It had been recognised by the PGA that a key reason for returning to Minnesota was the crowds and their enthusiasm. In a state gripped by extreme cold in the winter, the golf season tends to be well defined. Usually it runs from around April to October. In 2007 it was estimated that just under 750,000 Minnesotan golfers played just over eight million rounds. They love their golf.

After Poulter it was 2009's big wallets, Cabrera, Glover and Cink. I love to watch Cabrera because it's hard to imagine he gives a shit. Two guys in matching yellow shirts clearly feel the same way.

'Look at Cabrera. You know who he reminds me of? That guy, way back, really relaxed. Similar languid swing.'

'Julius Boros?'

'Yeah, that's him. Now there's a guy who really didn't care.'

Boros, the oldest winner of a Major, had been much in the golfing news this year when his record could have been surpassed by both Kenny Perry and Tom Watson. By way of some advice, Boros once said, 'By the time you get to your ball, if you don't know what to do with it, try another sport.'

I stay left of the 17th until Mickelson comes through and again the hill is full, Phil's fans following him religiously. I overhear a guy talking about Rory McIlroy, 'just turned twenty, out of Scotland', he says. This brings a smile to my face and, not that I'm at all bothered, makes up for the 30 or so times I've been asked if I am Irish during my trips to the States. Go Rory!

Mickelson seems out of sorts and who can blame him, he has other, bigger issues to focus upon. By now I've spent a lot of time around the corner of the course that contains 10, 16 and 17, and it's time to move on, especially with a view to this afternoon's games. I head down to the 8th green which lies at the junction of the 1st green, 2nd tee and 9th tee. It's a busy spot, as it's the second hole you come to after the entrance, and it's also close to the popular 7th green, the par-5 flanked by water.

At face value the 8th is a flat hole, with a slightly elevated tee, but the green is flanked by a series of small mounds, providing good views of the tee and the green. This, and the 17th I'd just come from, are the only two holes at Hazeltine that remain unchanged since 1987.

As I arrive, the game on the tee is Levet, Yang and Schneiter. Steve Schneiter is going high, and on his way home after this round. Not to pick on him in particular, but at 14 over par through 25 holes, this kind of performance is just fuel to the arguments that PGA professionals have no place in a Major championship, or even a high-class tournament. I don't agree. They've earned their places, and comprise just 20 players out of the starting 156. If Trevor Immelman and Paul Casey hadn't pulled out due to injury, 99 of the top 100 players in the world would have competed at Hazeltine. Before the PGA kicked off, Tiger described it as 'the deepest field' and added, 'you know if you win this championship, you've beaten the best field in all of golf.' In 2009, the pretender to the accolade of the fifth Major, The Players, had only 76 of the top 100 in its field. The numbers don't lie.

Two games later, Scott McCarron almost holes-in-one, and settles for a handy birdie two. As he leaves the green and the next game takes the tee, this corner is swarming with people and big cheers come from the first green. Phil Mickelson is now on the front nine and once again I'm engulfed by his fans.

As if I need reminding that Tiger will be teeing off soon, a few miles away, across the lake, I spot the Goodyear blimp heading our way in anticipation of the afternoon starting times. Just as I leave the 8th, Ishikawa almost holes his tee-shot and makes birdie. One of his playing partners, Adam Scott, is having another daymare, perhaps thinking too much of his girlfriend, tennis player Ana Ivanovic, and not enough about golf. He stumbles to a watery triple-bogey 6.

After grabbing some food, I head to the first tee, and again the hillside between the tee and practice putting green is solid with fans, bedecked in every colour imaginable, anxiously awaiting the best golfer in the world.

'Beemer!' shouts a fan as Rich Beem appears. Beemer is a real favourite, and for good reason. After winning the event here in 2002, he went on to build a relationship with the club, got honorary membership and fosters a series of matches and beers between Hazeltine and his buddies in El Paso. How many Major winners would do that?

'Yes, Steve! Go, Stevie!' Even Tiger's caddy is the subject of cheering and encouragement. Stevie doesn't foster a relationship with anyone.

They tee off, and although it's Friday afternoon, and there's load of golf to be played, an amazing sea of humanity cascades down the hillside at the 1st. Thousands of Woods acolytes stream towards the green. I get stopped in my tracks by marshals controlling the walkway from the putting green to the first tee. They tell us they are not opening the ropes and they decide to have a huddle and an impromptu meeting. Don't mind us, we just paid for our tickets. It's pretty annoying, especially when, by the time I've made it around the green and down the hill between the 1st and the 9th, Tiger has already played. And by the time I get past the bottleneck at 1, 8 and 9, I've seen one shot. I cross around 9 and over to the right of the 2nd hole.

Tiger bogeys the first hole – most unlike him – but he hits a decent tee shot at the 2nd and won't have any problems finding the green in two. Meanwhile Harrington hits a massive drive over the corner of the dogleg, stopping 375 yards from the tee, leaving a basic pitch up to the raised green on the 431-yard par-4. I watch from afar as the threesome makes collective pars.

As I wait by the side of the 3rd for the players to come back, I watch Alvaro Quiros tee off at the 2nd. I fancy on the angle he may drive the green, but he takes an iron and finds a nasty spot in the rough just shy of the bunker to the left of the fairway. Even though I am on the other side of the fairway I cannot see his ball at all, so I know it must, at the very least, be sitting down. He hits a fantastic shot out of the rough, high and flush, right for the pin, flying as if he's clipped it from the world's best lie. His ball comes to rest a matter of feet away, and the crowd go crazy.

'Did you see the speed of his downswing? Wow. Short backswing. VERY fast,' remarks the guy next to me to his buddies. He's not wrong. Quiros is exciting to watch, and perhaps a bit of a show pony, but it takes a lot of talent to hit it that well, that straight, out of that rough. It's just as well I watched that particular shot, because it remains the best I see for quite a while. Woods toddles along, playing cautiously optimistic golf which bears fruit as he picks some ripe ones off the birdie tree at 6 and 7. 'He's catching fire now', remarks a fellow spectator. I wouldn't go that far, but perhaps he's beginning to smoulder.

The rest of the afternoon is fairly anodyne, and eventually Tiger does what he does best, getting into the zone and reeling off birdies at 14, 15 and 16. Two things stick out from the rest of the round for me. Leaving the bedlam of the Woods game at 8, I make to cut my way around to the

10th. As I do so I have to wait at the 18th as Chad Campbell, Matthew Goggin and Peter Hanson tee off. While right behind me it's controlled pandemonium (if there is such a thing), and literally thousands of people are following Tiger's game, as I stand at the crossing I am the only person between my spot and the 18th tee 50 yards away. There's almost nobody watching these guys play. I'm only 80 yards from the marquee group, but I might as well be at the other side of the observable universe – I don't know how far that is, but I do know there isn't a yardage chart available.[1]

The other standout from that afternoon was a shot no one in the known universe knew was possible. Playing the 15th, Harrington had hit a drive of around 340 yards into one of the fairway bunkers down the left. This left him 301 yards to go. With his ball on the upslope at the front of the bunker, Paddy struck a monumental wood that climbed into the stratosphere, disappeared, and burst back into existence around 12 feet from the hole. Phenomenal. He didn't convert for eagle but the birdie was a nap. The guys on Sirius FM, the on-course radio, almost wet themselves at the result.

It was reported the next day that Tiger told Paddy he'd have paid to see that shot. 'You got 50 bucks?' came the Irishman's reply. Ominously, Tiger finished the second round with a 4-shot lead after a 2 under par 70. He was streets ahead of everybody else at getting round Hazeltine. It all looked very cosy.

PGA SATURDAY: SLIM'S OUTTA TOWN

In 1989, when England's Frank Bruno travelled to Las Vegas to take on Mike Tyson, Don King, boxing promoter and hair-care legend, was asked about the fight.

'What are the chances of a Frank Bruno win over Mike Tyson?'

'Slim and none. And Slim's outta town.'

1. For the record it's 4.81096425 × 1026 yards to the edge of the observable universe. That is a driver, a 3-wood, and a 9-iron for Quiros (assuming a neutral solar wind and a USGA / R&A conformant ball).

That was pretty much how I felt about Saturday and Sunday at Hazeltine. I awoke on the first day of the weekend in a bit of a funk. I just couldn't see how Tiger could lose. He'd won his last two events. He had won a total of five of the twelve events he'd played this year: a year he'd started as a cripple.

When he'd held a 36-hole lead in Majors his record was eight wins from eight. Tiger may have won his 2008 US Open on one leg, but on the weekend at Hazeltine, he was in danger of beating the entire field like a rented mule. It wasn't that I didn't want Tiger to win, I just wanted to see a good clean fight that would perhaps go to a points' decision. I didn't want a third round TKO.

Irish bookmaker, Paddy Power, had already paid out on Tiger. A canny spot of PR, as it even got a mention on the radio at the PGA. So some people didn't even care now if Tiger won, they'd banked their cash and could hope for any old outcome. Not a bad position to be in. It cost Paddy a total of £1.25 million for the early windfall, but no doubt they gained that and more in publicity and further bets. They had a reputation for doing this sort of thing, although not always to their benefit. A few years ago they paid out on Manchester United winning The Premiership, weeks before the season was over. They also paid out the night before Ireland voted on the European Community's Lisbon Treaty. Ireland voted 'no'; Power paid out on 'yes'. But this was Tiger, there was no way he was going to lose. After all, it had never happened before.

One thing I haven't yet revealed, dear reader, is that for the PGA I was accredited with a media pass and certain levels of access that were a real bonus, although none of this was inside the ropes. As with everything there is a hierarchy, and not everyone has those special armbands to get them on to the course proper. So the integrity of my spectating year was maintained, albeit with some access to the inside track.

I was fully aware that I might never get the chance to do it again, so it was nice to soak up the privilege of coming and going and seeing some of the familiar names and faces of the golf media, especially Frank

Nobilo and Kelly Tilghman of the Golf Channel. I always liked Frank as a player, a classic swing and an easy temperament. And Kelly is tasty.

The Media Centre is essentially split into five areas. The separate catering area (three free meals a day, a bachelor Scotsman's dream), and, under another roof, the PGA media office area; photographers' room; interview room; and a bigger press area that houses online, radio and TV press, with a massive scoreboard at the front flanked by two large TV screens.

As you enter the centre, all along the left side of the wall are the myriad press releases, factoid sheets, documents and manuals that are freely available. Any information you want, from the sublime to the ridiculous, is available, and if it isn't out there, just ask. Essentially this is how the media are able, at the drop of a hat, to come up with who-did-what-when-and-where.

Throughout the year I'd been lucky enough to get into all the media areas at some stage, and they all follow a similar pattern. My introduction to the photographers' area at Bethpage took both me and Ben aback – one guy was fast asleep, flat on his back in the middle of the floor, and another was similarly indisposed under a curtain. I couldn't tell you if it was drink, fatigue or an opportunistic power-nap. Not even a quick kick in the ribs could wake them.

Members of the media come and go all day, with security at the entrance starting around 05:30, catering for those who want to catch Tiger or have deadlines to meet in other time zones. Everyone has their own agenda to follow based on who's playing when and with whom, and what country they are from. It comes as no surprise that many, covering all types of media, follow Tiger, and that a lot of Japanese photographers go wherever their players are.

Regarding the various informational handouts that are available, they are a golfing anorak's wet dream. In one fell swoop a couple of things I picked up wiped out many books I'd bought and made redundant hours of web searching. I hadn't known in advance that I'd get credentials, so I just saw it all as a bonus. To give you an idea of what's available, here's a list off the top of my head.

Daily handouts, a mixture of planned and reactive, depending on what's happened during the championship – pin placements; hole yardages, usually exact par-3 measurements and any other changes; transcriptions of players' official interviews;[1] statements on any particular issues, for example player withdrawals; weather forecasts for the coming day and longer-range assessments for the rest of the week; formal press releases on certain points of interest, such as the Olympics; green-keeping and course superintendent information; player career facts and figures relative to what's happening in the event (these are ready in advance across a number of contenders, so it's all at the fingertips when any given player triumphs); guides for the media on how best to get round the course, including access and best vantage points; an entire list of stats of the previous day's play. And the list goes on.

Which doesn't even include some of the more formal handouts that one could pick up – the PGA of America media guide, including facts and figures on all their tournaments; PGA Championship player and history guide; spectator guide; PGA Championship journal; PGA Tour guide; Nationwide Tour guide; Hazeltine National G.C. guide; CBS broadcast guide; and numerous other local, national and international golf guides and magazines.

Basically, if there's information relevant to the championship or event, the chances are you'll have it at your fingertips. None of this writes the hundreds of articles produced, or drives the hundreds of hours of media footage churned out, but it allows the creators of all those things to spend their time and energy being creative, knowing whatever they need can be provided, rather than them having to chase the data themselves.

For many in the media, even for those who love golf, it's just another week. Another golf course, all part of the job, although the Majors do allow a chance to catch up with people they don't see every week. I wasn't accredited as a writer, as only those involved in reporting are given credentials. Instead I was lucky enough to be there as Alex Jackson's runner for the week, helping with photographic equipment, collecting

1. Worth noting that these are usually available, not just for the Majors, on the web at *www.asapsports.com*.

flashcards and downloading their contents. General gopher and dogs-body, and Alex was always good enough to make sure it didn't get in the way of my own project.

I did take the chance to attend a couple of official interviews, and earlier in the week it was a treat for a lifelong golf fan to be in the room listening to and photographing Tiger and Paddy Harrington.

The weather at the weekend saw a change, with the skies duller and the wind gustier. As the heat had continued to build across Minnesota, a storm was expected before the event's end on Sunday night. The forecast was gloomy for everyone but Tiger.

As things were a bit slow I decided to take a trip to the golf shop to have a look around. When I first saw the PGA Championship shop at Oakland Hills, I was staggered by its magnitude. A massive marquee that sold everything a golfer would want and more, all of it adorned with that year's event logo.

While The Masters and The Open stick with the same logo for every event – one iconic, the other much less so – I like the way both the US Open and PGA have different logos each year. This year's logo featured what is locally known as the image of 'the walking man', a silhouet-ted character, golf bag slung over his shoulder, walking the course. The image is based on a photograph taken of Les Bolstad, out playing one evening in the setting sun.

Bolstad is something of a legend in Minnesota, and the University of Minnesota's golf course is named after him, as is the college circuit's Big Ten Player of the Year Award. Bolstad won the fifth edition of the US Amateur Public Links Championship in 1926, played all four rounds of the 1930 US Open, the third leg of Bobby Jones' Grand Slam, and as the coach at the University of Minnesota oversaw the progress of lady golf-ing legends Patty Berg and Mickey Wright, as well as Tom Lehman. Even as an 80-year-old he regularly shot his age. Born in 1908, Bolstad passed away in 1998. A lot of history and a nice story behind a simple logo.

As well as the story behind the logo, Hazeltine itself has a place in US Major merchandising history, changing the face of how championship gifts were offered to the fans. In 1991 Hazeltine Club Professional Mike Schultz suggested that offering gifts in a department-store format would enhance both sales and the fans' shopping experience. He was right on the money, and that US Open had double the sales of Medinah the previous year. Since then, both the US Open and PGA have provided a custom-designed shop for each championship, and reaped the benefits.

Walking around the shop I'm again impressed by its scale, although now that I have been to a US Open, I would say that the USGA shop just edges it for the best retail experience of the Major year. Both shops are very similar, but to a hat fan, the sheer number on offer at Bethpage was astounding. Just browsing is a pleasurable experience, AC/DC playing from the speakers. As if the Aussie rockers aren't incongruous enough at a major championship, next up it's Madness with 'Our House'. Madness, indeed. Still, it beats the hell out of ads focusing on the elimination of bladder weakness.

As at the US Open there is a range of different manufacturers' merchandise on sale and I plump for a nice top that I'm not sure I'll wear too much in Scotland – the fabric features wicking technology to channel moisture away from the skin and keep one cool in hot weather: not usually a problem in Scotland, it has to be said. But at only $57 it's a bargain to take home in time for our next heat-wave in the year 2056.

After leaving the shop and checking my purchases for later collection, I head up to the first tee to have a chat with Alex Jackson, and to catch some of the early games in the second half of the draw. Rounding the back of the tee I spy Ritchie Blair and wish him the best for the weekend. Things don't go too well, as Richard Sterne, after getting to minus-1 for the championship, injures his wrist around the turn and reels off three sixes in a row – very good in cricket, very bad in Major golf. Sterne has to withdraw because of his injury.

Playing with Sterne is my favourite bomber, Dustin Johnson. Ritchie later tells me that he thinks he's the real deal. He hits it far, but he hits it straight, and great things would not be unexpected from the young man (I sound like my dad now). Certainly Johnson kills it down the first, the report of club head on ball more like a controlled explosion.

The next game up is Graeme McDowell and Hiroyuki Fujita. Watching Graeme is his dad, Kenny, whom I first met at Bethpage. Although I feel I am doing something special as a spectator, going to all the Majors in one year, for many on the golfing bandwagon it's just business as usual. Kenny tells me this is his second grand slam. I've lost count of the number of wives I've seen out on the course, some blending in to the background, others a bit more obvious. Bubba Watson's tall wife, Angie, is the easiest spot, her blonde hair atop wide shoulders befitting a former basketball player.

I get out on the course and take a look at local favourite and unofficial PGA ambassador this year, Minnesotan Tom Lehman. I've always liked Lehman's attitude to golf, a studied approach towards making things look relaxed and easy, much of which no doubt has to do with his friendly manner and slightly agricultural gait. I can never see Lehman without thinking of the Masters in 1994, when he ultimately was runner-up, two shots behind José-Maria Olazábal. Leaving the 10th tee, in the heat of battle, Tom looked into the TV camera, made that strange neck-movement he always has going on, and said, 'Phew, this is golf.' Simple.

What is it with that neck thing Lehman does?

Lehman is playing the 8th as I get to the hole, and he's being amply cheered on. He's not exactly firing on all cylinders and is sitting at plus-4 for the championship, although he was coming off a birdie at number 7. He's playing with Thongchai Jaidee.

'Who's that Tom's playing with?'

'Jaidee.'

'Who?'

'Jaidee.'

'JD. Jack Daniels, he's playing with Jack Daniels?'

Jack Daniels hits a lovely putt from 30 feet and almost pops it in. Meanwhile Lehman is surveying the result of a lovely tee shot into 8 feet left of the stick. He holes for a birdie 2, and the crowd go wild, cheering their local hero and talisman.

'Light 'em up, Tom,' cries one enthusiastic member of the throng.

We follow Tom up onto the 9th tee and I notice that he has an interesting mixture of powerful sponsors: Allianz (one of the world's biggest insurance groups), Taylor Made, Fairmont Hotels and God (his bag features the Christian fish rebus so favoured on rear bumpers). And I thought Tiger had some pretty big swingers in his corner.

Tom hits a cracking 3-wood drive up the 9th, and then flushes a short iron into 12 feet below the hole. I'm guessing I could be his talisman if he rolls this in and gets on a run. God's obviously looking the other way, as minutes later it's groans all round as he leaves his putt a full foot short.

I follow Tom for a few holes, but I'm mainly killing time. As I walk down the right of 11, I spot Henrik Stenson and Robert Allenby on 3, two of the best ball-strikers in the world. I stop to watch. Allenby flushes his driver down the 633-yard par-5, while Stenson takes a more unconventional approach. Knocking up a bit of turf, he places his ball on the slight knob, obviously looking for a lower trajectory and a bit of added impetus through the slight breeze. He's hitting driver and rips through the ball as if it's sitting up on a perfect tee. The ball hurtles through the air, straight down the middle. Impressive and ballsy at the same time. Sometimes these guys can really be depressingly efficient.

I decide to peel off, walk down the 4th and then cut up the 9th. On the 9th tee another impressive tee ball expert is readying himself for another bomb. Alvaro Quiros detonates a drive up the 432-yard hole, coming to rest about sixty paces from the front of the green.

'His clubhead speed is ridiculous,' says the guy next to me. And he's not joking. Quiros does possess a swing such that, if you blink at the top, you will not see his downswing, yet his poise and posture remain. He doesn't actually seem to hit it that hard, he just seems to coil his upper body and then uncoil through the ball: very, very quickly.

I get up to the 1st tee and it's not long until Tiger will fire away. Yang tees off in the company of Kaymer, both still in the hunt and with the possibility of turning their weeks into something good. Both have been in good form, especially Yang, who's had a pretty good run over the last two weeks, shooting 65, 69, 71, 67, 72, 72, 69 and 66 in his last eight rounds. He's 17-under for his last two tournaments. Only Tiger is better in the last fortnight.

Following this game are the Dane, Soren Kjeldsen, and Ernie Els. Ever since I heard Kjeldsen's name mispronounced *Kenjerson* at Augusta, the mispronunciations have been getting more varied. He's been called so many different names that he alone could make up half a Ryder Cup team. This week's radio announcers, who I think are great fun and usually amusing, have been having a hard time. At any given point Soren is *Kyeld-sen*, *Jeld-sen*, *Sheld-sen* or *Keld-sten*. After consulting Thomas Plenborg, a Professor at Copenhagen Business School, via text, I can confirm the correct pronunciation is close to *Kyeld-sin*, meaning son of Kjeld. The name Kjeld is a derivative of the Swedish for cauldron.

I watch the Dane and the Afrikaaner tee off, followed by Poulter and Westwood, Fisher and Harrington. The cream is rising to the top in the year's final Major. However Tiger's nearest challenger is four shots back, and it continues to look rather ominous. Playing with Tiger is Vijay Singh, and behind them are Lucas Glover and Brendan Jones, but I don't hang around to watch the final two groups tee off. I have another, more pressing, appointment.

I'd left the course because there was to be a light-hearted press conference in celebration of legendary US golf writer Dan Jenkins' 201st golf major. Dan Jenkins is not massively well-known outside the USA unless you're a real golf junky. I first heard of him when I read of his book, *The Dogged Victims of Inexorable Fate*. The titles of many of his works tell you he's a man with a rapier wit and keen eye for sport, particularly golf – *The Money-Whipped Steer-Job Three-Jack Give-Up Artist*; *You Call It Sports, But I Say It's a Jungle Out There*; *Bubba Talks: Of Life, Love, Sex, Whiskey, Politics, Foreigners, Teenagers, Movies, Food, Football, and Other Matters That Occasionally Matter*.

I first properly read stuff by Jenkins in *Golf Digest* magazine back in the late 1980s, and I still have one edition (December 1986) where he lists the best things in golf, but in his own inimitable and off-beat fashion. The entire list can be found in the collection that forms the book

Fairways & Greens, a *pot pourri* of mainly humorous takes on modern golf and many of its absurdities. Timing the conference ten minutes before Tiger's tee-off time wasn't the PGA's smartest move, but I could see Tiger any time and Jenkins fascinated and entertained in equal measure.

After the entertainment it was out to see The Man. Maybe it was just me and my project, a dark cloud hanging over it, but following the game was like a strange mix of ticker-tape parade and day of mourning, some of the crowd whooping it up and getting excited at Tiger's 4-shot lead, others respectfully following the match as if to mark the passing of the season's final Major.

Tiger missed a good birdie chance at the 3rd and progressed to the 4th, where play was backed up. I walked half the length of the hole, as previously I'd found an almost surreal spot where, despite standing in the trees with hundreds of spectators behind me and more in front, I could see the players on the slightly elevated tee and had a view to the green. Most fans just focused on the green, waiting for a ball to appear, and didn't realise they could see the action. One lady, however, was very keen to watch Tiger and taking no chances, as she was up on her husband's shoulders.

Tiger found the 4th green, but, bizarrely for him, 3-putted, something he doesn't do very often, never mind from so close.

Two guys next to me become animated for a few seconds. 'Oh, he three-jacked it,' said one, turning and looking at his buddy.

'Good. I really don't want him to run away with it.' For some reason, perhaps looking for validation – Forgive me, Father, for I have sinned and spoken out against The One – he looks at me.

I'm heartened for a few seconds. I'm not the only one out here who feels that way.

'Yeah. A few more of those in the next 24 hours will keep it interesting,' I say, even though I don't actually think that's going to happen.

I walk across to the 6th fairway, and watch the two games in front play the hole before Tiger and Vijay appear. Lucas Glover is Tiger's nearest challenger at 4-under, three shots behind, and he narrowly misses a birdie opportunity, shaving the hole. Hanging in there and playing well on a long golf course, Glover is living up nicely to the billing of US Open Champion. I know that Jim and Allen will be watching keenly on TV back home, enjoying their Clemson boy hanging tough.

Tiger and Vijay appear on the 6th tee, the radio telling me both had made par at the 5th, although Singh had missed a short try for bird. Perhaps this is playing on his mind as he plays a shot that would make a 10-handicapper cringe, a quick snipe or neck left that catches the boughs of the trees. For a minute I wonder if he's actually gone out-of-bounds, but then spot that he's bounced out into the middle of the fairway. Metronomic Woods finds the fairway.

Vijay now has about 250 yards to go, despite the hole only being 405 yards. This time his shot is much better, it's only a half-snipe, and again he hits the trees. By the time he finishes this hole he'll be wearing a checked shirt, a John Deere hat and asking his caddy to squeal like a pig. Again he finds the fairway, and the crowd claps and cheers his luck. Most club players with those shots would have been over the boundary fence, then in the shit. Life just isn't fair.

Singh narrowly misses his par (!) after a superb wedge in, just above the hole. Tiger narrowly misses birdie. It's not beyond reason that he could already have been six shots ahead if his putting game was playing its usual song. Depressing. 'Go Tiger!' someone irritatingly shouts.

Two groups of spectators who didn't look depressed were the couple of hundred people at two houses that lined the fairway up towards the 6th green, sitting on porches, verandas and by a swimming pool, drinks in hand, soaking up the atmosphere. Woods could have been ten shots ahead and they wouldn't have cared. I don't blame them. I too would have been focused on the social programme and just got ploughed; championship over.

Down the long 7th, the size of the crowd really becomes obvious, the fairway is thick with people down both sides. There must be about 5,000 following this march to glory. It's a wonder there isn't a jazz or Highland pipe band showing them the way. I stay up on the high ground well left of the ropes but with a clear view of all the proceedings. Tiger fails to make birdie, the result of a missed fairway, while Singh chips in to hole for eagle, a small spring in his step as he picks his ball out of the hole. Tiger's clearly not firing on all cylinders or, dare I say it, he's playing conservatively, the power of history and destiny on his side.

As they proceed to the next, I realise that I have been caught short, the two litres of cold drink I hoovered down now leaving me in a compromising position. The day hasn't got much warmer, and I need to go. I realise that by walking all the way to the Media Centre I will use no more time than queuing at the public facilities, and I can get food and watch some of the golf on TV. So I march up the hill, and by the time I approach the first tee I know what it's like to be on a flight from Honduras to Atlanta.

And then, as if by magic, a championship appeared. In the 45 minutes that I take to get to the WC and grab some lunch, the PGA has become like the Tour de France. A number of players break from the peloton in an effort to catch Lance, sorry, Tiger Woods. I couldn't believe it, but I had failed to see the writing on the wall, despite Tiger's missed putts. Of the top dozen players, only Tiger and Brendan Jones were not under par for the day.

Having been four shots ahead, Woods was now only one in front. Defending champion Padraig Harrington was 6-under and on fire, and a number of players had advanced to 5-under at some point, including Els, Singh and Glover. Both Henrik Stenson and Y.E. Yang were at minus-4. Who said this was the worst Major? Players were queuing up. All of a sudden, Tiger's invincibility was in question.

I couldn't wait to get out onto the course. I was glad to have left behind all the fun of a cortège. There was also the potential for an interesting scenario come nightfall. Tiger's record is eight from eight Majors after leading after the second round, but he's never won from behind after 54 holes in a Major. If he goes behind this evening, he's staring at maintaining that 36-hole record by doing something he has always previously failed to do.

I go straight for the 15th hole and my timing is almost perfect, as Kaymer and Yang are in the fairway, about 300 yards away, waiting to play their seconds. The German comes up short while Yang, only 5ft 8in but built like a piece of high-tensile steel cable, whips his ball through the back of the 642-yard par-5. I'm really keen to see Yang make his birdie, as he's only three shots back. Kaymer hits a poor chip, a bit heavy, and the guy in front of me says, 'He chunked it! That's fuh-nee.' Fair to say he didn't graduate *summa cum laude* from Harvard. Yang chips down to about 6 feet right of the stick; no gimme.

Kaymer comes good, and much to the delight of the crowd rolls in a 15-footer for birdie. Next up, it's Mister Yang. He slides his testy, quick putt into the middle and punches the air! Quite the live wire, he picks his ball out of the hole and punches the air with both hands and arms, getting the crowd right on side, encouraging them to yell and to cheer by raising his arms again and again. I didn't have the Korean down as a showman, but 90 minutes ago this championship's atmosphere was flatter than Kansas, now we're all cheering and whooping, Yang is beaming and he throws his ball into the small bleacher behind the green. In seconds we've gone from Boredom Central to a Minnesota Twins baseball game, as the fans strike up the classic baseball refrain, 'Take Me Out to the Old Ball Game'. On their feet, cheering and clapping, lapping up Yang's delight, they melodically tell us,

> *'Take me out to the ball game,*
> *Take me out with the crowd.*
> *Buy me some peanuts and cracker jack,*
> *I don't care if I never get back,*
> *Let me root, root, root for the home team,*
> *If they don't win it's a shame.*
> *For it's one, two, three strikes, you're out,*
> *At the old ball game.*
> *For it's one, two, three strikes, you're out,*
> *At the old ball game.'*

All of a sudden the PGA has become a New York US Open and we're loving Yang's showboating. He's now only two back from Tiger.

In the next game it's Soren Whathisname and Ernie Els, the big South African only two back and in danger of reliving past glories. Kjeldsen just misses his birdie effort, and as Ernie lines up his putt, there's a massive crack right behind me and then another, although Els seems oblivious, wrapped up in the moment of his putt. We all look round, and up a pine tree there's a young boy, keen to get a view. An official arrives and tells him to get down, creating further cracking and splintering. He's climbing down but I'm now slightly nervous. It would have been an idea at least to allow Els to putt first. As I wait for a sudden noise, Els comfortably holes and again the crowd is ecstatic.

'Let's go Ernie, let's go Ernie. Let's go Ernie, let's go Ernie...' the crowd in the bleacher cheers. They have a tune for every occasion, weddings and bar mitzvahs most welcome.

I decide that I'll follow Ernie for the next couple of holes, and as he walks off the back of the 15th green, down the hill towards the 16th tee on the lake, we cheer, clap and encourage him. He nods, murmurs thanks and gives a thumbs-up. It now feels as if Slim is heading back to town. I'm energised, it's threatening to be a great day on Sunday. Just then, a massive cheer from back down the fairway. Harrington has birdied the 14th and pulled alongside Tiger at minus-7. Wow. The PGA has exploded into life, a post-Tiger mushroom cloud.

Els hits a good drive down the 16th, but it rolls out and comes to rest on the collar betwixt fairway and rough. It's an awkward lie, especially on a hole flanked by water on three sides. His wife, Liesl, walks by with some friends, notebook in hand, charting Ernie's round. Ernie tweaks his approach, missing left and making bogey. He then bogeys in, walking off the final green deflated, admitting later his mind was ahead of itself. He hadn't stayed in the moment.

Ernie's bogeys seem to have a domino effect, creating a worrying pattern back down the field, except for two men – Tiger Woods and Yang. The magician, Woods, chips in at the 14th for birdie, having hit a poor shot to settle on the fringe. At almost the same time, Harrington fails to birdie the long 15th. Yang birdied the 16th too, after his histrionics at the 15th, and Woods pars in.

I'd decided to follow Woods and Singh for their last couple of holes, but at the 17th it gets rather dark, and the skies look ominous. There's a crack of thunder and it starts to rain, a storm is on its way. Given the unfortunate death of a fan back in 1991 at Hazeltine, there's a big premium on safety, and many take it into their own hands, thousands streaming across the course for the exit. Fortunately I have the sanctuary of the Media Centre and head up the hill at the 1st, the rain starting to get bigger, and surely a massive downpour is only minutes away.

Later, the draw for the final round of the final Major of the year is an interesting one, and there's plenty of class to suggest a good day on Sunday is in prospect, provided the weather holds up. Everyone's fear is that there's a delay and we're into Monday. Tiger leads at minus-8, and five shots back Ernie Els plays with Alvaro Quiros, who's one shot further adrift. US Open champ Lucas Glover goes with the Dane of many names, Soren Kjeldsen, and Harrington and Stenson provide much quality and could pull each other along on the last day, Harrington seeking a successful defence.

The final pairing is Tiger and Y.E. Yang. Would Yang's presence allow some of the others to sneak under Tiger's radar? Would Yang himself, only two back, come through and challenge? I didn't imagine so, but I did think that the power of the eastern mindset and the self-belief that Yang could take into Sunday would make it interesting. For once, in the final round, it felt as if Tiger had some real competition.

Slim was back in town.

PGA SUNDAY: THE SPELL IS BROKEN

From arriving in Augusta in the dark on a Wednesday evening to getting to Hazeltine and having a great week, it all seemed no time at all. I'd met lots of good people and drank a lot less beer than I thought I would – I'd spent more time at the golf than I had in bars. Surely it wasn't meant to be like this?

On Sunday at Hazeltine I planned to get down for the start of play, but when I awoke at 05:20 the rain was bouncing outside and there were rumbles of thunder in the distance. I went back to bed. Sean O'Hair would just have to tee off without me.

It'd been a great year of close Majors, but Tiger was involved in a final round showdown for the first time. He'd been on the fringes at the Masters and the US Open, but hadn't really threatened, continuing his inability to win a Major from behind in the final round. By failing to win the US Open at Bethpage, he was without a Major for the first time in four years, and we all knew he wanted some Major silverware. Badly. Also, by getting to Major win number 15, he'd be within a single season of beating Jack Nicklaus' record of 18 professional Majors. That would set him up for a sweep of Majors in 2010 to beat Jack's record in grand style. An academic at Berkeley, Jennifer Brown, had shown that when Tiger's in the field, the top players in the world score worse than when he's not. The PGA was his for the taking.

I walked up to the course with Steve and his family, pleased at the fact that the skies seemed to be clearing and it was looking like a nice day, although I had a waterproof top on for the first time during PGA week. We parted ways by the first fairway, as I hadn't decided what I was going to do, but I knew one thing, I needed some breakfast.

After eating it was time to head out, although first of all I checked out the play-off holes. Two out of three Majors so far this year had gone to an extra-time shoot-out, and perhaps cruel fate would again play a hand. However, the definition of the play-off holes to be used was in the kind of wording that only a Lehman Brothers securities analyst or Enron accountant would understand.

'In the event of a tie for first place after 72 holes, there will be a three-hole aggregate score play-off on Holes No. 16, 17 and 18.' Okay, that much was simple. I was following it up to this point.

'If a tie still remains, there will be a sudden death, hole-by-hole play-off beginning on No.18, and if a tie remains, there will be a hole-by-hole play-off beginning on No. 10.' I think they meant the next two holes would be sudden death over 18 then 10, although repeating the words 'hole-by-hole' made it very hard reading and totally misleading. Somebody somewhere was having a laugh. And they continued to do so.

'If a tie remains, the progression of play-off holes will be Nos. 17, 18, 10, 17 and 18 repeated until a winner is determined.' By this time I had lost the will to live. If they have to read this out later over the PA system, there'll be hysteria and mass panic. Aside from the shocking English, the logic seemed nutty, too. They'd play 17, 18, 10, 17, 18, then go back to 17th, when the 10th tee was right there. I was now hoping it really wouldn't go to a play-off, as only the truly gifted would understand the sequence. Stick this in *Rain Man 2*, and even Raymond Babbitt would struggle with it.

I'd bumped into Alfie Lau over breakfast and suggested that we take a walk out to the 14th, as it and the 15th could be pivotal, presenting two eagle opportunities late in the day. Someone a few shots back could catapult themselves into contention with two stellar holes, so it would be interesting to see how they played that morning.

Sean O'Hair had already completed his round, whipping through his eighteen holes in a mere 133 minutes. Playing alone, O'Hair was in the danger of losing his tag as one of the slowest players on tour. Glaciers have been known to melt quicker than his usual game. He was only marginally faster than the 1950s. The joke on tour is that his real name is Sean Hair, but they added the 'oh' while waiting for him to putt. He'd gone round so fast, that by the time we got to the 15th at 10:55, the game behind him was on the green.

En route, we noticed the sucker pin seen at the 16th, cut middle right. Although technically 21 yards from the front and five from the right, if you took the direct route to the pin, it was actually only on the green by around six yards. Later, it could be tears at bedtime for someone.

When we arrived at the 14th, Alfie put his empty bottle of Gatorade to good use. He used it as a pillow, lay down and went to sleep. I stood up near the green with a decent view of the tee. The hole showed that it could offer some intrigue. At 301 yards in total, and 288 yards to the front, it was more of a tough par-3 for the world's best, although we did see a mixed bag, so it was bogeyable, too. Of the 14 players I watched go through, two knocked it in close, but failed to convert for eagle. David Smail missed from around 18 feet; Kenny Perry did the same, hitting a woeful putt from around 15 feet. Meanwhile a few others missed the green well right, including Grant Sturgeon, who I thought for a second had popped his tee shot over the perimeter fence.

After watching Perry miss, we decided to follow the game in front, Rory Sabbatini and Geoff Ogilvy. Sabo had his wife following him and she didn't seem to be too impressed with someone in the gallery, pointing and scowling at him. Amy Sabbatini is not known for her forgiving nature, and she was pulling faces like the guy was Ted Bundy. Mrs Sabo once wore a top that read, 'Keep Up', protesting about Nick Faldo's slow play. Faldo commented later that it was a shame she had to bring their sexual problems to the course. She certainly looks like the kind of woman that when she demands something, she gets it.

It's now approaching lunchtime, and as we meander back to the range, it's obvious that Minnesota has once again come out in its thousands to watch the best golfers the planet has to offer. People are queuing for seats at the 9th and 18th greens already, so a seat there later is going to be out of the question. Alfie heads off as I make my way up past the first tee, and it's all I can do to make headway, as the hill is mobbed.

I round the side of the clubhouse, and the fans are going wild, cheering and shouting. Not at me, of course. Tiger and Stevie Williams appear from their car, Tiger in his customary Sunday red. Children scurry excitedly along the railing dividing them from the players, hoping for a signature. Tiger acknowledges the crowd but is otherwise unmoved. He's here to win, and only to win. There's plenty of history to be made today aside from his 15th Major. Victory at Hazeltine will make Tiger the joint most winning player in PGA history, with five titles alongside Walter Hagen and Jack Nicklaus. It will also make Tiger the first man in history to win a Major every year for five years. He will feel destiny is on his side.

After noshing with the media crew, I get back to the first tee to catch the main challengers, and I plan to follow Els and Quiros once they have teed off. As ever, Quiros is Mister Long off the tee, carrying it 345 yards, leaving him a short club to the green and a good birdie chance. However, both he and Els make par, although that's a steady start for the last day of a Major. In the games behind, Lucas Glover pars, Kjeldsen bogeys, and in similar fashion, Stenson pars and Harrington bogeys. And then it's Woods and Yang on the first tee.

The scene is like a Cecil B. De Mille biblical epic. It had been lashing down when the penultimate group played the 1st, but atop the hill, in brilliant sunshine, I can see The Chosen One standing above all others on the elevated tee. Although he's about 350 yards away, I can see Tiger clearly, the red shirt dancing in the sun, a beacon of danger for other golfers.

The championship leader, uniquely among the Majors, has the honour on the first tee, so is not the last player to tee off in round four. The crowd is vast and, like the recent downpour, also of biblical proportions; thousands and thousands seem to have gathered all along the 490-yard hole. Countless others, like me, are not on the ropes, but standing on higher ground up towards a tented hospitality area. It's easily the biggest crowd assembled for the Major year. This is Tiger's moment.

Woods finds the fairway and ominously strikes a lovely approach iron to around 10 feet.

'Roar, Tiger, roar,' shouts the guy next to me. Thousands of others encourage Tiger on his walk to the green.

Classic Tiger would roll the putt in and be off and running. But he misses, looking bemused at the aberration.

'Oh, no!' is one response, heavy with sarcasm, clearly wanting a game of it today. Yang missed his birdie try prior to Tiger, but put a good stroke on it and did not look tentative.

Both he and Yang par the first two holes while, up ahead, young Lucas Glover birdies 3 and 5 to move to within two of Tiger.

I walk from number 1 round to the 3rd, waiting for Woods and Yang to reappear. The junction at the 8th tee and 7th green is also brimming with people, and passing through the mass of humanity is like trying to get to the stage during a rock concert without the flying beers overhead.

Although Woods had missed at one, he has plenty of time to get into his stride. *It's what he does.* Yang birdies the 3rd but Tiger fails on this one, again missing a good chance. I take up my comfortable position amid the trees down the right of number 4 and wait for them to play.

As the players wait for the game in front fully to clear, the pin flutters in the light breeze, then is still, then flutters again, creating indecision. It's Tiger's turn to play, and he steps off his ball a couple of times, unsure exactly what he's trying to do. Indecision and an inability to visualise one's shot is a crucial error at all levels of golf, but in a Major it can be the difference between winning and losing, especially coming down the stretch. However, the great man hits a lovely shot onto the green, not far from the pin, and will have chance for birdie, a chance to get ahead again by two.

In some sort of perverse parallel to the Saturday, Tiger not only fails to birdie, he three putts. His ball striking appears imperious, affording opportunity after opportunity, but he cannot buy a putt. Welcome to the real world, Mister Woods. He slips back to 7-under, only one ahead of his playing partner and Harrington.

Waiting in the corner at the 6th hole for Tiger and Yang to appear, I decide to follow Harrington down the par-5 7th. Rather inexplicably, they're not opening the walkway that leads from that point next to the 7th tee down the fairway. I can understand that they are trying to control the crowds, but I don't see the point when it means that anyone and everyone following Tiger will be corralled in this spot, followed by an exodus of thousands when Woods and Yang do get through. I cheat and use my media pass to get across the roped-off corridor.

What I see in the next 15 minutes threatens to change the complexion of the entire day and restore the status quo. I grab an iced lemonade, and before I can say 'global warming' and enjoy my $5 purchase, Paddy Harrington and my lemonade begin to melt. Harrington's transformation is more bitter and much less enjoyable. I'm watching Yang and Woods at the 7th green, the former way right on the hill, the latter in line with the pin, a birdie chance, when I hear on the radio that the Irishman has knocked his tee shot in the water at the 8th. As I look to my left, I see

Harrington back on one of the front tees, having taken a drop. I can then tell that through the ball on his next shot he's reacted to having a ball in the right-hand water and yanked it left. You know the rest, or at least the result – a quintuple bogey 8. Horrid, and the worst thing to happen to Irish sport since Shergar was turned into low-grade dog food. For the second time in a week, Harrington's put the carrot in the nose of the snowman. I'm shocked, as it feels like we're back in familiar territory and Tiger will coast to victory. Not after only seven holes. Please.

Part of my disappointment was that I was sure that Yang had taken a drop to the right of the 7th, but either he hadn't or it was a free one, and he almost birdied. When Tiger bogeyed the 8th, he and the Korean were equal and it was now basically head-to-head: arguably the best golfer of all time against the winner of this year's Honda Classic, a farmer's son from Korea.

'Go Eldrick,' someone shouts – using Tiger's given name as a form of encouragement, or ridicule, depending on your viewpoint – as he walks to the 9th tee. It's hotting up, and I take my waterproof top off.

I make my way behind 9 and across 18, heading for 10, only to find the equivalent of the entire population of India has either had the same idea or been waiting here all day for Woods and Yang. It's a great place to stand to look at the backs of people's heads, but not much else, so I march down into the bottleneck at 10 green, 16 green and 11 tee. A game walks by, heading to the 17th tee, but I don't even take any notice of who they are. All but Woods and Yang are now superfluous. I get up to the left side of the 11th, and wait for our gladiators to appear.

Just after two o'clock, with the sun beating down and a glorious day now in full swing, Tiger's ball appears opposite me, 40 feet away, sitting pretty in the fairway. Yang is not as long and won't have the chance to get on the 606-yard par-5 in two. Could this be the pivotal hole, as it was in 2002? Back then, Rich Beem found the green in two and holed for eagle. He went on to beat Tiger by a single shot.

'Run out and get it, Tracy, you'll get on TV. Then end up in jail.' Tracy decided to leave Tiger's ball alone and he duly walked up, pulled a club and smoked it – a 3-wood? – onto the front of the green, much to the delight of the crowd in the bleacher greenside. Yang had laid up, short and left, and I watched from nearby as he hit a tentative pitch. Mmmm. Surely Tiger could smell blood? He wasn't far away for eagle. But when both players two-jiggled we were in familiar territory: Tiger was 1 ahead, six holes to play, and Yang had hit a poor pitch, a first sign of nerves.

Up 12 Tiger pulled his tee-shot into the rough, and was near Yang, who was on the fairway. This time I was about 20 feet away from Tiger and Stevie Williams, almost close enough to smell their sweat and hear their hearts beat. I couldn't quite make out their conversation, but there was a brief discussion on club and shot choices. When Tiger hit, it was like an air-raid siren had gone off, followed by panic. People immediately lurched left, others started running, most cheered, hollered or whooped. His ball seemed to go left, hooking, and he missed the green.

'Go, Tiger!'

'You got it!'

'Go for the throat, Tiger!'

Just some of the things shouted as people scattered, and all as Yang was in pre-shot mode. Tiger had complained that an official spoiled the battle between himself and Harrington at Firestone the week before, but I wonder how many times he's complained about, or even been conscious of, his fans and the gallery in general, indirectly interfering with the final stages of a Major? Of course, this isn't his fault, whether he notices or not.

I was pretty annoyed. Yang was one shot back and every shot was now the most important of his life, yet the majority of the crowd were behaving as if they were at a football game, carried away by the excitement of Tiger winning in their own backyard. Yang didn't appear to notice as one guy bellowed across the gallery, 'Sinkowski!? Sinkowski!?'

'Yo! I'm here.' The guy in front of me put his arm up, signalling he hadn't disappeared. It's nice to know that two men can be so close one can't live without the other while watching a golf tournament. The crowd was now so pro-Tiger, they appeared to have forgotten there was still a lot of golf ahead and another player involved.

Yang made a pretty average swing, a bit shorter and with a tad more body through the ball. I thought he'd pulled the ass off it, but was glad to hear via the radio he'd found the left side of the green. Tiger bogeyed the hardest hole of the week and it was level once more.

Down in the corner, where 12 green, 13 and 14 and 15 tee were, it was pandemonium between shots, anxious fans scurrying to get a view of Tiger. One of the most impressive shots of the week is Tiger's tee-shot at the 13th. Fresh off a bogey, five holes to play in a Major championship down a long par-3 that, this day, tee to hole, measures 240 yards, Woods cuts a towering hold-up shot, probably with a 2-iron, into around twenty feet. It's the kind of shot most players would be delighted to hit once, anywhere, any time, but in the heat of battle it's an impressive reminder of Tiger's mental strength and golfing ability.

Both players par the tricky 13th, but Tiger, yet again, misses a birdie chance. Level with five holes to go. The 14th is now a very different spectator proposition than it was late morning. Fans are concentrated all along the home stretch, and in this corner it's only one way from here – back and down along the 15th. As soon as the players had struck their tee shots at the previous hole, half the gallery turns on its heels and runs to the ropes at 14. I can't quite see the pin, but I can see the tee and the front portion of the green.

Yang hits a good shot, finding the fringe at the top left of the right-hand bunker. He's maybe 45 feet from the pin, and has hit a better shot than most of the earlier players who weren't even in the game. Woods finds the bunker. I watch as Tiger splashes out, coming to rest around 10 feet from the hole. It's a good shot, but by no means a gimme birdie.

I had resisted coming into this section of the course on previous days because it tended to be very busy, and I'm keen to get out, not wanting to be stranded behind the masses ahead of me and already on the 15th. I watch Yang eye up his chip, and then decide to take a walk forward, as I can't see the bottom of the pin anyway.

Just as I round the next tee, Yang unleashes hell, holing his pitch for an eagle. The bleacher, the thousands behind the green, the countless others in the vicinity with radios and hand-held TVs, all erupt, shouting and cheering madly, as if they've just seen a last-second touchdown to win the Superbowl. It feels like an unprecedented show of emotion that, although not directed against Tiger, is hardly in his favour. For the first time since the Masters, almost instantaneously, I break out in goose pimples. I even think I have bumps on the soles of my feet. I feel cold and fuzzy: history beckons either way.

And now we have it. Tiger is behind with only four holes left in a Major. I can't even recall him having fallen back when leading after 54 holes; falling behind is usually someone else's job. Steadfastly, though, Woods holes to drop only one back.

Thousands stream up the 15th, many staring dreamily at other fans, eyes wide in wonderment. Just as Phil and Tiger went at it on Augusta National's back nine, there's a collective suspension of disbelief, as if we are unsure if we are dreaming or watching a film. Can this really be happening?

As I look back to see the players tee off, I make eye contact with a fellow fan.

'Wow! What about Yang, man? When do you ever see someone stare down the beast?'

'This *is* golf,' was my pert reply.

The noise and delirium of the crowd has all of a sudden become more egalitarian. No longer are they behind just one of the fighters, they're behind both, and now it's the fight that seems to matter, not who wins. In contrast, up at the 18th – Steve would tell me later – where the crowds are not swept away by post-chip hysteria, there are moans and groans all round, most of the fans rooting for Tiger. I've now been given what I want, a good clean fight . . . to the death.

'This is awesome,' says another guy as he runs past me. Thousands line the 642-yard 15th as both players find the fairway. Yang's chip has electrified the crowd, a high voltage jolt has doubled everyone's speed and volume. Everywhere people scramble for a view. I step under the ropes lining the 11th and position myself on top of a bunker, which gives me a view of the players. I'm the first or second to take up this stance and by the time Tiger plays, about a hundred of us are standing on this single mound, jostling for position, like schoolchildren trying to catch a glimpse of the President or the Queen.

Tiger hits a poor second, taking it a bit heavy, and it comes up short and left. Most unlike him, and he probably regards it as total garbage. A birdie or eagle here would put him back on terms, or even ahead.

Chaos is far too strong a word, but it gives a flavour of the energy levels of the crowd, which are increasing exponentially with each passing hole; as fewer holes are left, thousands are tagging onto this final match. A marshal in a buggy appears and tells us to get inside the ropes. I do duck under and back alongside the 15th, but countless others are scurrying across and down the fairway, totally absorbed in locating their next vantage-point. A few run through a bunker.

This poor marshal is up against it, and he's trying to round up the fans like a shepherd trying to control a herd of sheep which have overdosed on amphetamines. He has no chance, and a bizarre ballet takes place, he jolting back and forth in his buggy, turning left and right, chasing people down. Nobody means any harm, we all just want to see the final holes of this historic championship. He looks totally stressed, but everybody else sees it as light relief.

Both players par the 15th, and standing to the left of 16 my heart is in my mouth. Yang is on the cusp of history, and I wouldn't mind seeing him do it. All I can see is water, grasses, rough, a creek and a small bit of fairway. He hits his shot and it disappears into the sky above the water. The few seconds feel like a minute, and I'm as uptight as I would be if I was watching a good friend challenge for the championship. Torture. His ball appears in the fairway. Woods is also on the short stuff, and it's him to play. He pulls his approach, and as he leans and grimaces, there's deathly silence. Two poor shots in as many holes.

Yang is next. Remember that sucker pin, middle right? He swings, and as soon as the ball leaves the club head he gives it the long look, not sure, hoping against hope that it's okay. He leans left, his body language indicating he doesn't want the ball to go right. His ball lands right in line with the pin and a massive cheer goes up. A nail positioned above the coffin, hammer in hand.

Both players par as I look down the hill from one of the forward tees on the 11th. The 16th is in the corner, thousands of people down and around the final part of the hole, anxious for a view. I walk up to the middle left of 17, with a view of both tee and green, left and right. I've stood here at some point every day, but now it has real purpose. Tiger is one behind. Two holes to play.

People stream past me, others stop and stand. Most are animated, some are contemplative. It's a walk of around 200 yards to the tee from the 16th green. This provides much time for the players to think of what's just been and what's to come. It's never easy to control one's mind and stay in the present at the best of times, much less so when there is an extended period between holes. Tiger is nowhere to be seen. He's gone to the toilet. I wonder to myself if he really needed to go, or was he giving Yang some time to think? Was he psyching himself up for the defence of his perfect record?

I also wonder if either player is aware that in 1991, in his playoff against Payne Stewart, Scott Simpson pulled his approach well left and into the water. And he had to take a drop left of the pond, leaving a horrendous pitch down and across to a narrow target. Probably neither player was conscious of this, but I was fully aware that anything could happen. This was Major golf.

Again it was all I could do to watch. Yang put a good swing on his tee ball and found the middle of the green. It was a miracle he could even swing at all. Tiger hit his best shot of the day, a high iron shot that looked to be all over the pin like a cheap suit: it was long and came to rest in the gnarly rough behind the fringe. Not far from the pin, but with a tricky pitch to be negotiated. Advantage Yang.

I move up near the green, almost at the spot where Simpson had fatefully pitched in 1991, but I'm about eighth row from the front. I listen on the radio and also turn to the portable TV around my neck. Tiger's chip is, at best, mediocre. Yang hits a poor putt and comes up well short. HE'S LET TIGER IN. Time and time again this happens. The tension around the green is unbearable. It doesn't matter who you are supporting, the entire championship is hanging in the balance.

It's just before 18:00 on a lovely Sunday afternoon. There's not a cloud in the sky and the heat of the day has yet to subside. Thousands of people surround the 17th and you could hear a pin drop. Tiger misses, his putt just skimming the left edge. I feel drained even watching this, the suspense almost too much to take. A few people crowd round me, looking at my TV, anxious to see what Yang does. He almost holes his putt, but it stops on the right lip of the hole. Two seconds later I get the chance to watch the time-delayed transmission on TV: so close but so far. One shot in it. One regulation hole to go.

The 18th was always going to be problematic for me as a spectator since it's up a hill, with the green at the top. I head straight up, hoping I might be able to use my media badge to get to the back of the green. I listen on the radio as, along with hundreds and thousands of others, I scurry upwards. Both players have hit the fairway, Yang up on the left. As I get to about 100 yards shy of the green, I can see up the hill and onto the putting surface. I hadn't realised this was possible before. But there's still not a view of the bottom of the pin, so I press on.

Thousands of people are standing in this area, and for several minutes and about 50 yards there is just a single lane of people pressing their way through. I'm sure at one point I won't be able to go any further, that I'll have to stop and give up. Five minutes later, however, I break through, then start running while listening to Yang's second on the radio. He launches a utility 3-iron; when it lands the noise is deafening, and the radio guys go ballistic. Like his chip at 14 I don't actually see it, but the sound generated is like a bomb blast, rippling and distorting the air all around. I cheer as I run. Yang has done it, surely?

As Tiger then just misses the green, I'm convinced Y.E. Yang has done it. I am not allowed in behind the green, but I notice that the marshals usually in place behind the stands have gone, no doubt to watch the action. I clamber up the steps as fast as I can, making it to the third step from the top. I grab the railing beside those seated and stick my foot on a single supporting horizontal bar. Hoisting myself up, I have a clear view of all the play.

Tiger and Yang are contemplating their next moves. Somewhere in the stand is Steve and his family. He tells me later that they could see Yang play his second shot, but it disappeared from view when it cleared the tree, before it landed just shy of the flag and terrified the hole. Tom Lehman was right – this is golf.

When Tiger misses his chip, there is no doubt that many in the stand are disappointed. Yang steps up, and amazingly rolls his putt in.

'Yes,' I shout loudly and long, punching the air. History. Game over. The first Asian winner of a men's Major, and Tiger's spell is broken. Some people look at me as if I've committed the ultimate sin, rooting against Tiger. But the finish is immense, and people everywhere are shouting and screaming; thousands of others also love what Yang has done.

Yang runs off the green, and like a circus strongman picks up his tour bag and lifts it over his head: the most unique of celebrations.

'Y.E.Yang! Y.E.Yang! Y.E.Yang!' the fans begin to chant, embracing the winner as their own. A hero.

'Y.E.Yang! Y.E.Yang! Y.E.Yang!'

Epilogue
The Mystic Chords of Memory

The spectator has a perfect right to his opinion. It is only when he begins to act as if it were of value that you are justified in correcting his mistake.

Horace G. Hutchinson, *Hints on Golf*, 1886

And then it was over. After 19 weeks, golf's Majors were in abeyance for another year, until the bandwagon would roll into Augusta for the golfing rites of spring and the birth of the next set of Major champions. Many are called, few are chosen. In the years since the first Open Championship, only 198 players have won Majors, fewer than most club memberships. This is what makes the likes of Jack Nicklaus and Tiger Woods and all the other Major winners so special, they've done things nobody is meant to be able to do.

Two months after the PGA I sat down to watch the Presidents Cup on TV. As I viewed the twelve best players from the USA against the eleven best and Adam Scott from the Rest of the World, I found myself wishing I was there as the teams did battle, followed by thousands of fans. It evoked the memories and the emotions, the sights and the sounds that I had experienced at The Masters Tournament, the US Open, The Open, and the PGA Championship. I'll never be able to watch these great championships on TV now without thinking of my year – the superb golf, the many, varied and wonderful fans, the jokes, the laughter, the pain and the heartache: Major golf has it all.

The Masters doesn't feel like a Major. Inexorably it is something other, it's The Masters. Clifford Roberts and Bobby Jones' brainchild spawned a perfect offspring. Short of the Four Horsemen of the Apocalypse riding up Magnolia Lane in early April, I don't believe it's possible to have a bad Masters Tournament as a patron. The cold and rain would dampen the spirit, but one would see the splendour and the beauty through different eyes, the way one sees mist and rain across a splendid Norwegian fjord.

Augusta National is the real world magnified and perfected beyond our golfing dreams. If the powers-that-be allowed, The Masters Tournament would be the ultimate Harvard Business Review case study, where no stone is left unturned in the quest for perfection and a desire to please. It is as if some benevolent higher being has invited you to golf's greatest garden party. And yet, perhaps the greatest paradox, if you can source a ticket at face value, it's far and away the cheapest Major to attend – $200 for four days of drama and excitement, rising to fever pitch on Sunday afternoon.

At his inauguration speech in 1861, Abraham Lincoln spoke of what held America together, the 'mystic chords of memory'. Augusta resounds to these chords, the echoes of golfing times past, present and even future. Each new year, you know that great things will happen once again on the rolling hills of the old Fruitland Nurseries.

The other Majors can't compete with Augusta National, but they don't have to. They each have their own special meaning, and are run by organisations for titles that originated in very different ways. The US Open is the first Major chance for Joe Public to see his golfing heroes in the flesh, and boy, does Joe get behind the players. I'll be laughing for years to come at the US Open crowd and their spontaneity. The terrible weather at Bethpage somehow added to the experience, emphasising the privilege of being at the USA's National Championship. A New York US Open is a unique event, and maybe, just maybe, I need to give the Californian version a shot.

At The Open Championship, whether in Scotland or England,

classic golf is always nearby. To visit The Open is to step back in time. You can walk and play the same links courses that the greatest trod – the Tom Morrises, Harry Vardon, Bobby Jones, Ben Hogan (only once, but what a visit), Arnold Palmer, Jack Nicklaus, Seve Ballesteros, Nick Faldo, Tiger Woods. All these great players have lifted the Claret Jug. Is it any wonder many consider it *the* championship to win, a chance to join the game's greatest.

The courses have remained largely unchanged over the years. Some have been lengthened and new bunkers added, but they are not stretched massively because links golf's greatest defence is the weather; the light or strong wind; rain; the cold or heat; every day the courses change. The unpredictability of the conditions means that no single type of game is good enough to win. Imagination and power, touch and cunning, brute force and desire, all are required.

The PGA of America has taken its championship to 25 of the USA's 50 states. Ordinarily Minnesota would not have been on my travel list, but to enjoy great Midwest hospitality was a pleasure and a privilege. Next time it's Wisconsin, and it will be interesting to see where the centenary championship will take place in 2016. America has so many classy golf courses, it's a tough call.

I saw history made on the plains, the world's best player run out of town by Yang. The PGA Championship is a great one, maligned by forces in the media who choose to look elsewhere. Players queue up to win it and recent finales show that it's much desired – Yang, Harrington, Tiger, Tiger, Phil Mickelson and Vijay Singh. In what part of those events did guys not look interested, and at what point did the runners-up look happy to go home with fat cheques but no trophy?

The PGA is a happy, inclusive Major. The US summer holidays meant Hazeltine was awash with kids in a way Bethpage could not be in mid-June. Many golfing insiders consider the PGA to be the best run Major, put together by a professional organisation. Given that Hazeltine had been effectively classed in 1970 as ruined cow pasture and cornfields in the middle of nowhere, it was great to see a course universally embraced by players and fans. It was long and tough, but fair.

223

If you're a golfer or just a fan, I'd urge you take your next trip to one of golf's great championships. Each is different, unique. Sometimes it felt like hard work, but so is anything that's really worth doing. Seeing the world's best in your own backyard is something, seeing them in someone else's is even better. It's 150 years since Willie Park won that first Major at Prestwick in 1860 – what better time to start your journey.

Acknowledgements

Many people helped make my year and added to my experiences, but without some, in particular, it might not have been possible. So a big thanks to Art Benton, David Fleming and Craig Harrow for smoothing the way, as well as the team at Birlinn Publishing, specifically Peter Burns, Kenny Redpath, Tom Johnstone and Neville Moir.

Others were only too happy to help me as the project took shape, and their insight and the time they made available were gratefully received, especially when they had so much else going on in their own lives. Rees Jones, Ritchie Blair, Raymond Russell, Tom Brakke and Alex Jackson all went out of their way to assist me where possible, and I won't easily forget their giving natures. And a special thanks to Steve, Nic, Colleen and Becca Weiler for putting up with me in Chaska.

A number of friends provided encouragement and allowed me to believe I could succeed with this project, despite my never having undertaken anything of this magnitude. Without the gentle enthusiasm of Craig Munro, Ewan Thomson, Edward Thomson, Calum Callan, Scott Howie, Iain Robertson and J. Allan Thomson, I might never have given this a bash.

I also want to thank my reviewers whose cold insight and keen minds provided objective analysis and elucidating feedback. As well some of those already mentioned, it's thanks to Andrew Lochhead, Guy Linkleter, Dave Kemp and Alan Reid.

And a quick thank you to Allan Sheriffs, David Allan and Nicole Allan for giving me some work during this project *and* allowing me to fit in my writing where possible.

Many thanks to the people I met throughout my trip, who gave their time to chat and shoot the breeze. And apologies to those of you whom

I have forgotten to include below. It felt like hundreds were keen to help. In no particular order – Simon Leschallas, Garry Harvey, Peter Graham, Murray Stevenson, Gavin Lawrie and Andy Robertson; the marshals I spoke to at Augusta National; John Sullivan, Greg Weiler and Bill Sider; Jim Douglas, Allen Smith and Joe Falce; Rob Matre; Jeff Sorg; Ken Olsen and Chuck Giorgi; Andrew Cotter and Cameron Murray; Michael Brown; Ben Fontaine; Alan Tait; Mannie Garcia; Ken Grant; Billy Foster; Craig Connolly; The Irvine Boys; Dave Gorman; Alfie Lau; Gabe Lopez; Charles Miers and Kirk Hutchison; Elaine Harris; Diane Jackson and Steve Weisser; Bob Smiley; Jim Chatman; Michael Mac-Dougall and John Paramor; Oliver Katcher; Morton Dewar and Mitch Cumstein; Maurice Hastie; Gene Mattare; John Huggan; Rick Anderson; Kenneth Reid (and his mate Peter); Gordon Sherry; Roy Murray; Guy Redford, Ricky Hall and Kerry Haigh.

See you on the fairways.

Appendix
Attendance and Travel Tips

Useful travel and accommodation websites for all the majors:

www.expedia.co.uk
www.expedia.com
www.lastminute.com
www.virginatlantic.com
www.carhire3000.com
www.internetcarhire.co.uk

Ticket websites (on the open market) for US events:

www.stubhub.com
www.gotickets.com

THE MASTERS TOURNAMENT

Played each year at Augusta National, Augusta, Georgia, finishing on the second Sunday in April. Practice tickets can be applied for, via a lottery, by writing a letter with your name, address, email address, daytime telephone number and Social Security number (if you're a US citizen) to

Masters Tournament, Practice Rounds, PO Box 2047,
Augusta, GA 30903-2047

www.masters.com; *www.augusta.com*; *www.atlanta.net*;
www.exploregeorgia.org

Future dates:

2011, April 4-10; **2012**, April 2-8;
2013, April 8-14; **2014**, April 7-13

THE US OPEN CHAMPIONSHIP

Played at a selection of top-flight golf courses throughout the United States. There is no official rota of US Open sites, but regular repeat venues are generally recognised as Shinnecock Hills, Pebble Beach, Pinehurst No.2 and, latterly, Bethpage Black. Other regular stops are Oakmont, Oak Hill, Olympic and Congressional. The tournament finishes on the third Sunday in June, coinciding with Father's Day in the USA.

www.usga.org; www.usopen.com; www.discoveramerica.com

Future dates:

2011, June 13-19, Congressional, MD
2012, April 11-17, Olympic, CA
2013, June 10-16. Merion, PA
2014, June 9-15, Pinehurst No.2, NC
2015, June 15-21, Chambers Bay, WA
2016, June 13-19, Oakmont, PA

THE OPEN CHAMPIONSHIP

The standard rota for The Open covers England and Scotland, with every fifth year being held at the Old Course, St Andrews, Fife, Scotland (next in 2010). Other Scottish venues: Carnoustie, Muirfield, Royal Troon, and Turnberry. Sites in England are Royal Birkdale, Royal Liverpool (aka Hoylake), Royal Lytham & St. Annes, and Royal St. George's (aka Sandwich). The second day at The Open always includes the third Friday in July.

www.randa.org; www.opengolf.com; www.visitscotland.com
www.enjoyengland.com; www.visitbritain.com

Future dates:

2010, July 12-18, St Andrews
2011, July 11-17, Royal St George's
2012, July 16-22, Royal Lytham,
2013, July TBC, Muirfield
2014, July TBC, Royal Liverpool

THE PGA CHAMPIONSHIP

The PGA is the championship most likely to add contemporary venues, for example Whistling Straits, Kiawah Island and Valhalla. The centenary championship in 2016 will be held at the A.W. Tillinghast classic, Baltusrol's Lower Course, in New Jersey. The PGA is usually held four weeks after The Open, but sometimes deviates from this.

The PGA of America's website, *www.pga.com*, will allow you to link to the address for current and future PGAs. All of the US Open and general sites above are good for the PGA, too.

Future dates:

2010 August 9-15, Whistling Straits, WIS
2011 August 8-14, Atlanta Athletic Club, GA
2012 August TBC, Kiawah Island, SC
2013 August TBC, Oak Hill, NY
2014 August TBC, Valhalla, KY
2015 August TBC, Whistling Straits, WIS
2016 August TBC, Baltusrol, NJ

And if you want to follow the press conferences from the above and many other tournaments around the world, reading what main contenders, leaders and the other big stories have to say, try *www.asapsports.com*.